BUILDING IDAHO

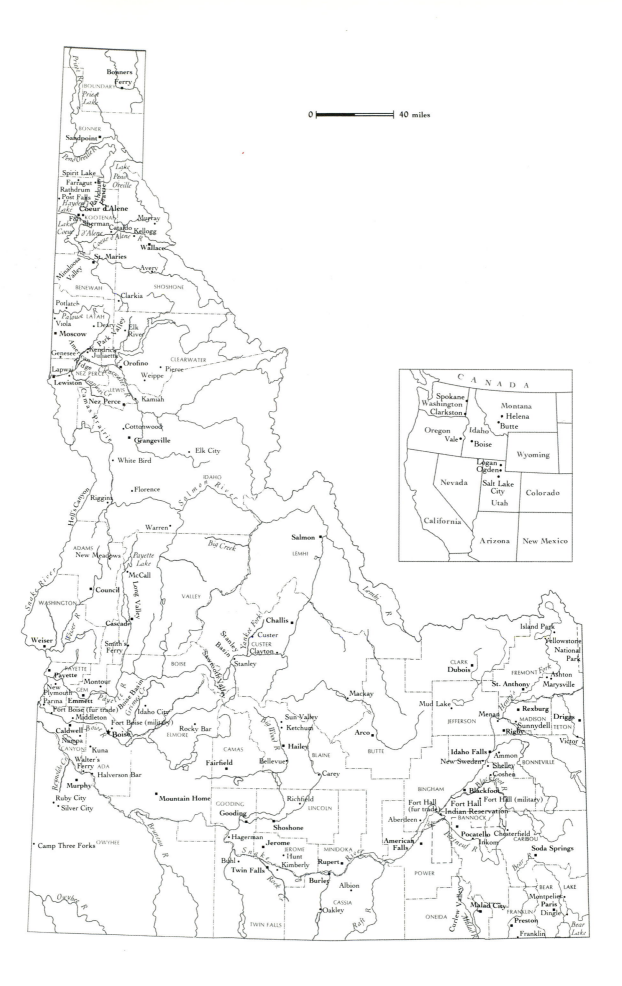

BUILDING IDAHO

An Architectural History

Jennifer Eastman Attebery

University of Idaho Press
Moscow, Idaho

First published 1991 by the University of Idaho Press, Moscow, Idaho 83843.
©1991 by the Idaho State Historical Society
Foreword ©1991 by the Idaho Centennial Foundation
Published with the assistance of the Idaho Centennial Commission.

Printed in the United States of America
95 94 93 92 91   5 4 3 2 1

Library of Congress Cataloging-in-Publication Data
Attebery, Jennifer Eastman, 1951–
    Building Idaho : an architectural history / Jennifer Eastman
Attebery.
        p.   cm.
    Includes bibliographical references and index.
    ISBN 0-89301-139-8
    1. Architecture — Idaho. I. Title.
NA730.I2A88 1990
720'.9796 — dc20   90-36717
                                                    CIP

To my parents
Bob and Ruby Eastman

Contents

Foreword

Appreciation and systematic study of Idaho's built environment is a relatively recent development, sparked in large measure by federal legislation and funding. The Historic Sites Act of 1935 authorized a program for identifying and marking National Historic Landmarks. Only two Idaho buildings studied by the National Park Service were accorded this distinction—the United States Assay Office in Boise, and the state's oldest surviving building, the Mission of the Sacred Heart to the Coeur d'Alenes at Cataldo.

The National Historic Preservation Act of 1966 broadened the concept of historic sites designation to include those of state and local significance, and an executive order issued by President Richard Nixon in 1971 further emphasized the federal government's responsibility to identify and preserve sites and structures of significance to Americans. None of these federal acts required the preservation of private property, unless federal grants had been accepted by owners. Federal agencies were required to perform certain studies and reviews before listed federal properties could be destroyed.

When the executive director of Boise's Redevelopment Agency, operating under the federal Urban Renewal program, was asked in 1969 which historic buildings in downtown Boise's redevelopment area were going to be saved, he answered, "What historic buildings? Nobody told me there were any historic buildings in Boise." This he said despite the fact that the Historic Preservation Act of 1966, in place for three years, required that studies be done to protect structures of state and local significance and that some of the city's century-old Main Street buildings were still standing. That no such studies had been done suggests the general lack of interest in Idaho's architectural heritage prevalent at the time. True, there had been one volunteer association of Boise women with the unfortunate acronym of SOB (Save Our Buildings), but apparently the city's redevelopment agency had not taken their concerns seriously in its planning.

Funding of Idaho's Historic Preservation Office in the State Historical Society began in 1970, and the staff began a statewide survey of historic sites of all kinds. From the beginning it was decided to record on film and with field notes every aspect of Idaho's built environment—not just conspicuous landmarks such as mansions and courthouses. We collected and recorded information about barns, fences, hay derricks, mine structures, railway buildings, bridges, and every kind of vernacular building done without benefit of architects. We also published information sheets on significant commercial buildings in Idaho cities, some of them threatened by Urban Renewal projects or other proposed development.

The study of Idaho's architectural heritage began in earnest with the availability of annual grants through the National Park Service. An inventory of sites and structures in each of Idaho's forty-four counties grew from hundreds to thousands of individual listings. Those deemed to be of outstanding state or local significance have been researched in detail and recorded in the National Register of Historic Places.

Educational efforts by the Idaho State Historical Society and other organizations to raise the consciousness of Idahoans to their architectural heritage have included illustrated lectures in all parts of the state to civic clubs and local historical societies. The first college courses devoted exclusively to American architecture were offered at Boise State University beginning in 1970. The University of Idaho's architectural curriculum, offered first in 1923, like that of Idaho State University later, included the history of architecture primarily as a world survey. Although faculty members at both schools pursued their own studies of local vernacular architecture, that of Palouse country barns, for example, bibliographical materials are scarce.

Jennifer Eastman Attebery's work is a landmark in its field. It fills a long-felt need for a readable, informative, and carefully researched history of Idaho architecture and should stimulate further research and writing on a variety of special topics it suggests. It is also a worthy and lasting legacy of the Idaho centennial celebration, the special occasion of its publication.

Arthur A. Hart, Director Emeritus
Idaho State Historical Society

Introduction

August . . . . 3ᵈ Came to Fort Hall, this morning distance eight miles. A cool breeze made our ride very pleasant. . . . was much cheered with a view of the Fort at a considerable distance. Any thing that looks like a house makes us glad.
— Narcissa Prentiss Whitman, *My Journal, 1836*

(Previous page)William Tappan sketched Fort Hall in 1849, depicting the palisadelike outer wall and blockhouses (corner fortifications) as adobe structures. (ISHS 1254-C.)

Today you can recapture Narcissa Prentiss Whitman's sense of unoccupied wilderness only from the air.[1] Flying over Idaho affords a spectacular but deceptive view of the region. In the fabric of the state's folds, faults, lava intrusions, glaciations, and river valleys, habitation appears sparse and insignificant. It is only during descent that you begin to note houses, farms, factories, and main streets as foreground. As mountain and plain recede into a scenic backdrop, the extent to which Idahoans have reshaped the landscape becomes visible, significant, and inescapable. The view from the air is a humbling geographical lesson; that from the ground, a historical lesson of a heritage in which can be found both pride and humility.

Shaping the landscape to human needs — building Idaho — has been underway for millennia. There is evidence of the human hand at work in Idaho 14,000 years ago. But it is only within the past 130 years that human habitation has worked dramatic changes in the Idaho landscape. Beginning in 1860 — a quarter century after Narcissa Whitman traveled the mostly unoccupied Snake River Plain — miners, merchants, farmers, ranchers, and soldiers came to the region now called Idaho to search for gold, sell goods to the gold seekers, establish Mormon villages, or enforce federal law. They brought to the sagebrush desert and rocky mountains of Idaho a notion of civilization — home, church, school, main street — that rapidly transformed the landscape. Whitman had been glad to see a house in 1836. Within a few years of the Idaho gold rush, thousands of buildings and tents sheltered the territory's several thousand white residents.[2]

Idahoans celebrated the construction of buildings as evidence that their architectural heritage could be transplanted in the arid West. The proper role of a newspaper editor was to note the completion of fine new residences and substantial, brick commercial buildings. It was likewise the duty of business clubs to promote a town with photographs of its architectural masterpieces as well as statistics attesting to its salubrious climate and its economic prospects. Idahoville was Anytown, U.S.A., complete with classical business fronts, tree-lined residential neighborhoods, Italianate schools, and Gothic Revival churches. Anything that looked like the streetscapes of Illinois made Idahoans glad.

The familiar landscape was a comforting measure of prosperity, but it was after all only a desert mirage, a reflection of some faraway midwestern or California town. Behind the business block's false front, the building was made of logs. Behind the brick-veneered bank was a lava rock building. The church's porch columns were pine logs. The brick house was adobe. It is these differences, evidence of unique, regional traditions, that Idahoans should celebrate.

The history of Idaho architecture is a story of traditions transplanted and transformed. Transformations of that heritage began when immigrants first reached the Snake River Plain and have continued as each new generation of builders confronts the regional environment, physical and social. Climate, geology, topography, native flora and fauna, the migration of peoples, stylistic trends, the availability of shipped materials, the introduction of new inventions, the development of federal programs, and cycles of economic prosperity and recession have all played a part in the development of a regional architectural tradition. Always in the foreground, though, were the builder and the materials at hand.

Geography was of primary importance in the period before mining and Mormon settlement, discussed in chapter 1. Most of this era is unknown except as represented in a few excavated archaeological sites. The architecture of prehistoric peoples and of the several Native American groups in the Idaho region was dependent upon local materials, and these peoples developed considerable expertise in their use. The few white settlements in the pre-gold-rush era were equally dependent upon the local environment. Fur traders and missionaries constructed compounds in which they experimented with the construction systems they knew, using the local materials that were most comparable to those of their homeland.

After the fur-trade and missionary era had passed, Idaho Territory saw twenty years of relative isolation before railroad construction made the Midwest and the West Coast more accessible. As discussed in chapter 2, miners and Mormons brought with them an architectural tradition that they adapted to the region's new conditions. By the end of this era several standard forms had emerged as the most common architectural solutions.

With railroad links to the rest of the United States, the Idaho builder had access to shipped building materials, and pattern books wielded new influence. New residential neighborhoods developed along streetcar lines. Main streets and residential neighborhoods displayed the architectural styles of the day, whereas farms and ranches continued to utilize traditional forms and materials. In this period, discussed in chapter 3, the state gained a few professional architects who designed up-to-date buildings for the growing urban centers.

After the turn of the century and until the agricultural depression of the 1920s, Idaho's architecture reflected the economic prosperity that resulted from an expanded lumber industry in northern Idaho and newly irrigated lands in southern Idaho. As described in chapter 4, Idaho's towns were reshaped by architects trained in Beaux Arts classicism. Streetscapes imitated the Renaissance Revival architecture of Portland, San Francisco, Salt Lake City, and Denver. Territorial and county buildings were replaced with larger and more efficient classical buildings. Farmsteads proliferated, and company towns were built. All this prosperity greatly boosted the practice of architecture, attracting new architects to the state and producing major commissions to support them.

The countryside absorbed some of its architectural trends from the city, but more profound influences included innovations in agricultural technology, changes in the farm economy, and differences in climate and soil types from region to region. Considered in chapter 5 are Idaho's rural builders and the architecture they designed and constructed in the period 1880 to 1920.

Depression years in Idaho began even before the crash of 1929. The state suffered greatly from the agricultural depression of the 1920s, and the period from 1920 through World War II saw a drastic reduction in private construction around the state. However, this was also the era of cooperative government programs. Although few new farms, residences, and business blocks were added to Idaho towns in this era, numerous public buildings were constructed, as discussed in chapter 6.

Stagnation was followed by a period of postwar expansion that coincided with Modernism. Idaho's architectural heritage was often replaced, sometimes rebuilt, and occasionally restored during the postwar era under the public's shifting attitude toward regional culture, including old buildings. Business blocks were masked with aluminum; old residential areas were lost to commercial expansion, often in the form of strip development; and farms were consolidated into large sprinkler-irrigated acreage. Very different in their ultimate results, both modernism and historic preservation, described in chapter 7, were attempts to follow national trends to effect progressive change.

If there are any all-embracing trends spanning these eras in the building of Idaho, they are the use of local materials and an aesthetic of plainness and spaciousness.

Utilization of indigenous building materials spans early periods when using local materials was simple necessity and later periods when their use was a matter of intentional, aesthetic choice. Noteworthy is the distinctive use of native wood and stone in Nez Perce sweathouses, old and new; in miners' log cabins and in the rustic log cabins used as second homes in resort towns like McCall; in the pioneer stone meetinghouses of southeast Idaho and the 1920s basalt bungalows of Jerome.

Austerity and pragmatism are characteristic of Idaho architecture from early days to the current generation. The exuberant Bannock Hotel, Boise Natatorium, and Normal Hill neighborhood are exceptions in the story of Idaho architecture. More representative are farmsteads like the Stricker Ranch, company towns like Potlatch, or brick and stone commercial blocks like those in Shoshone. Vernacular architecture has flourished in Idaho while elite design has had hard times. It was important for main street to suggest a midwestern hometown, but it was not necessary to express the spirit of its buildings by duplicating every terra-cotta embellishment. Idaho buildings are small: low in height, slight in massing, and spaced generously apart from each other. Spaciousness is so basic to the Idaho landscape that the Idahoan abroad is struck by the claustrophobic closeness and height of buildings in places like Indiana or Rhode Island, where culture seems all too present, the environment tamed. As if to remind themselves of the frontier past, Idahoans elect to preserve a view of the mountains or desert — the homeless wilderness — just outside town.

It would be difficult to generalize any further about Idaho architecture without adding a cautionary phrase: "except in the north, where thus and such is the case," or "with the exception of southeast Idaho." Regional divisions underlie every facet of life in Idaho: affiliations with political, religious, or ethnic groups; allegiance to a particular university or college; concern about regional industries, the regional hospital that serves the citizenry. The popular commonplace that Idaho has three capitals — Spokane, Boise, and Salt Lake City — is accurate, if perhaps an oversimplification. Northern Idaho looks to Spokane and beyond to Seattle and the Washington coast; southwestern Idaho, including Boise, looks to Portland and the Willamette Valley and also to California; and southeastern Idaho looks to Salt Lake City and beyond to Denver and the

Midwest. The central Idaho mountains and south-central Idaho (the area around Twin Falls), ringed by these other areas, have complex allegiances that also include Montana and Nevada. Regional trends are apparent in every era of Idaho architecture. Mormon settlers from Utah brought distinctive house types to southeast Idaho. Scandinavians in Long Valley and in northern Idaho brought special log construction techniques to those areas. Ranchers in Owyhee County built log, willow, and mud buildings similar to those of Nevada. In the 1980s, urban renewal in Boise has tapped the Post-Modernist ideas of architects working in Portland and Seattle. The regional character underlies every attempt to describe what is Idahoan, and is a subtheme throughout this effort to describe Idaho architecture.

This volume summarizes what is currently known about Idaho architecture and attempts to present new perspectives on the development of Idaho architecture, with emphasis on builders, designers, and their materials. The book is not intended as a guide to styles and types or as a tour guide. Many Idahoans will be disappointed not to find their favorite buildings discussed or pictured here, for I have selected buildings primarily on the basis of their usefulness as examples of the trends in and influences on Idaho architecture. Buildings that are still standing in 1989 are discussed in the text in present tense; demolished buildings are discussed in past tense.

The photographs and drawings operate in lieu of a glossary to illustrate styles and types. For style categories I have relied primarily on *Architecture Oregon Style*, which adapts American stylistic terminology to the Pacific Northwest, but I depart from that guide in my discussion of two Queen Anne modes, Stick and Shingle, categories originated by Vincent J. Scully, Jr., that I found useful for interpreting houses of the 1880s and 1890s. For categories of house types I have adopted Thomas Carter and Peter Goss's typology in *Utah's Historic Architecture, 1847–1940*, which adapts house typology to western architecture.[3]

The bibliography is a summary of secondary sources having to do with Idaho architecture. I owe a deep debt to the writers listed there for their groundbreaking work on various aspects of Idaho architecture. Arthur A. Hart has earned the unofficial title of Dean of Idaho Architectural History through his twenty-year career of studying Idaho buildings. I have benefited greatly from his work and from the work of the architectural historians who have worked for the state historic preservation office: Don Hibbard, Patricia Wright, Susanne Lichtenstein, Lisa B. Reitzes, Kathleen Watt, and current staff members Elizabeth Egleston and Nancy F. Renk. To Merle W. Wells I owe thanks for years of patient tutelage in the art of writing history.

Many colleagues and friends have assisted

me in bringing this project to completion. I would like to thank Arthur A. Hart for suggesting the project and Thomas J. Green and David Crowder for making it possible. Brian Attebery, Merle W. Wells, and Elizabeth Egleston read drafts of the manuscript, and I am grateful for their thoughtful comments, emendations, and suggestions. I would also like to thank Arthur A. Hart, Thomas J. Green, Kathleen Watt, Donald W. Watts, and Ann Swanson for their comments and corrections.

Many friends and fellow staff members at the Idaho State Historical Society helped me find sources, sometimes in odd corners. I would especially like to thank Lois Palmgren for her assistance in locating items in the society files. I also received help from Donald W. Watts, Ann Swanson, Frederick L. Walters, Merle W. Wells, Louie W. Attebery, Ron Hatzenbuehler, Mary Reed, Bobbi Rahder, Madeline Buckendorf, Ruth Hall, Doris Camp, Keith Petersen, Kathleen Carney, Gary Bettis, Elizabeth Jacox, Larry Jones, Guila Ford, John Yandell, Judy Austin, Marjorie Williams, Ken Swanson, Fred Fritchman, Jerry Ostermiller, Carol Cole, and Rick Greenfield. The special collections staffs at the

Idaho State University and University of Idaho libraries were very helpful in tracking down sources for me, as were the staffs at the Idaho State Library, Latah County Historical Society, the Idaho Bureau of Occupational Licenses, and the office of the Idaho Chapter, American Institute of Architects. Jim McDonald helped locate materials at Targhee National Forest. Thanks are also due the architectural firms that kindly allowed me to inspect their private collections: Sundberg and Associates, Idaho Falls; Wallace-Hudson and Associates, Pocatello; and Hummel LaMarche Hunsucker Architects PA, Boise.

The staff at the University of Idaho Press has brought the project to final fruition with great dispatch. I would like to thank the director of the Press, James J. Heaney, and especially Karla Fromm, who designed it, and Norma B. Mikkelsen, who edited it, for their part in shaping this book.

To my family and friends I owe thanks for morale boosting and for their kind hospitality in my numerous trips across the state. Finally, I would like to thank my daughter Stina and husband Brian for their creative support.

The activity that is the subject of this publication has been funded in part with federal funds from the National Park Service, U.S. Department of the Interior. However, the contents and opinions do not necessarily reflect the views or policy of the Department of the Interior nor does the mention of trade names or commercial products constitute endorsement or recommendation by the Department of the Interior.

Notes

1. Narcissa Prentiss Whitman, *My Journal, 1836*, 2d ed., ed. Lawrence L. Dodd (Fairfield, Washington: Ye Galleon Press, 1984), 20.

2. According to Merrill D. Beal and Merle W. Wells, 7,453 votes were cast in Idaho Territory's first congressional election of 2 December 1863; *History of Idaho*, 3 vols. (New York: Lewis Historical Publishing Co., 1959), 1:341. At that time the territory included present-day Montana and practically all of Wyoming. In the 1870 census Idaho Territory had 17,804 people, including those residents of southeast Idaho who thought they were part of Utah Territory.

3. Rosalind Clark, *Architecture Oregon Style* (Portland, Oregon: Professional Book Center, 1983); Vincent J. Scully, Jr., *The Shingle Style and the Stick Style: Architectural Theory and Design from Downing to the Origins of Wright*, rev. ed. (New Haven: Yale University Press, 1971); and Thomas Carter and Peter Goss, *Utah's Historic Architecture, 1847–1940: A Guide* (Salt Lake City: University of Utah Press, 1988).

1

The Materials and Strategies of Shelter, Architecture before 1860

We here, the people, ask thee rock and earth of the sweathouse to bear our petitions to the sun, moon and stars and through these to the Great Master Spirit. Grant us food, wealth, health, shelter and care.
—Kutenai sweat-bath prayer

A simple dome-shaped building of saplings covered with mats, the Kutenai sweathouse might seem a humble place for petitions to the heavens.[1] The sweathouse is, however, an important Native American building type, the only one that the several Idaho tribes had in common. With its covering of mats, skin, dirt, or bark, the sweathouse was part of the natural and spiritual landscapes. Its builders were mindful of the natural ecology as it fulfilled spiritual needs as well as economic ones. Humankind was only one rather clever player in the order of things; its architecture was properly adapted to the environment.[2] In construction and purpose the sweathouse exemplifies the difference between Native American and white architecture. The architecture of the fur trappers and missionaries was an architecture subject to, rather than adapted to, its environment. Attempting to construct buildings based on their idea of what buildings should look like, the whites who came to the region after 1805 saw local materials as restrictions on what could be done. In either case, the materials at hand were crucial to the final results. Even today, the state's remarkably varied environment is a basis for everything Idahoans do and make, but the link with environment was much more evident in the period before 1860.

A large state of about 84,000 square miles, with an awkward panhandled shape, Idaho has mountains up to 12,662 feet in elevation;

valleys as low as 710 feet above sea level; soils ranging from the rocklands of the Snake River lava plain to the fertile, arable soil of the Palouse; and a complex pattern of vegetation and geological zones.[3] Precipitation and temperature range widely. Mountainous areas can experience temperatures as low as sixty degrees below zero Fahrenheit and can receive up to fifty inches of precipitation per year, most of it as snow. Lower elevations can experience the opposite extremes, summer temperatures

up to a record 118 degrees Fahrenheit and only about seven inches of annual precipitation.

Idaho's variability is the result of its complex geography. River drainages and the mountainous terrain between watersheds divide the state into southern, central, and northern regions as well as numerous subregions. The southern half of the state is dominated by the high lava plain through which the Snake River arcs southwest, west, and

E. Jane Gay documented the pole framework of a Nez Perce sweathouse and a finished structure in her photographs taken during the early 1890s. (ISHS 63-221.103 and 63-221.25.)

northwest, collecting tributaries from the surrounding hills and mountains. These tributaries form a series of approximately north-south trenches funneling water to the Snake through the canyons and valleys of the Henrys Fork, Blackfoot, Portneuf, Raft, Big Wood, Bruneau, Boise, Owyhee, Payette, and Weiser rivers. Only a small corner of southeast Idaho is not part of the Snake's vast watershed; the Bear River circles through Bear Lake, Caribou, and Franklin counties to make that area part of the Salt Lake basin, and the Curlew and Malad valleys of Oneida County also drain southward.

The central mass of the state is dominated by the Salmon River Mountains, which with the Wallowa Mountains to the west form an obstacle to the Snake as it flows through the 8,000-foot-deep Hell's Canyon before the Salmon River joins it at the southern tip of Nez Perce County. Northern Idaho, drained by the Clearwater, Coeur d'Alene-Spokane, Clark Fork-Pend Oreille, and Kootenai river systems, is a moist region of lakes, coves, and massive round-topped mountains shaped by glaciation.

Diversity in topography, soils, vegetation, precipitation, and temperature has given Idahoans a wide choice of building materials. In the Idaho highlands the native fauna includes large mammals such as deer and bison, whose hides were used by Native American builders.[4] The native vegetation includes desert brushes and shrubs, such as the willow, and

dryland grasses like Great Basin rye, and the softwood trees that grow on the slopes of Idaho's mountains.

A number of indigenous trees have been used for construction, including cottonwood, western red cedar (giant arborvitae), grand and subalpine fir, Engelmann spruce, Rocky Mountain Douglas fir, western larch (tamarack), western white pine (Idaho white pine), and ponderosa pine (yellow pine). Idaho's most commercially valuable trees are the western white pine and ponderosa pine stands. Both woods are lightweight and easily worked; their uses include moldings and paneling as well as dimensional lumber. The relatively heavy western larch wood is rot resistant, making it useful for pilings as well as lumber. Other woods are known for their strength (Engelmann spruce), durability (juniper), straight trunks (lodgepole pine), and good splitting ability (western red cedar). Western red cedar has a red-brown heartwood resistant to decay and useful for siding, molding, and shakes or shingles. Whether commercially valuable or not, all of these woods have been put to use by local builders. Construction of pioneer buildings with cottonwood, for example, was as ubiquitous as the tree itself, which grows in combination with willows along the state's rivers and streams in all but the highest vegetation zones.

Idaho is famous for its metal deposits, but equally rich and more significant for builders were the state's nonmetallic mineral deposits:

building stone and the soil itself.[5] With a few major exceptions these materials have not been exploited commercially because of marketing and transportation problems, but their use in local construction has been extensive. Adobe mud, in bulk or in bricks, liquifies in a wet climate, but was able to withstand the dry climate of southern Idaho. Mud was used for mortar as well as bricks when adequate lime sources could not be located. Clay for the manufacture of fired brick is found in nearly every Idaho county, the best deposits lying in northern Idaho, especially in Latah County. Builders of the 1860s searched out lime deposits suitable for mortar, which are relatively rare in much of Idaho. Idaho lime was also mined for the manufacture of cement; major plants were on Pend Oreille Lake and at Orofino in northern Idaho and at Inkom in southeastern Idaho.

Stone is a readily available and popular building material in Idaho. Although stone was not favored by Native American builders, who preferred light and portable materials, the permanency of stone was valued by white settlers. Historian Arthur A. Hart notes "the frequency with which local stone was used"[6] in the Pacific Northwest east of the Cascade Range. In southeast Idaho, the availability of easily workable local stone, coupled with the Mormon preference for using substantial building materials such as stone, brick, or heavy timbers, has produced a landscape rich in stone buildings. Idaho stone ranges widely,

The Potlatch Lumber Company mill at Potlatch produced railroad ties, lath, box stock, and dimensional lumber (boards cut to standard measurements). From 1906 to 1981 the mill supplied national markets with its white-pine products. (Latah County Historical Society.)

Boise sandstone, quarried at Table Rock and elsewhere in the Boise foothills, has been used for buildings throughout the West. (ISHS 73-2.31/D.)

from lightweight perlite used for manufacturing plaster aggregate and light building block to the dark basalt used extensively throughout south-central Idaho for farmhouses and outbuildings.

Most celebrated of Idaho building stone is Boise sandstone quarried at Table Rock and other locations along the Boise front. Light gray, yellowish, or reddish and easily dressed and carved, Boise sandstone has been used in numerous Boise buildings, including the earliest buildings at military Fort Boise (1864). The stone is also one of the few building materials aside from timber that has found an out of state market. Boise sandstone has been used throughout the western states for the construction of railroad stations, commercial blocks, and institutional buildings. Perhaps the farthest the stone has been transported for construction is New Haven, Connecticut, where Boise sandstone was used for the Harkness Memorial at Yale University.

Boise sandstone and deposits at Dingle and near Salmon that have had limited local use are the few genuine sandstones found in Idaho. Often called "sandstone" is volcanic tuff, a consolidation of volcanic ash with clay minerals. Under the stress of a moist climate and frequent freezing and thawing, tuff is not a desirable building material, for the freeze-thaw cycle causes the stone to swell and break. In the dry Idaho climate, however, tuff has proven acceptable. Tuff deposits near Challis, Clayton, Lewiston, Albion, Sunny-

dell, Menan, and Reynolds Creek have produced stone for local buildings of all kinds. Many have stood for a century, partly because of climate but also because of the stone's ability to harden with exposure to the air. The stone is favored by builders for its easy workability and for its variety of hues, which have been used by southeastern Idaho builders to produce quoining and other decorative designs.

Stone produced by volcanic flows includes two popular materials: dark grey or black basalt and the lighter grey or pink rhyolite. Both are common building materials in southern Idaho. Rhyolite has been quarried at Goshen, Prospect, Rigby, and Rexburg; basalt at Idaho Falls, Warren (near Nampa), Cottonwood, Coeur d'Alene, Lewiston, and Twin Falls. The volcanic deposits are so common that establishing temporary quarries close to

Four to five thousand years ago prehistoric peoples built semisubterranean dwellings that archaeologists call pit houses. The drawing shows a cross section of a pit house supported by a pole framework that is attached to a larger center post. The house is covered with grass thatch. In the center of the packed earth floor is a fire. (Drawing by Cheryl Marshall.)

the building site has proven to be the most expedient and inexpensive way to extract the stone.

A few building stones occur only locally and therefore have had limited regional use. Cobblestone occurs in the glaciated Clark Fork valley and Rathdrum Prairie and appears in a few buildings there. Cobbles also were used along the Boise River; one example is the herringbone cellar walls of the Montgomery house (circa 1870) in Middleton. Boulders deposited by the Bonneville flood in the Pleistocene epoch were the basis for a regional prehistoric form, the pole and rock shelters of Gooding County. Marble deposits suitable for construction occur in Nez Perce County and southeast Idaho, but have been used in few buildings. The Supreme Court Building (1968–1970) in Boise is veneered with marble from southeast Idaho. Granite quarries in Boise and Lewiston have supplied granite for minor decorative use, such as the entrances to commercial blocks. Stone from near Oakley has also been used for buildings at least since the 1950s. The Teater studio (1953–1957) is an example that exploits the stone's warm color and thin stratification.

Even with the addition of imported and synthetic materials like cast-iron building fronts, mail-order millwork, prefabricated aluminum-frame windows and mobile homes, these native materials — especially wood products — continue today to provide a substantial portion of the building materials for Idaho ar-

chitecture. For the greatest part of the state's architectural history they were the only building materials. Even so, remarkably complex technologies were used in Idaho before railroad transportation made alternative materials easier and cheaper to obtain.

Every group to come into the Idaho region has had its own idea of what shelter is and has used the materials differently. Out of the abundance and variety of materials, each group has limited itself to using a few materials worked in a few ways. The area now called Idaho has been inhabited for about 14,000 years, but information about the architecture of most of that period is available only through the observations of archaeologists who have methodically excavated some of the state's prehistoric sites.[7] The most common house type that has been unearthed in Idaho is the pit house. In northern Idaho, these houses were constructed slightly earlier than 5000 B.P. (before the present), and their construction and use continued in several phases into historic times, when Indians and whites first met. Pit houses had round or oval plans about six meters in diameter. They were dug into the ground, usually to about a half meter, and had dirt floors. Poles and grasses such as Great Basin rye formed a roof. Sometimes posts sunk into the floor added additional roof support.

On the Snake River Plain of southern Idaho, pit houses were built as far east as Hagerman. The prehistoric peoples of south-

ern Idaho used pit houses as early as 5000–4000 B.P. They abandoned the house type around 1200–1000 B.P., when they began building pole and thatch houses, a house type identical to the southern Idaho wickiup of historic times. The southern Idaho pit house resembles that of northern Idaho except in its generally smaller size.

The pole and thatch wickiup is the only prehistoric house type that has been found in southeast Idaho. Wickiups were also used farther south, in the Great Basin. Their simple framework consisted of flexible poles stuck in the ground in a circular or an oval plan about three meters in diameter. These poles were then brought together at the top of the house to form a dome or cone, which was covered with grass thatch or mats. The earthen floor, slightly excavated, was only a quarter meter below ground level.

Written records about shelters begin in 1805 with the first visits to the Idaho region by white explorers and trappers. At that time six groups lived in the area: the Shoshoni and Northern Paiute (primarily Bannock) in the Snake Plain–Great Basin culture area of southern Idaho and the Nez Perce, Coeur d'Alene, Kalispel, and Kutenai in the Plateau culture area of central and northern Idaho. Each group used natural materials somewhat differently, producing a number of distinct regional building types.[8]

In the Plateau culture area the longhouse was the most popular dwelling before the

Tipis made of poles covered with hide or canvas were the principal dwellings for the Native American groups that used horses. On the Fort Hall reservation, a group of Shoshoni, Bannock, and whites posed beside winter tipis and one summer tipi covered with brush. (ISHS 77-155.20/B.)

Plateau groups acquired horses and changed their life-style accordingly. The longhouse was a gable structure of poles covered with woven mats or bark. Hearths spaced along the center of the longhouse provided heat and light for each family using the house. Longhouses could be as long as 100 feet, housing ten families. For summer shelter the northern peoples built conical lodges out of poles covered with woven mats. These accommodated the mobility required for tasks like gathering food. Other Plateau shelters included specialized buildings for menstrual seclusion, giving birth, and sweat bathing. Less elaborate than the longhouse, these dome-shaped structures were fashioned of poles covered with woven mats or bark. After acquiring horses in the early eighteenth century from the Shoshoni, the Plateau tribes were increasingly influenced by Plains Indian traditions. Among other items, they adopted the Plains tipi, a portable conical structure of poles covered with animal hide.

The Native Americans of the Snake Plain–Great Basin culture area knew about and admired the longhouses of the Plateau peoples, but they did not build them. Instead they built shelters identical to the prehistoric pole and thatch house, and some of the Northern Paiute used the form until contact with incoming white settlers. The Shoshoni were Idaho's earliest mounted peoples, and after they acquired horses they made a simple transition from the conical pole and thatch house to the

buffalo house, a conical pole and buffalo-hide tipi. Buffalo became extinct in southeast Idaho by about 1840 and in the Montana hunting grounds used by the Fort Hall Indians by 1880. During the same period, trade with whites provided a new material: canvas. The buffalo house was gradually replaced with the pole and canvas tipi. The Snake Plain–Great Basin tradition included menstrual and sweat lodges quite similar to those of the Plateau. It also included the use of caves for shelter and the construction of temporary sun and wind shelters of thin willow poles fashioned into a lean-to or tripodal framework

with a covering of brush or a blanket.

The peoples who displaced the Native American groups brought with them a building tradition that contrasted sharply with Indian traditions. The native architecture relied primarily upon earthen, vegetal, and animal materials that are pliable and can be worked into geometric shapes based on circular and other curved figures. The white tradition relied on hard materials like wood and stone that can be worked into a square or rectangular geometry. The native construction was labor- and energy-efficient, and the final product was usually light and transportable or simply temporary; the white architecture involved labor- and energy-intensive construction, and the product was not easily moved, although not always regarded as permanent either.

Some types of precontact Indian architecture are constructed to this day in Idaho, especially buildings for celebrations or spiritual observances. At modern-day Fort Hall, for example, the Shoshoni have constructed canvas tipis and Sun Dance lodges for spiritual use. The Nez Perce adapted part of their architectural heritage to modern needs in the contemporary sweathouse, an aboveground, blanket-covered version that preserves the sweathouse's domic structure and many of the practical and spiritual functions of the sweat bath. Modern Nez Perce added a nearby wooden frame shelter to their sweathouses, lending the architecture unaccustomed "permanency and comfort," as noted by anthropologist Deward E. Walker, Jr.[9] However, as in all other lifeways, white traditions came to dominate, transforming the Idaho landscape. White architecture has been adopted by the Native American peoples for most everyday uses.

The Indians' adoption of white architecture was a result of many concurrent pressures. Extinction of the buffalo was just one way the new white presence restricted access to the resources traditionally used for shelter, clothing, food, and spiritual life. The Indians also had to cope with treaty restrictions on their terri-

tory and with increased competition for resources, both from whites and from other tribes. At the same time, they encountered encouragement, chiefly from Indian agents and missionaries, to learn carpentry. In some places this encouragement was accompanied by promises to provide milled lumber to Indians wanting to build, although in many cases the attempts to fulfill those promises were halfhearted.

The most effective agents of change were the missionaries. At their Protestant mission at Lapwai, Henry and Eliza Spalding encouraged the Nez Perce to take up agriculture and domestic sciences and to build permanent shelters. A few Nez Perce did follow their advice, which was partly founded on a concern that the Nez Perce could not survive the coming onslaught of white settlers without adapting to an agrarian livelihood. Thus, when United States Indian agent A. J. Cain came to Lapwai in 1859, eleven years after the Spaldings had abandoned the mission as a result of the Whitman Massacre, he found a few hundred acres being farmed, an orchard, and at least one cabin said to have been built by Reuben, a Christianized Nez Perce.[10]

Christianized Nez Perce at Kamiah constructed a wooden frame church in 1874. Its Greek Revival style, altered to Gothic Revival in 1890, clearly reflected the adoption of a white architectural vocabulary. The Coeur d'Alene received similar encouragement to adopt white forms from the Jesuits at the Mis-

sion of the Sacred Heart, where an Indian village included a mixture of tipis, longhouses, and log cabins and where Native Americans provided the labor to build the mission church. The shift to white patterns proceeded more slowly among other groups. Some of the nontreaty Nez Perce (those who did not consider the treaty that reduced the Nez Perce reservation to be valid for their territories) learned carpentry during their exile on the Oklahoma reservation after the Nez Perce War of 1877. Some bands of Shoshoni, isolated in what is now Idaho wilderness, were able to preserve their traditional life-style until the turn of the century.

The years between Lewis and Clark's entry into Idaho in 1805 and 1860, when E. D. Pierce discovered gold at Orofino and Mormon settlers established the town of Franklin, saw little white occupation. Those settlements that were established, isolated and nearly self-sufficient, can be regarded as the testing ground for adaptation of white architecture to the new region. During this period, settlement took the form of whole compounds — missions or forts — within which was a marked variety of materials and structure. These compounds were isolated from each other by distance and by the rivalry among different religious groups and fur-trapping companies, but they still had a common basis in Euroamerican tradition. The Spaldings' mission is usually noted for its varied architecture, but the mission was only one very well documented example of

Nez Perce posed for E. Jane Gay in front of their Greek Revival style church at Kamiah. Greek Revival features in the Nez Perce building included the location of the entrance on the gable end of the building, its moderately pitched gable roof, gable returns at the eaves that suggest a triangular pediment, and simple molded window heads that suggest entablatures (in a Greek temple, the horizontal beam above the columns). (ISHS 63-221.90d.)

Pièce sur pièce (right) was a French Canadian construction method used by both the North West Company and the Hudson's Bay Company for their fur-trade establishments in the Pacific Northwest. Called Red River style by Hudson's Bay personnel, *pièce sur pièce* consisted of horizontal timbers that were fit into grooves cut into vertical uprights. The drawing shows a top and side view. (Drawing by Cheryl Marshall.)

these early self-contained settlements. Other compounds included Asa and Sarah Smith's Protestant mission at Kamiah, the Coeur d'Alene Mission of the Sacred Heart at its 1842 and 1846 locations near present-day St. Maries and Cataldo, the Mormon Salmon River mission in the Lemhi Valley, and the several forts and temporary shelters established by trappers.

Experimentation with local materials was

an important aspect of these early settlements. The missionaries and fur trappers worked with adobe, local woods and grasses, and native stone to test the practicality of these materials in the regional climate. Following these early experiments, certain materials were discarded from the repertoire and certain ones favored. By the time miners and Mormon settlers entered the area, the most practical means of building had been worked out, al-

though at some places the lag between forts and missions and later settlement meant that the exchange of knowledge was indirect.

The fur-trade forts were the earliest white constructions in Idaho. David Thompson of the North West Company built his Kullyspell House on Lake Pend Oreille in 1809. The trade house was probably built with the French Canadian *pièce sur pièce* construction (horizontal timbers fit into the grooves of a vertical timber framework) that was typically used by the North West Company. In his journal Thompson complained that the site "had no blue clay which is so very necessary for plaistering between the Logs of the House and especially the roofing."[11] The pole roof was covered with a mud and grass mixture, and the same mixture was used in a cat and clay chimney (a chimney constructed with a pole framework filled in with plaster). Thompson also described a similar storehouse.

Kullyspell was the first of several places where trappers and missionaries raised buildings known only from descriptions in journals and letters. Most of these sites have no aboveground remains, nor has there been sufficient archaeological investigation to suggest much about the kind of construction. The list includes Donald Mackenzie's Astorian fur-trade post of 1812, established on the Clearwater River five miles above its confluence with the Snake. The post consisted of a store and two houses constructed with driftwood. Clay was

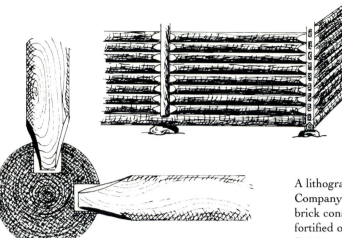

A lithograph of Fort Boise by E. Weber and Company of Baltimore (below) suggests the adobe brick construction of its buildings, chimneys, fortified outer wall, and blockhouses. (ISHS 1254-D-1.)

used to plaster chimneys and roofs. Mackenzie's group abandoned the post, burning its buildings, in order to convey news of the War of 1812 to the West Coast.[12]

Also noteworthy are Andrew Henry's winter fort on the upper Snake River, built in 1810, and John Reid's short-lived post built in 1813 on the south bank of Boise River near the later fur-trade fort called Fort Boise. Construction at these places is not clearly documented.[13]

Fur traders established two important settlement centers in southern Idaho. Fur-trade posts on the Boise River — Fort Boise —

and the Snake River — Fort Hall — established two hubs for travel and trade on the Snake River Plain that eventually became important Oregon Trail stopovers. Fort Hall was established by Nathaniel Wyeth in July of 1834; Fort Boise, by Thomas McKay in the same year. Both were independent operations with ties to the Hudson's Bay Company. Like other Company forts in the Pacific Northwest, they were rectangular compounds with buildings ranged around the interior walls and blockhouses at the corners. Fort Boise was adobe, a departure from the Company's usual use of wood construction for buildings and pali-

sades. Journalist W. A. Goulder wrote of an 1845 visit to Fort Boise:

The fort was a large quadrangular structure, built of adobe, inclosing quite an area, and within the thick walls were some rude dwellings and shops, which sheltered traders and artisans, who passed the long, weary years here in the heart of the remote wilderness, engaged in hunting and trapping and in trading with the Indians.[14]

Although Fort Hall was apparently quite similar to Fort Boise in form, it was constructed with a combination of cottonwood and adobe.

In log construction (right), horizontal timbers, hewn or round, are stacked and notched together at the building's corners. Notches are cut with many configurations, from the square notching shown here to round, V-shaped, and dovetail-shaped joints. (Drawing by Cheryl Marshall.)

Christian Nez Perce near Lapwai and Kamiah combined their traditional culture with techniques adopted from the whites. Here a member of the Lawyer family winnows grain using a woven basket in a farmyard that includes a log outbuilding. (ISHS 63-221.4a; E. Jane Gay, photographer.)

The descriptions of early visitors to the fort agree that the palisade was constructed of vertical cottonwood logs set about two and one-half feet into the ground and extending to a height of about fifteen feet. On the interior were log buildings with adobe-plastered chimneys and roofs. When Narcissa Prentiss Whitman stayed at Fort Hall in 1836 she saw

buildings of the Fort . . . made of hewed logs roof covered with mud bricks, chimney & fireplaces also of the same. No windows except a square hole in the roof, & in the bastion a few port holes large enough for guns only. The buildings are all enclosed in a strong log wall.[15]

By 1849, however, the fort apparently had undergone some rebuilding or plastering with adobe. Maj. Osborne Cross visited Fort Hall in August 1849 and described it as a clay construction; and a drawing by George Gibbs, of Cross's company, depicts Fort Hall as adobe. A later inventory by the Hudson's Bay Company included four adobe buildings and a wall thirteen feet high and nineteen inches thick, which was quite likely adobe.

The construction of Forts Boise and Hall proved that exposed adobe could be used with some success in southern Idaho, and Fort Hall's cottonwood log construction presaged the most common form of pioneer building to be used in the next few decades. But both con-

structions had their limitations. Both forts were greatly damaged in the spring floods of 1853.[16]

The self-sufficiency of the fur-trade compounds was partly a matter of necessity. Shipments of supplies were expensive and delayed by the difficulties of prerailroad travel. Fur traders had to spend part of their time hunting for food. But the building of agricultural compounds by the missionaries was a matter of mission strategy as well as survival. In order to Christianize the Indians, Protestant and Catholic alike assumed that Native Americans would have to drop their nomadic economy, which was based on buffalo hunting, camas digging, salmon fishing, and other seasonal hunting and gathering. Simply from a practical point of view, the missionaries could not easily convert a person who lived near the mission for only part of the year.

The Spaldings' mission to the Nez Perce, established in 1836 on Lapwai Creek, eventually included at least eleven buildings, which Henry Spalding constructed with the help of the Nez Perce, his fellow missionaries, and the few travelers who stayed at Lapwai for a season.[17] After living briefly in a pole and hide tipi, Spalding constructed his first house in 1836. It was, apparently, a *pièce sur pièce* building with a roof of wood, grass, and clay. Lumber for the building was pit-sawed by the Nez Perce.

In 1838 the Spaldings moved the Lapwai mission downstream to the mouth of Lapwai

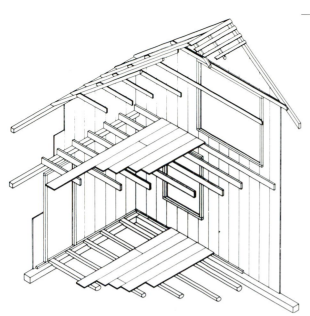

Creek, where Henry gradually built up a sizable collection of buildings. Ironically, he accomplished some of the most ambitious construction over the period 1840 to 1844, years in which his relationship with his Oregon mission colleagues and with the Nez Perce was strained and continuation of the Lapwai mission was uncertain. With the 1838 move, Spalding built a new house, this one a log building of hewn cedar (probably western red cedar) and pine timbers. Rather than use basalt for the foundation (which was readily available near the building site and which he did use for a chimney foundation in the student dormitory) he built the house with a cobblestone foundation. There were two chimneys, on the south and north gable ends. The north chimney was a wattle and daub structure, with wattle fashioned of woven laths split from conifers and adobe from the banks of Lapwai Creek mixed with grass. Excavations have shown that Spalding had access to some imported materials: window glass and machine-cut square nails. In his inventory of the Lapwai mission Spalding wrote that the roof was "lathed & wattled,"[18] suggesting that woven pieces of wood formed part of the roofing, which was coated with adobe.

Gradually, Spalding improved his house. In 1840, after his sawmill was working, he added a planed board floor; in 1842 he added boards to the roofing; and in 1844 he plastered the building, interior and exterior. His formula for plaster is left to us on the flyleaf of a note-

book: three parts clay, two parts ash, and one part sand. Historical photographs of the ruins of this building depict its long front wall with a centered door flanked by windows, a facade characteristic of traditional house types of the late nineteenth century.

Spalding went on to complete a number of major projects before he and Eliza were forced to abandon Lapwai. They included a student dormitory connected to the house by a breezeway, a blacksmith shop, two school buildings, a meetinghouse, two printshops, a spinning and weaving workshop, a poultry house, a multipurpose building used as a summer kitchen/shop/storeroom/granary/wood house, and a blockhouse that was erected following the Whitman Massacre of 1847.

While it would be inappropriate to call Spalding's building career at Lapwai sophisticated or expert, his constructions put the lie to a popular misconception about frontier architecture: that the earliest buildings were fashioned with only a few simple tools. Spalding left a tool list in his 1849 inventory of equipment left behind at Lapwai. The list included the essentials of a carpenter's tool kit: broadaxes, narrow axes, and adzes; pit, whip-, and crosscut saws; crowbars; augers and braces and bits; gouges, chisels, and drawknives; planes of many kinds, including tongue and groove; rasps, sawmill files, and small files; and squares and gauges.[19]

After 1840 most of Spalding's buildings incorporated milled lumber, but his materials

and construction techniques continued to be quite varied. Spalding erected frame buildings in which the panels were filled with an adobe and grass aggregate or with wattle and daub. It is difficult to know for certain what framing system Spalding used, but his inventory descriptions suggest that he used either heavy braced-timber framing or a lighter framing system with vertical posts set into sill and plate and spaced a few feet apart. It is possible that the buildings sided with cedar were box-constructed (vertical boards nailed to sill and plate). Spalding also used log construction in his cedar and pine house and in the blockhouse.

Spalding's experiments with adobe daub, basalt, cobblestone, cedar, and pine were successful adaptations of regional materials. The one material that proved impractical for the northern Idaho region was adobe brick. Spalding may have been inspired to experiment with adobe brick by its promotion in agricultural publications of the 1830s. However, he did not follow suggestions to cover the adobe with clapboards, and his two adobe buildings, the 1838 blacksmith shop and the 1839 printshop, were destroyed in a February 1840 rainstorm. Spalding replaced the printshop with a clapboarded frame structure.

The Spaldings' fellow missionaries Asa and Sarah Smith came to Kamiah in 1839 and lived among the Nez Perce for a little less than two years.[20] The Kamiah mission remained a smaller and more isolated settlement than

Lapwai, and the scholarly Smith was not inclined to promote the agrarian life after the manner of Spalding. Indeed, he was critical of Spalding's elaborate construction plans for Lapwai. By September 1840 the mission had only a few acres under cultivation. Asa characterized their first shelter at Kamiah as a "rude hut hastily built."[21] It was, however, quite similar to the Spaldings' first house: a *pièce sur pièce* structure with a dirt roof and without windows or flooring. The Smiths' second house was identical in construction— "built with posts grooved & set in the ground & filled with split cedar"[22]—but had the added luxury of flooring and windows. Roofing for this second house was also dirt. As drawn by Sarah Smith, its two-room plan suggests the traditional Anglo-American hall and parlor plan. The Kamiah mission also included a grass lodge built by the Nez Perce for Smith to use as a meetinghouse and a two-room house for fellow missionary Cornelius Rogers.

The 1855 Mormon mission to the Shoshoni, Bannock, Nez Perce, and Flathead Indians was located eighteen miles southeast of the present town of Salmon. Shorter lived than the Spalding mission, the Lemhi mission nonetheless had similar aims and similar problems. Like Spalding, the Mormons attempted to build up agricultural settlements designed to teach the Indians farming and to instill in them a desire for a settled life. And, as with the Spalding mission, the strategy ultimately failed, although quite substantial white settle-

ments were built and ultimately abandoned.[23] In fact, Brigham Young decided in 1857 that Fort Lemhi should become a permanent Mormon settlement in addition to its missionary purpose. As originally laid out, the Mormon mission bore a resemblance to those Mormon settlements in Utah and southeast Idaho that began as forts. The mission was enclosed by a timber stockade within which log cabins were located along the interior walls. There was also a corral constructed with two-foot-thick walls of adobe mixed with stones and grass. The settlement later acquired a blacksmith shop, a sawmill, and irrigated fields.

Coeur d'Alene Mission of the Sacred Heart

One of Father Nicholas Point's many drawings from his tenure in the Northwest depicted the chapel at the first Mission of the Sacred Heart, near present-day St. Maries. Surrounding the building were Coeur d'Alene longhouses and log buildings and pole fences adopted from white tradition. (New Mission Establishment in 1846 among the Pointed-Hearts, a sketch by Nicholas Point; Pierre Jean de Smet Papers, Washington State University Libraries.)

was the most sophisticated of these missionary attempts to convert Native Americans to Christianity by fostering an agrarian economy. From its founding by Father Nicholas Point in 1842, the Sacred Heart mission was planned like the Jesuit reductions (agrarian mission villages) of the brotherhood's earlier work in South America. Point's drawing for the first mission site, Mission Point near present-day St. Maries, depicts an axial plan with neat ranks of Coeur d'Alene dwellings and a church dominating the central axis. This proposed "Plan du Village des Coeurs-d'alênes"[24] was realized only in part at the mission's two locations. Point and the Coeurs

At the Mission of the Sacred Heart the Jesuits used braced-timber frame construction for their church building. A framework of heavy timbers was fashioned with mortise and tenon joints (the end of one timber is shaped to fit into a hole cut in a second timber). The structure was braced with diagonal timbers. Panels between timbers were filled with wattle (woven poles and twisted straw) and daub (mud applied over the wattle). (ISHS 75-228.7/G.)

d'Alenes erected a chapel at Mission Point during Holy Week, 1843. According to Point, between Holy Week and the tribes' dispersal later that spring to collect roots (probably camas roots), progress toward establishing the reduction included allotting public and private lands and planting seed. Father Point wrote in his memoirs:

At the end of October, over a hundred families were gathered in the vicinity of the church to the construction of which almost all had contributed in one way or another. To see these poor little thatched huts huddled around the chapel brought to one's mind the pelican in the desert.[25]

At the mission's 1846 location, about twenty miles east of Lake Coeur d'Alene near present-day Cataldo, the Coeur d'Alene Mission of the Sacred Heart was more completely realized. The first structure at the mission was a temporary chapel. In 1850 Father Antonio Ravalli came to the mission from St. Mary's mission (now in Montana) to supervise construction of a permanent church building. The compound grew to include a parsonage next to the church, a dormitory for the brothers, a cabin for travelers, a kitchen, and outbuildings for blacksmithing, harnessmaking, storage, baking, carpentry, and housing poultry. There were also a gristmill, a barn, a tool building, several cabins for Indians, and sev-

eral small buildings whose function remains unknown. The reduction had a cemetery, pasture, fields, and—centrally located—a large mission cross. For their many buildings the Jesuits used log construction and braced-timber frame construction secured with wooden pegs. They experimented with local stone for foundations, mud from deposits along the Coeur d'Alene River (used both as mortar and as daub), wattle woven of poles and twisted straw, and local woods. The presence of flat glass in excavations suggests that some construction supplies were imported. Unlike Spalding, the Jesuits did not use cobblestones, nor did they have a sawmill for lumber. They made the same discovery that Spalding did in their use of adobe. The wattle and daub panels of the Sacred Heart church building eroded sufficiently in the building's first few years to prompt the brothers to side the building in 1865.[26]

While Spalding and the other missionaries and fur trappers were not trained architects or builders, the Jesuits came to the Northwest with considerable expertise. It is not surprising, then, that they produced what was probably the first architecturally sophisticated building in the area, the Sacred Heart church building. Father Ravalli, the principal designer for the building, was born in Ferrara, Italy. Joining the Society of Jesus in 1827, he studied art, mechanics, and many other subjects in Italy before being ordained a priest in 1843 and joining Father Pierre-Jean De

Smet's mission to the Oregon country. Here his architectural knowledge was put to use by the brothers in a number of locations. Ravalli was at the Sacred Heart mission beginning in 1850, and the mission church was essentially completed on the exterior by 1853 when John Mix Stanley drew a view of the mission as part of a federal expedition.[27] Father Ravalli went on to design buildings at St. Ignatius mission and at St. Mary's mission in Montana,[28] but finishing work at Sacred Heart continued for some time. In 1859 Father Joseph Joset wrote of the mission:

> No one sees our church without testifying his astonishment. . . . If it were finished, it would be a handsome church even in Europe. . . . It is a great grief to us that we cannot finish it. There are two fine altars, with handsome pictures of the Sacred Heart and of the Blessed Virgin, but all the rest is naked, without doors, windows, or flooring, and not being framed in on the outside, I fear it will rot before it is completed.[29]

Other Jesuits took a hand in the building's design. As originally built, the church's timber frame and wattle and daub panels were left exposed. In 1865 Father Joseph Caruana sided the building with clapboards and finished the interior with pine. Brother Francis Huybrechts assembled the wooden ceiling panels, each of them incorporating a different baroque design. Throughout construction, the

In his design for the church at Mission of the Sacred Heart, Father Ravalli recreated the baroque features of Italian churches using local materials. The wooden false front forms a curved baroque pediment embellished with urns. Below the pediment is a portico (columned porch) with classical columns supporting an entablature. The photograph shows the building after its 1976 restoration. (ISHS 1985-5.35/a.)

Coeur d'Alenes provided free labor for the building.

Given its place and time, the Sacred Heart church was a remarkable accomplishment. Ravalli's design reflects the Jesuit tradition exemplified in *Il Gesu,* the Jesuit's Roman church. Using a wooden false front and massive timbers for columns, he created a facade dominated by a curved baroque gable above a columned classical portico. On the interior there are decorative wood carvings and painting simulating marble, creating from simple materials a resplendent baroque character.

Today little remains of the early forts and missions to represent the efforts of Spalding, Wyeth, McKay, Thompson, and their fellows. In fact, the Cataldo church building, designated a National Historic Landmark for its architectural values and its historical importance, is a rare survival. On the surface, this elaborately styled building would appear unrepresentative. In many respects, however, the mission church does represent white architecture from this era in Idaho history. The church was substantially built with a European-derived structural system but using materials available near the building site. It was part of a larger compound within which there was considerable variety of materials and construction. Its style was based on the traditions of its builders.

Because the architecture of the fur trappers and missionaries is known principally from their writings, it is difficult to say much about the style and forms of their buildings and much easier to generalize about materials, structure, and the circumstances of construction. The trappers and missionaries uncovered usable local stone deposits. They discovered the failings of exposed adobe north of the arid Snake River Plain as well as its limitations in the south. They introduced several Indian groups to carpentry and to Euroamerican house forms like the log cabin. They demonstrated the workability of local woods like red cedar and pine. Wood, a staple for the structure of prehistoric and Native American architecture, became the basic material for white architecture throughout the region, augmented by local stone where it was available.

In the midst of all this experimentation, the trappers and missionaries also held to tradition. Building widely separated compounds, they nonetheless used a remarkably similar architectural vocabulary chosen out of French Canadian, Hudson's Bay, and American frontier traditions. These standard forms included the palisade, a few wooden framing systems, and special uses for adobe. At Forts Boise, Hall, and Lemhi, they built square or rectangular enclosures for their settlement compounds—a descendant of the American colonial palisade—constructed of vertical timbers sunk into the ground or, in the unusual cases of Forts Boise and Hall as rebuilt, of adobe. Even the Mission of the Sacred Heart had a fence marking off the boundary between reduction and wilderness. At Lapwai and Ca-

taldo they used frame construction with wattle and daub paneling—a construction common in colonial New England and known throughout Europe. At Kullyspell, Lapwai, and Kamiah they used a French-American form, *pièce sur pièce* construction (called Red River style by the Hudson's Bay Company) with easily split cedar. At Lapwai, Fort Hall, Lemhi, and Cataldo they used log construction of cedar, pine, or cottonwood. And at all the missions and forts, adobe—usually in combination with grasses or cobbles—was a plaster substitute for roofing, chimneys, or walls. In fact, the cat and clay chimney with a wooden framework and adobe daub and the wooden pole roof with an adobe plaster seem to have been standard practices of the era. Did the fur trappers and missionaries build using traditional house types like the hall and parlor house, or popular styles like Greek Revival? One can only assume that they were as tradition-bound with regard to form and style as they were in matters of construction and that a suggestion of style may have appeared in such matters as massing, roof pitch, and gable orientation.

When Father Pierre-Jean De Smet visited the Sacred Heart mission in 1858–1859 he remarked that the church there "would be a credit to any civilized country."[30] Clearly the point of reference for the white builders of this period was the world outside the region. Standards for construction and style came from without; only the materials were indigenous.

The sweathouse, longhouse, pit house, and tipi — the truly indigenous forms of the Native American tradition — were abandoned in this era and with them the spiritual link between geography and humankind.

Notes

1. Epigraph quoted from Ronald E. McFarland and William Studebaker, *Idaho's Poetry: A Centennial Anthology* (Moscow, Idaho: University of Idaho Press, 1988), 27.

2. Deward E. Walker, Jr., describes sweathouses of the Kutenai and other tribes in *Indians of Idaho* (Moscow, Idaho: University of Idaho Press, 1978), 34, 46, 53, 55, 76, 82. Walker discusses the spiritual and practical role of the sweathouse in Nez Perce culture in his article, "The Nez Perce Sweat Bath Complex: An Acculturational Analysis," *Southwestern Journal of Anthropology* 22 (1966):133–71. The degree to which the Plains tipi was adapted to its environment is discussed by Carroll Van West in "Acculturation by Design: Architectural Determinism and the Montana Indian Reservations, 1870–1930," *Great Plains Quarterly* 7, no. 2 (Spring 1987):97–100.

3. Information about Idaho geography can be found in the following sources: Harry H. Caldwell, ed., *Idaho Economic Atlas* (Moscow, Idaho: Idaho Bureau of Mines and Geology, 1970); *The Compact Atlas of Idaho* (Moscow, Idaho: Center for Business Development and Research and Cart-O-Graphics, 1983); *Idaho Almanac* (Boise: Office of the Governor and Division of Tourism and Industrial Development, 1977); and David J. Stevlingson, *Climates of the States: Idaho*, Climatography of the United States, no. 60–10 (Washington, D.C.: U.S. Commerce Department, Weather Bureau, December 1959).

4. The indigenous flora and fauna of Idaho are described in Rexford F. Daubenmire, "Plant Geography of Idaho," in *Flora of Idaho*, ed. Ray J. Davis (Provo, Utah:

Brigham Young University Press, 1952), 1–17; and F. D. Johnson, *Native Trees of Idaho*, Idaho Agricultural Extension Service Bulletin, no. 289 (Moscow, Idaho: University of Idaho, January 1966).

5. Soil and stone deposits in Idaho and their use in construction are discussed in R. R. Asher, *Volcanic Construction Materials in Idaho*, Idaho Bureau of Mines and Geology Pamphlet, no. 135 (Moscow, Idaho: 1965); Charles H. Behre, Jr., "Volcanic Tuffs and Sandstones Used as Building Stones in the Upper Salmon River Valley, Idaho," in *Contributions to Economic Geology, 1929*, U.S. Geological Survey Bulletin 811, ed. G. F. Loughlin, G. R. Mansfield, and E. F. Burchard (Washington, D.C., 1930), 237–48; "Idaho Building Stone," in *Twenty-Sixth Annual Report of the Mining Industry of Idaho for the Year 1924* ([Boise]: Idaho Inspector of Mines, [1924]), 16–19; G. F. Loughlin, "Idaho," in *Mineral Resources of the United States*, 2 pts. (Washington, D.C.: U.S. Geological Survey, 1914), 2:1,376–87; Clyde P. Ross and J. Donald Forrester, *Outline of the Geology of Idaho*, Idaho Bureau of Mines and Geology Bulletin, no. 15 (Moscow, Idaho, May 1958); and Sylvia H. Ross and Carl N. Savage, *Idaho Earth Science: Geology, Fossils, Climate, Water, and Soils*, Earth Science Series, no. 1 (Moscow, Idaho: Idaho Bureau of Mines and Geology, 1967).

6. Arthur A. Hart, "Farm and Ranch Buildings East of the Cascades," in *Space, Style and Structure: Building in Northwest America*, 2 vols., ed. Thomas Vaughn and Virginia Guest Ferriday (Portland, Oregon: Oregon Historical Society, 1974), 1:244.

7. For information about the architecture of Idaho's prehistoric peoples I am indebted to Kenneth M. Ames, "Instability in Prehistoric Residential Patterns on the Intermontane Plateau" (Paper delivered at the Northwest Anthropological Conference, Tacoma, Washington, 1988); and Thomas J. Green, "Aboriginal Residential Structures in Southern Idaho" (Paper delivered at the Great Basin Anthropological Conference, Park City, Utah, 1988).

8. Basic information about Idaho Indian groups and their architecture is in Walker, *Indians of Idaho*. Changes in Indian culture with white contact are documented by Sven Liljeblad in *The Idaho Indians in Transition, 1805–1960* (Pocatello, Idaho: The Idaho State University Museum, 1972); and "Indian Peoples in Idaho," Intermountain West Collection, Eli M. Oboler Library, Idaho State University, Pocatello, Idaho. The E. Jane Gay Photograph Collection, Idaho State Historical Society (hereafter ISHS), Boise, is a good source for Nez Perce architecture influenced by white contact. The First Presbyterian Church at Kamiah, built by the Nez Perce, is documented by Merle W. Wells in a National Register of Historic Places nomination form on file at ISHS, Boise. Examples of modern Nez Perce architecture can be found in Allen P. Slickpoo's *Noon Nee-Me-Poo (We, the Nez Perces): Culture and History of the Nez Perces* ([Lapwai, Idaho]: Nez Perce Tribe of Idaho, 1973), 72, 196–99, 238, 260, 261; and in Walker, "Nez Perce Sweat Bath Complex."

9. Walker, "Nez Perce Sweat Bath Complex," 154.

10. Erwin N. Thompson, *Historic Resource Study, Spalding Area: Nez Perce National Historical Park/Idaho* (Denver: U.S. Department of Interior, National Park Service, September 1972), 86. The Whitman Massacre of November 1847 brought Marcus and Narcissa Whitman's mission at Waiilatpu (in present-day Washington) to a tragic end. Suspecting Marcus of witchcraft, the Cayuse killed the Whitmans and twelve other whites.

11. Richard Glover, ed., *David Thompson's Narrative of His Explorations in Western America, 1784–1812* (Toronto: The Champlain Society, 1962), 297. See also Merle W. Wells, "'A House for Trading': David Thompson on Pend d'Oreille Lake," *Idaho Yesterdays* 3, no. 3 (Fall 1959): 22–26.

12. A. W. Thompson, "New Light on Donald Mackenzie's Post on the Clearwater, 1812–13," *Idaho Yesterdays* 18, no. 3 (Fall 1974):25–27.

13. Merrill D. Beal, *A History of Southeastern Idaho* (Caldwell, Idaho: The Caxton Printers, 1942), 89; and

"Fort Boise: From Imperial Outpost to Historic Site," *Idaho Yesterdays* 6, no. 1 (Spring 1962):16.

14. W. A. Goulder, *Reminiscences: Incidents in the Life of a Pioneer in Oregon and Idaho* (Boise: Timothy Regan, 1909; reprint edition, Moscow, Idaho: University of Idaho Press, 1990), 122.

15. Narcissa Prentiss Whitman, *My Journal, 1836,* 2d ed., ed. Lawrence L. Dodd (Fairfield, Washington: Ye Galleon Press, 1984), 22.

16. For more information about the construction of Forts Hall and Boise, see Richard G. Beidleman, "Nathaniel Wyeth's Fort Hall," *Oregon Historical Quarterly* 58, no. 3 (September 1957):225–26; Jennie Broughton Brown, *Fort Hall on the Oregon Trail: A Historical Study* (Caldwell, Idaho: The Caxton Printers, 1932), 164, 266, 289, 311, 343–44; "Fort Boise: From Imperial Outpost to Historic Site," *Idaho Yesterdays* 6, no. 1 (Spring 1962): 14–16, 33–39; "Fort Hall, 1834–1856," *Idaho Yesterdays* 12, no. 2 (Summer 1968):28–31; Arthur A. Hart, "Fur Trade Posts and Early Missions," in *Space, Style and Structure,* 1:39; and Osborne Russell, *Journal of a Trapper: Or Nine Years in the Rocky Mountains, 1834–1843* (Boise: Syms-York Company, 1921), 11.

17. Construction at Lapwai is richly documented in a variety of primary sources. These references are compiled in Thompson, *Historic Resource Study, Spalding Area.* Further documentation of construction at the Spalding mission is available in David H. Chance and Jennifer V. Chance, *Exploratory Excavations at Spalding Mission, 1973,* University

of Idaho Anthropological Research Manuscript Series, no. 14 (Moscow, Idaho, 1974), 89–90, 99–105. For a summary of publications promoting adobe construction in the 1830s and 1840s, see Richard Pieper, "Earthen Architecture in New York State," abstract in *Perspectives in Vernacular Architecture, III,* ed. Thomas Carter and Bernard L. Herman (Columbia: University of Missouri Press, 1989), 237–38.

18. Clifford Merrill Drury, ed., *The Diaries and Letters of Henry H. Spalding and Asa Bowen Smith Relating to the Nez Perce Mission, 1838–1842,* Northwest Historical Series, no. 4 (Glendale, California: The Arthur H. Clark Company, 1958), 361.

19. Ibid., 359–66.

20. Information about construction at Kamiah is culled from the Smiths' writings, ibid., 103, 113, 118, 121–22, 184.

21. Ibid., 121.

22. Ibid., 122.

23. Lawrence G. Coates discusses the parallels between Protestant and Mormon missionary strategy in "The Spalding-Whitman and Lemhi Missions: A Comparison," *Idaho Yesterdays* 31, no. 1–2 (Spring/Summer 1987):43. More about the Salmon River mission is available in Beal, *History of Southeastern Idaho,* 136–52; John D. Nash, "The Salmon River Mission of 1855," *Idaho Yesterdays* 11, no. 1 (Spring 1967):22–31; and "Salmon River Mission," Idaho Historic Sites Series, no. 3 (Boise: ISHS, n.d.).

24. Nicholas Point, S.J., *Wilderness Kingdom: Indian Life*

in the Rocky Mountains, 1840–1847, trans. Joseph P. Donnelly, S.J. (New York: Holt, Rinehart and Winston, 1967), plate 58.

25. Ibid., 94. See also page 79 for a description of the reduction.

26. Observations about the construction of the buildings at Cataldo can be found in Harold Allen, *Father Ravalli's Missions* (Chicago: The School of the Art Institute of Chicago, 1972), 18–29; and George Fielder and Roderick Sprague, *Test Excavations at the Coeur d'Alene Mission of the Sacred Heart, Cataldo, Idaho, 1973,* University of Idaho Anthropological Research Manuscript Series, no. 13 (Moscow, Idaho, 1974), 11–24, 40–44. The mission church has been documented by the Historic American Buildings Survey, HABS ID-1, copies on file at the Library of Congress, Washington, D.C., and ISHS, Boise.

27. *Reports of Explorations and Surveys,* vol. 12, book 1, 36th Cong., 1st sess., S. Exec. Doc. 133 (Washington, D.C.: Thomas H. Ford, 1860), pl. 35 opposite 133; reproduced in Allen, *Father Ravalli's Missions,* 24.

28. Details of Father Ravalli's career are in Allen, *Father Ravalli's Missions,* 9–21.

29. Quoted in Pierre-Jean De Smet, S.J., *New Indian Sketches* (1865; facsimile reproduction, Seattle, Washington: The Shorey Bookstore, 1971), 66.

30. Hiram Martin Chittenden and Alfred Talbot Richardson, *Life, Letters and Travels of Father Pierre-Jean De Smet, S.J., 1801–1873,* 4 vols.(1905; reprint ed., New York: Arno Press and The New York Times, 1969), 2:760.

2

In Search of Materials and Builders, 1860–1879

Fort Boise, Idaho Territory
July 27, 1863

My darling little daughter:

By the last express, I received your letter. . . . I will not be able to get a Newfoundland dog for Jackey, as this place is too hot for wooly dogs to live here. They are only good in places where we have plenty of rain & very little dry weather. This place is a good deal like Texas. The air is dry and hot & we always have a slight breeze blowing. The new fort is getting along slowly, but we are almost ready to go to work in earnest. The saw mill was started yesterday & will commence sawing at once. The adobe yard is ready & we can now burn lime whenever we need it. The Quarter Master's corral is about two thirds done. The blacksmith shop will be finished, when we get shingles to cover it. The bakehouse is being built now & will soon be ready to run. We have given a contract to some people to cut & stack us all the hay on a large island. We have also given a contract to some people, to make shingles & when the saw-mill gets to running well, we will be able to go to work and build quarters for officers & men to live in. The quarters for officers and men, are to be built of sandstone. The quarters for the laundresses will be built of logs. I think that I will have all the houses we will need this year, built before snow falls & next year — if any more people come here, we can build houses for them. I believe that all kinds of vegetables can be raised here next year. Tell Lieut. Means & Moss, to save me all kind of seed for my garden next year; as I am too poor to buy any seed & we must have some vegetables next year to keep off the scurvy.

When he set out to establish a United States military post near the Boise Basin gold mines, Maj. Pinckney Lugenbeel had to solve the problems encountered by every settler new to the territory.[1] How was he to build a fort where there were—as yet—no sawmills, no brickyards, no quarries, no blacksmith shops, no kilns, and few if any professional builders or architects? In Lugenbeel's letter to his daughter he described with some satisfaction the completion of part of the task before him. He had, by the end of July 1863, set up a mule-powered sawmill, located adobe mud and set up a yard for making adobe bricks, found lime and built a lime kiln, built a blacksmith shop, and located a source of good sandstone in the Boise foothills. Later that year he was fortunate to have a knowledgeable brickmaker and -layer, an Englishman named Charles May, come down from the Boise Basin to lay sandstone for the quartermaster's building, completed 1864.[2]

Like Lugenbeel, settlers came to Idaho Territory equipped with tools and an idea of what a building should look like. But in order to translate their architectural traditions into whole buildings the settlers found it was necessary first to seek sources of raw materials, then to extract and process them into building materials. Finally, settlers who were not experienced in construction had to locate workers who knew how to lay a masonry wall or frame a wooden structure. The chief architec-

tural problem of the era was the search for materials and builders.

After E. D. Pierce's gold discovery at Orofino and the Mormon establishment of Franklin, both in 1860, the region soon to become Idaho Territory experienced a rapid influx of settlers from west and east at once. To the Idaho gold mines came disappointed forty-niners, a mixture of Americans, Chinese, Mexicans, and Europeans. To southeast Idaho came Mormon town builders from Utah Territory, a mixture of northeasterners, mid-westerners, and converts from western and northern Europe. As different as their motivations were, both miners and Mormons brought into the region a vocabulary of constructions and styles derived from the eastern and midwestern United States and parts of Europe. Their traditions included several building types and architectural styles and numerous technologies for building with logs, stone, milled lumber, and brick. By 1879 major settlement centers were established, a sense of white cultural regions began to emerge, and in each of those regions Idaho architecture began to demonstrate standardized trends.

Northern, central, and southwestern Idaho first developed as mining areas, and the boom-bust mining economy supported four principal settlement forms: mining camps; supply towns; isolated farms, ranches, and way stations that supplied the mining population with fresh meat and produce; and government cen-

Masonry construction with Boise sandstone was used for the quartermaster's office at military Fort Boise, shown here in about 1890. Mason Charles May laid up the ashlar (cut) stone in randomly coursed rows. (National Archives 92-F-10-11.)

ters such as the military forts and Indian agencies established to control the conflicts that arose with containment of the Indian population on restricted portions of their territory. By the 1870 census, communities had formed in and around the Clearwater mines, the Salmon River mines, Boise Basin, Jordan Creek, the middle and south forks of the Boise River, the upper Salmon, and Stanley Basin.

The early mining camps contained nothing as stylistically sophisticated or as substantially built as the Sacred Heart mission church, or even as Spalding's more haphazard constructions. The missionaries, building with a purpose that looked ahead to permanent farm settlements of Christianized Indians, built as substantially as they could. But in their first years many of the mining camps, built by temporary exploiters of the streams and hillsides, were little more than main streets lined with tents and one-story log, box, or frame constructed shelters. Many of the camps never grew beyond those limits.

The uniformity of mining camps is not surprising when one considers that—due to the nature of prospecting—the inhabitants shifted rapidly and widely from place to place and therefore shared ideas and information with their immediate predecessors, the missionaries and trappers, and among themselves. This cosmopolitan pool of wealth seekers took ideas about expedient shelter from California north to British Columbia and Alaska and east to Montana, the Dakotas, and Colorado. In the process a standard form emerged for the mining camp.

Created in the midst of mining claims, haphazard settlement, and steep topography, the mining town nevertheless was a ghost image of the ingrained American grid plan, with a main street of gable-fronted buildings side by side along a more or less consistent setback. Camps were laid out in the scanty flatland along stream beds. The lack of flatland and pressure to use it for mining rather than town building made the camps crowded and compact. A measure of their impermanence was the tendency literally to undermine buildings, leading to the collapse of some. That this common mining camp streetscape appeared throughout Idaho's mining regions is documented in numerous historical photographs and in early descriptions. Reports of Orofino, Pierce City, Florence, and Idaho City describe a long main street with frame and log houses ranged along it. A San Francisco *Daily Alta California* correspondent, C. Aubrey Angelo, wrote of Idaho City in 1863, "the principal street, as yet unnamed, is one mile and a quarter in length by ninety feet wide [perhaps an exaggeration], and from one end to the other is a continued line of frame buildings."[3] Within a few years Idaho City and other successful mining camps, like Silver City, became cosmopolitan centers with some of the territory's most impressive buildings.

Although many of the mining camps were doomed to shrink as the most accessible and most cheaply processed ore was eventually mined out, the service communities, farms, and ranches survived to form permanent settlements. Originally, though, they were little more substantial than the mining camps. Lewiston began as a tent town. Boise buildings were "built mostly of adobe, logs or boards, the doors of which opened on the street with the proverbial latch string hanging down."[4] These settlements were laid out near rivers or creeks, often where two streams ran together or at the point where a creek entered a valley.

A service town's grid plan usually paralleled a creek or river. It included a main street for commerce crossed by numbered, lettered, or named streets. The first service towns were only a few blocks in size, their residential neighborhoods close to a main street. Residential yards could be quite large, often including agricultural uses such as pastureland or orchards. Along the main street, though, buildings were spaced closely together to approximate an urban streetscape, however modest their size and style.[5]

Farms, ranches, and way stations were located convenient to water, arable land, range, and transportation routes. Often a single establishment, like the Mitchell, Marsh and Ireton ranch on the Payette River near present-day Emmett, served more than one purpose, operating as ranch and way station in one. Water and timber were important considerations in locating a farm or ranch. Like

the towns, these were often established at the point where a stream entered its alluvial plain or on a major stream, providing for small littoral irrigation systems. The former were prime flatland locations, close to timber and guaranteed a water supply throughout the year.

The layout of farms and ranches varied considerably. The house was usually set separately from barnyard and corrals. The one outbuilding that might be close to the house, other than an outhouse, was a cellar, often built into a hillside. The farmyard, consisting of outbuildings, pasture, corrals, and orchards, could be to the rear or side of the house or across a lane or road. Farmyards had numerous small outbuildings serving specialized functions—chicken house, horse barn, cow barn, silo—and arranged in various configurations around the farmyard—linear, L, or rectangular plans, for example. A ranch might have upper and lower pastures, each with dwellings, outbuildings, and corrals. An upper, or summer, pasture was typically located near a spring.[6]

In contrast to the mining areas, southeast Idaho was developed as a frontier of northern Utah. Mormon settlers came into southeast Idaho from Utah to establish Mormon villages, a distinct type of cooperative settlement that grouped farm families together in a grid-plan town and allotted the surrounding, untenanted land for farming. By the time Mormons established Franklin in 1860, a strategy

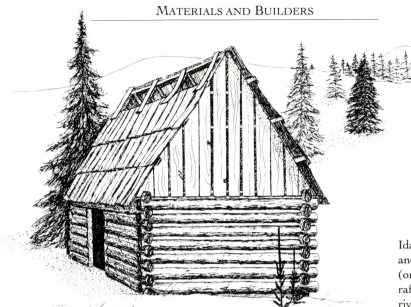

Idaho miners built simple cabins with round logs and simple corner notching. This is a single-cell (one room) house with round notching and a rafter roof structure covered with shakes (hand-riven shingles). (Drawing by Cheryl Marshall.)

for settlement had been worked out in numerous Utah communities. Using the findings of reconnaissance parties, Brigham Young decided the locations of new villages, called individuals with the skills needed, and sent out the settlement parties. On site, each group first established a fort, a square of log houses with or without a palisade, then platted the village and parceled out village lots and arable fields surrounding the village. Finally, in the first years of settlement an irrigation system was established to support agriculture and lumber and flour mills, and other industries were established to make the village self-supporting.

The Mormon village plat was based on Joseph Smith's ideal town, the City of Zion. Villages were a mile square and laid out parallel with section lines, therefore aligned with compass directions. Two principal streets crossed at a central square where land was allotted for public and church buildings. Businesses were located nearby, and residential lots were found on the numbered streets, which were aligned with the two principal streets. The Mormon village plan was derived from the English system, followed in colonial New England, of allotment of lands in a village for residential use and of lands outside the village for farming. Farmers lived in the village rather than on isolated farms. Their village lots included space for specialized agricultural uses. A Mormon farmer might own a quarter- or half-block, for example, with one or more

houses located on its corners and with the interior of the lot devoted to small outbuildings and fenced yards for chickens, pigs, horses, or milk cows. This Mormon village plan is still visible in early Mormon settlements like Franklin and Paris.[7]

The mining towns, service communities, and Mormon villages had diverse origins and distinct plans, but their architecture had much in common. The miners, farmers, ranchers, and Mormons sought out the same materials, built in similar styles, and used similar house plans. One can best compare their buildings by looking at the way each group used available materials. What did they use for temporary shelter? How did they build with log timbers, with adobe bricks, with stone, with milled lumber, and with fired brick?

All over Idaho temporary shelters like dugouts and tents were commonly used. In fact, tents were probably the most common shelters for the miners of the 1860s, especially for those wintering elsewhere and working their claims only when water was available in the wet spring and early summer months. "We have no *other* place to stick our heads but, in this country, where the climate is so mild, a tent answers a very good purpose, and hundreds there are among us, who occupy them during a quarter of the year," C. N. Teeter wrote of his accommodations in Idaho City during June 1864.[8]

Most settlers, including the miners who intended to stay more than a season, eventually

built more permanent shelter. Many undertook construction by themselves or with the help of neighbors. If the miners took the advice of guidebooks like John L. Campbell's *Six Months in the New Gold-diggings*, they came to the territory equipped with a few basic woodworking tools. Campbell prescribed axes, a handsaw, a drawknife, chisels, augers, a hatchet, a hammer, and ten pounds of machine-cut nails as well as a tent and cast-iron stove.[9] The Mormons came well prepared for construction. Often settlement parties included skilled builders like Lorenzo Hatch, a Franklin pioneer who combined carpentry with farming and serving as a bishop. By 1870, according to one count, Idaho Territory had 160 people supporting themselves in the construction trades.[10]

The Idaho environment offered carpenters plenty of wood suitable for building. Even in the desert areas of the south, timber could be hauled from mountain creek canyons; and settlers did that heavy labor, for their architectural tradition was predominantly based on wood. Building with wood took several forms, but one of the earliest put to use throughout the territory was log construction.[11]

Especially during the 1860s the log cabin was a staple, used for institutional and commercial buildings as well as for housing. In the mining camps the cabin was expediently constructed with round timbers, pine or cottonwood, joined with the simpler corner-notching systems—round, V, or square notches. Often

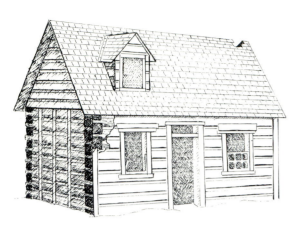

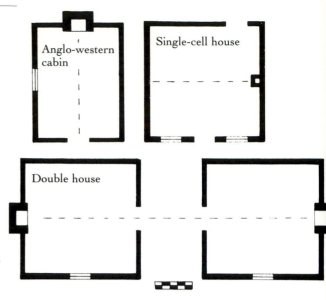

Substantial log buildings can be found in the Mormon villages of southeast Idaho. This single-cell example (left) in Paris has a dormered half-story, hewn logs framed together with square notching, and milled clapboard siding, window and door moldings, and shingles. (Drawing by Cheryl Marshall.)

Traditional house plans of the 1860s and 1870s (right) included the Anglo-western cabin, the single-cell house, and the double house. The Anglo-western cabin was one room with its front wall on the gable end of the house. The single-cell house was one room with its front wall on the lateral (long, nongable) end of the house. The double house consisted of two one-room units with a breezeway between, all under one long roof. (Drawings by Cheryl Marshall.)

the miners employed a gable and roof system purely of logs—log purlins and gables—covered with split shakes, a roof material readily available in western red cedar areas.

Outside of the mining frontier, log construction served as both temporary and more durable shelter and took a slightly more substantial form than in the mining camps. Log construction was used for way stations like the 1870s Fry trading post in Bonners Ferry and the Rock Creek (later Stricker) stage station (1865); military posts like Fort Hall (1870) and Camp Three Forks in Owyhee County (1866) housed troops in log buildings; and log construction was used at the Lapwai Indian Agency. Early farms and ranches in the Boise and Weiser river valleys and in the Owyhee rangeland were built with horizontal logs. In supply towns like Boise and Lewiston some of the earliest houses were log. Log construction was most prevalent, however, in the Mormon settlements of southeast Idaho. Not only were most of the first buildings in a Mormon village built with horizontal log timbers, but log construction also continued to serve there as a major construction throughout the nineteenth century.

Most of the log buildings in Mormon villages and service towns were constructed with round timbers, but some had hewn timbers instead, and those were usually notched together using corner timbering that required more skill and produced a tighter, stronger structure than the mining cabin: V notching,

square notching (sometimes secured on the interior of the notch with wooden pegs), and half- and full-dovetail notching. The dirt and pole roof that had been used by the missionaries and trappers had become a standard practice in the arid inland West. It was used by townspeople, farmers, and ranchers (Mormon and non-Mormon) for a first roof that could later be replaced with shingles. One Oregon Trail immigrant noted of the Mormons in Bear River valley that

> they live in little villages, built of pine logs covered with poles first, then grass, over which is thrown several inches of clay and gravel precisely after the style of every building we have seen on the road after leaving Big and Little Blue in Nebraska Territory, except a few buildings in Kearney and Bridger.[12]

In the Boise Valley, Junius Wright built his winter cabin near present-day Caldwell with a roof of "split poles and hay and covered the hay with dirt to hold it down," finding that "many of the settlers along the river had built their cabins in this way and [I] thought it safe to try it."[13]

Wherever they were built, log houses of this era were usually modest one-room buildings. In fact, building with logs, especially cottonwood or lodgepole, lent itself to the one-room plan of about sixteen feet on a side. The earliest and roughest shelters had a single room entered on the gable end of the building, a

plan sometimes called the Anglo-western cabin. Many miners' cabins, the Sleight cabin in Paris (circa 1863), the first log cabins in Franklin, and Wright's house near Caldwell were examples of this simple house plan. Wright clearly described how space could be allotted in such a plan.

> We planned for a log cabin about 16 feet square, placed close up against the hill with a door in the west end and a chimney made of canyon rock at the east end with a wide fire place for cooking and loafing and spinning yarns for pastime in the evening. . . . At the door in the west end we curtained off a sleeping room on one side for myself and wife and on the other side a room for Joel Richards and Mr. Payne [fellow travelers]. The other part was our sitting room and parlor.[14]

A few settlers instead built log double houses (sometimes called dogtrot houses). The double house was a form from the southern United States in which two square rooms separated by a breezeway were joined under a single gable roof. As rough as these shelters may appear to us today, they were regarded as comfortable by their occupants, who described their log houses as commodious, substantial, dry, and strong.

Another common house type—the single-cell plan—also consisted of one square room, but the front door was on the longer, nongable side of the house. The O'Farrell and Coston

Carpenters skilled in log construction built the 1862 Shoshone County Courthouse at Pierce with hewn logs framed together with half-dovetail joints (notches cut at a slant so that the butt ends of the logs have the profile of half a dove's tail). The front wall of the building, shown here, has a braced-timber frame. (ISHS 79-5.157/r.)

houses of Boise (both 1863), the first of Charles Rich's houses in Paris (circa 1864), the Johnston brothers' house near present-day Caldwell (1864), and the Gilmore ranch house in Owyhee County (1878) are all examples of this house plan.

The roughest of the log buildings could be constructed quickly and with few tools. Craftsmanlike log buildings were built, though, for structures intended to play a permanent and central role in a community. The 1862 Shoshone County Courthouse at Pierce, one of the few mining-camp survivors, is just such an exception. It was constructed for $3,700 by builders N. Keith and R. C. Reed, whose names appear on the building specifications, dated July 26, 1862.[15] Built twenty by thirty feet, the courthouse combines log and braced-frame construction. Three walls are formed of hewn white-pine timbers laid horizontally and notched together with half-dovetail corners. The fourth wall, the front, is a heavy braced-frame construction with its plate and sill beams notched into the side walls. On all four walls, the top rank of timbers is further secured with wooden pegs driven vertically through the corner joints. Similarly substantial hewn-log buildings were constructed to serve as a school in Florence (1864) and as a jail at Buena Vista in Boise Basin (1864), another public building that was built under contract.

The prevalence of log construction has provided the chief symbol of pioneer life, but the

log cabin was only one of the options used by white settlers. Adobe and stone masonry were early alternatives to log construction. Neither material was used much in northern Idaho. In the south, though, stone and adobe found specialized uses.

Sun-dried adobe bricks were put to use principally during the 1860s. In Boise, the 1863 Cyrus Jacobs store was built with adobe brick, as was Thomas E. Logan's house, an 1865 adobe that he purchased from Boise businessman James Crawford in 1868. Other

The Logan house in Boise (below) was built with small sun-baked bricks made from local adobe deposits mixed with manure and twigs. The walls of the building are three withes (brick thicknesses) deep. (ISHS 72-100.91.)

One of Idaho's finest examples of the Greek Revival style is the Lorenzo Hatch house in Franklin (below, right). The builder used local stone to create outset quoins at the building's corners. Along the eaves are wooden dentils (toothlike projections). Eave returns at the bottom of the front gable turn the gable space into a triangular pediment reminiscent of the Greek temples that inspired Greek Revival. It was typical for a Greek Revival house to have its front wall on the gable end of the building. (ISHS 72-100.33/E; Arthur A. Hart, photographer.)

adobe buildings existed in Boise, and at least one adobe was constructed at Walter's Ferry, located on the Snake River near present-day Murphy. And Charles Rich built four adobe brick houses in the 1870s for those of his wives that accompanied him to Paris. Even in the arid southern Idaho climate adobe buildings developed moisture problems, and by 1865 Boise's adobes were being rebuilt with stone foundations.[16] In the Logan house, moisture problems were solved with an exterior coat of red oil-based paint, first applied sometime before 1872.

The Logan house and the Walter's Ferry building illustrate some typical features of adobe construction and some departures as well. Both are small, one-story buildings. The fourteen-inch adobe walls of the Logan house were built with three withes of small adobes about the size of standard fired brick and molded in sand-dusted molds (a technique used for fired brick but unusual for adobes). The adobes in the Walter's Ferry building more nearly approximate the normal size of adobe bricks, which are generally larger than fired brick. The adobe of both buildings came from near the building site, yielding bricks with a low clay content (less than 10 percent). The Logan adobes were strengthened with manure and twigs and were laid up with adobe mortar, typical of adobe buildings generally. Also typical is the Walter's Ferry roof system, a rafter roof sitting directly on plates that rest on the lateral walls of the building.[17]

Stone construction also served specialized uses in southwestern and southeastern Idaho. In the southeast, stone was used quite early for houses as well as commercial and institutional buildings as an alternative to log or adobe construction. All three materials fulfilled the Mormon settlers' preference for substantial housing materials. In any call for would-be settlers Brigham Young included artisans of various skilled trades. A Mormon village usually had at least one person knowledgeable in stonework and a corp of residents ready for cooperative labor. In addition, southeastern Idaho had several deposits of easily worked tuff, which lent itself to frontier exploitation. In southwestern Idaho, however,

stone construction required a large financial investment and skilled labor. In that quarter of the state, stone was reserved for institutional or commercial construction.

The stone houses of Franklin exemplify the remarkably early and finely crafted stonework of the Mormons. They include the 1865 Doney house, designed in the Greek Revival style; the James Chadwick house, built about 1870; the 1872 Lorenzo Hatch house, also Greek Revival style; and the 1875 Lafayette Hatch house. These and other southeastern Idaho houses of the era demonstrate a clear link with Utah tradition not only in their use of stone but also in their traditional house plans, which were as basic to Mormon life as

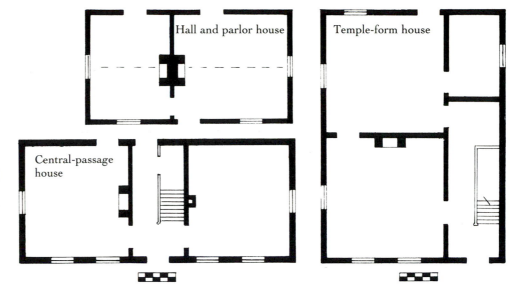

Three common mid-nineteenth-century traditional house plans constructed in southeast Idaho were the hall and parlor house, the central-passage house, and the temple-form house (right). The hall and parlor house had two rooms, one square and one rectangular, alongside each other. The central-passage house had a central hallway flanked by square rooms. Both plans had entrances on a lateral wall. The temple-form house had a gable front and a floor plan with a side hallway. (Drawings by Cheryl Marshall.)

the ranch style house is to us today. They included the single-cell plan, the hall and parlor plan, the central-passage plan, and the temple-form plan. This last house plan derived from housing traditions in New England and upstate New York and almost always was used with the Greek Revival style. The Lorenzo Hatch house was a classic example of this characteristic pairing of the temple-form plan with the Greek Revival style. The building's ashlar stone finish, quoining, gable returns, denticulated eaves, and gable front make it the state's best survival of the Greek Revival style.

In southwest Idaho, occasional uses of

stone included cobblestone cellars, such as those at the Mitchell, Marsh and Ireton ranch (circa 1863) and at the Montgomery house, Middleton (circa 1870), and a few scattered business and institutional buildings, such as the E. J. Curtis law office (1868) and the Broadbent store (1869), both in Boise, and the Owyhee County Courthouse (circa 1870) in Silver City. But this era also saw the first use of Boise sandstone to build a handful of the state's most substantial early buildings. They were made possible through federal funding of a military fort, a penitentiary, and an assay office.

The earliest of these government projects

was Fort Boise, where the efforts of Maj. Pinckney Lugenbeel and his successors eventually led to construction of a full complement of stone, brick, and frame buildings on officers' row. The fort's first buildings include Charles May's sandstone officer's house (Building No. 1) and the quartermaster building, both completed in 1864.[18]

Charles May was also the successful bidder for construction of the 1871 Idaho penitentiary, which he built using Boise sandstone quarried on the penitentiary grounds. In fact, the territorial assembly's deliberations over a site for the penitentiary included the proximity of stone that could be quarried. As with construction of Fort Boise, the building schedule was slowed by extracting and preparing materials. And some materials had to be shipped. When May's bid of $34,745 was accepted in October 1869, superintendent of construction Thomas Donaldson arranged a twelve-month contract for completion of the building, writing to Secretary of the Interior Jacob D. Cox that

winter is already on us, and for six months there can be no brick or stone laid. The stone will be cut and the brick burned during the winter. The iron, cement and materials for plumbing must come from Chicago. It will be at least 10 months from this date before the building is completed, I have made it twelve months for safety.[19]

Lime also had to be shipped from Oregon, and

A 1912 photograph of the Idaho penitentiary shows the Mansard roof of the first building on the site, constructed by Charles May from 1869 to 1871. (An identical building constructed to match the original structure appears in the center of the photograph.) The Mansard roof, a characteristic of the Second Empire style, is shallow except at the roof edge, where a steeply pitched section of roof is penetrated by dormer windows. (ISHS 68.57-26/b.)

a blacksmith shop had to be set up at the site to accomplish some of the ironwork. Specifications called for two-foot-thick rubble masonry walls laid up with lime mortar, three tiers of brick cells with thirteen-inch-thick walls, and seasoned pine woodwork, including tongue and groove ceilings and gallery floors. The block of six-by-eight by eight-foot cells was surrounded by an iron gallery and stairs. On the exterior this solid building suggested the Second Empire, or Mansard, style with its segmental window arches and dormers set into a Mansard roof.

The most elaborate Boise sandstone building of the era is the assay office (1872) designed for Idaho Territory by Alfred B. Mullett, U. S. Treasury Department architect, just two years before he left that office for private practice. Mullett favored the Second Empire style in his designs for public buildings across the nation, but for the Idaho assay office he used a subdued, classical Italianate design. The cubical, two-story building has stone quoining, denticulated eaves, and a bracketed cupola atop its pyramidal roof. Its interior plan provided first-floor space for the federal assayer's office and laboratory and second-floor living quarters.[20]

Stonework lent itself to the simple lines, plain texture, symmetrical facades, and temple-form or cubical massing of the Greek Revival style and of the Second Empire and Italianate styles in their classical phases. Although Greek Revival was outmoded by the

1870s, the Second Empire and Italianate styles of the penitentiary and assay office were not. Federal funding of those buildings provided a link with national building trends, however modest their regional expression. The assay office was probably the inspiration for Joseph Bown's Italianate sandstone house built in 1879 on his ranch north of Boise. The Bown house duplicates the assay office's cubical massing and its cupola. The Italianate style became quite popular for Boise housing during the 1870s, and the Italianate style Russell and Pinney houses also mimicked the assay office's massing; but a house like Bown's, built of stone, was unusual in the Boise Valley.[21]

Buildings constructed with milled lumber

Alfred B. Mullett's design for the assay office at Boise was Italianate, as expressed in the building's cubical shape, segmental window arches (arches that are segments of a circle), and bracketed cupola centered on the pyramid-shaped roof. Quoins, denticulated eaves, and heavy bracketed pediments over the entrance and second-story window link the building with classicism (motifs from the architecture of classical Greece and Rome). (ISHS 70-169.5.)

were debatably weaker, less weatherproof, and more subject to the frequent town fires than a building like the Pierce courthouse, but they required a complex technology and expensive materials and allowed for stylistic flourishes through the application of band-sawed trim. Therefore, they were regarded as desirable. Log cabins were used for a season; frame houses were built by those few who actually profited from the mines — the mine owner, the freighter, the merchant, the banker, the lawyer.

The availability of lumber is a surprising fact of the mining frontier.[22] Sawmills were established within the first year of most mining camps. Mills were in operation in Pierce and Orofino by 1861, in Lewiston by 1862, in Elk City by 1863, and on Grimes Creek near the Boise Basin by the spring of 1863. Lafayette Cartee also had his Rocky Bar sawmill going by 1863. In the mining towns and their supply communities, lumber buildings appeared alongside the tent and the log cabin. In the Mormon villages sawmills were established somewhat later, and frame construction appeared during the 1870s.

Milled lumber was used for both box construction and balloon frame construction. Box construction, also called plank framing, was a method of building a wall solely with milled boards attached to a plate at the top and a sill at the bottom. An English technique that was widespread in parts of New England, box construction was probably brought to the

West by the many northeasterners of the gold-fields and the Willamette Valley, who would have known the construction from their home region. The technique was also described in contemporary construction manuals like *The Immigrant Builder.*[23] The method was easy, allowing the relatively untutored to put up a satisfactory building quite rapidly. Its frequency in Idaho is simply unknown; it is even possible that box construction was as popular as log construction. Box construction has been found in the ranch house at the Mitchell, Marsh and Ireton ranch, built near present-day Emmett in 1865, in the 1867 St. Joseph's

Catholic Church in Idaho City, and in the 1872 addition to the Thomas E. Logan house, Boise. At Lapwai Indian Agency, box construction was employed for teachers' housing, and box-constructed houses were built by the agency for the Nez Perce.[24]

With the exception of log and stone construction in southeastern Idaho, balloon frame construction rivaled all other methods for popularity throughout the state.[25] The light-weight yet sturdy structure of a frame building recommended it, as did its economic use of wood. But the popularity of frame construction probably owed as much to the ease

The builder of the Collings house in Paris (1876) combined the hall and parlor house plan with motifs from the Greek Revival style: eave returns and a garland molding under the front eaves (where roof meets wall). (ISHS 84-5.11.)

Boise carpenters of the 1870s built a number of ornate houses using Gothic Revival or Italianate trim. The George W. Russell house on Warm Springs Avenue expressed the Italianate style in its cubical massing, bracketed eaves, and pyramidal roof with a cupola. (ISHS 80-5.217.)

with which a variety of architectural styles could be rendered in wood. These early frame buildings were typically quite simple versions of the Greek, Gothic, or Italianate styles, or blends of the three. Few expressed style through complex massing; whatever their style or function, they were generally one- or two-story boxes with gable roofs and gable-front plans. Charles Nelson Teeter describes this typical plan in a letter from Idaho City:

Imagine you see a house 14 by 20 feet in size standing with end fronting the south upon one of the principal streets of the city running east and west. Said house is a frame building with a pair of sash doors and a large window in front below, and also a large window in front above.[26]

Two important exceptions were the lateral-front, hall and parlor house type, favored by the Mormons and also evident in the supply towns, and some of Boise's finest houses, which expressed Picturesque ideals with more complex massing. Frame architecture of this era tended toward a few standard forms. They were the Greek Revival style house; the Gothic Revival or Italianate house; and the Greek or Gothic Revival style institutional building.

Alongside the Greek Revival stone houses of a Mormon village were a few frame houses expressing the same style in their general massing, roof pitch, and simple milled details, such as pedimented window heads and gable

returns. The Collings house in Paris (1876) is an example. References to Greek Revival appear in the house's symmetrical facade, returned eaves on its side gables, and an under-eave garland molding along the front wall.[27] In the mining towns, such simple references to Greek Revival can also be found on both log and frame houses.

The Gothic Revival and Italianate styles were used for frame houses primarily in the mining towns and supply centers. In Boise a number of important examples existed in the town's first pretentious residential section

along Grove Street. In the houses of the capital city's prominent families is the first evidence that architectural stylebooks wielded some influence on Idaho architecture of the 1870s. Gothic Revival appeared in the Cartee, Nye, and Lemp houses; Italianate in the Russell, Kelly, and Pinney houses; and all of these buildings exhibited some cross-pollination between the two styles, whose popularity overlapped in Idaho. Beneath their band-sawed bargeboards, brackets, porch trim, and pierced aprons these houses had the standard vernacular plans of contemporary pattern

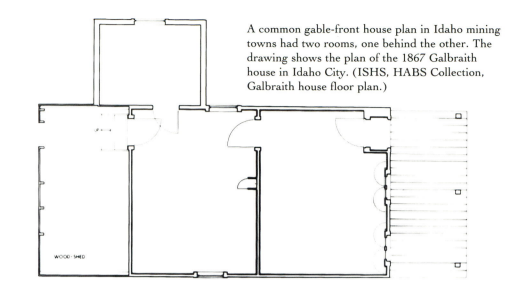

A common gable-front house plan in Idaho mining towns had two rooms, one behind the other. The drawing shows the plan of the 1867 Galbraith house in Idaho City. (ISHS, HABS Collection, Galbraith house floor plan.)

The William H. Nye house in Boise, shown here in an 1884 lithograph from Elliott's *History of Idaho Territory* (San Francisco: Wallace W. Elliott & Co., 1884) had Gothic Revival style bargeboards (ornamental boards along the roof line) and porch trim. (ISHS 2126.)

books like Andrew Jackson Downing's *Cottage Residences* and Henry Hudson Holly's *Country Seats*.[28]

Boise's ornate wooden houses of the 1870s had few counterparts. The average Idahoan lived in a building like the Galbraith house (1867) in Idaho City or the Adelmann house (circa 1878) in Boise. These two buildings represent two standard two-room house plans to which Gothic or Italianate ornamentation could be applied. In the Galbraith house one room sits behind the other. Its three-bay, gable-end facade would be reminiscent of Greek Revival but for the Gothic bargeboard

and window heads. This house plan, with or without ornamentation, appeared throughout Idaho's mining towns. In the Adelmann house two small rooms, one square and one narrower, sit side by side to create a hall and parlor plan. Its plan, its three-bay lateral facade, and its turned porch posts that are reminiscent of the Gothic Revival are features that appear in numerous supply-town houses.[29]

Frame hotels, boardinghouses, and barracks of this era were nearly identical to single-family residences. In Coeur d'Alene, the Fort Sherman officers' quarters (circa 1878), its central-hall plan built to U. S. War

Department standards, drew upon the Gothic Revival and Italianate styles for its porch and window details. The earlier Fort Lapwai officers' quarters (1866) has a simpler Greek Revival facade. These buildings and hotels like the Overland House (1864) and Hart's Exchange (1866), both in Boise, and the Luna House in Lewiston (a log building) were like oversize houses in external form and style.

Frame construction was used for institutional buildings all over Idaho during this era. Most of these buildings were simple two-story rectangular boxes with a gable front and Greek Revival or Gothic Revival ornamentation. On churches, schools, and town halls, a steeple or bell tower might be added to the front wall of the building. On fraternal buildings a stairway might be added to the side wall for separate access to a second-story lodge. Few of these buildings had the false fronts that are generally associated with frontier architecture. The false front, a way of mimicking masonry with a frame building, was more appropriate for the Italianate style than it was for the Greek and Gothic Revivals, styles that made good use of a pitched roof line. During this period, Italianate had not yet reached the peak of its popularity in Idaho.

Many of the institutional buildings mixed Greek and Gothic motifs. The box-constructed St. Joseph's church in Idaho City is a good example. Its gable returns and pedimental window heads suggest Greek Revival, but the building's steep roof suggests the

Institutional buildings of the 1860s and 1870s were simple gable-front buildings with Greek or Gothic Revival style trim. The carpenter for Idaho City's Masonic Hall, built in 1865, drew on Greek Revival style for the building's entablaturelike moldings and window heads and for its thick columns and pilasters (flat attached columns). (ISHS 60-99.14.)

Gothic. Sometimes Greek Revival churches were later remodeled to Gothic, as in the Kamiah Presbyterian Church, remodeled in 1890 under the supervision of anthropologist Alice Fletcher and her companion Jane Gay.[30] Greek and Gothic Revival churches were built by Protestant and Catholic congregations throughout northern, central, and southwestern Idaho: St. Michael's Episcopal, Boise (1866); St. Joseph's, Idaho City (1867); the Kamiah Presbyterian Church (1874); St. Joseph's Mission Church near Lapwai (1874);

the Boise Methodist Church (1876). In the Fort Sherman Chapel (1879) the U. S. War Department used a style preferred by low-church groups, the Romanesque Revival. The chapel has round-arched windows and wall buttresses fashioned of wood.

Fraternal temples or lodges of the 1860s and 1870s were typically two-story frame buildings with commercial space on a lower story and a meeting hall on the upper. Their very plain use of Greek Revival details, limited to porch columns, gable returns, and win-

dow pediments, reflects the Enlightenment origins of the fraternal orders. Examples include the 1874 Salmon Odd Fellows Hall, the 1875 Odd Fellows Hall in Idaho City, the 1865 Idaho City Masonic Hall, Silver City's 1869 Masonic Hall, and the 1870 Good Templars' Hall in Boise.

Bricks were available in a few of Idaho's early mining towns, but brickmaking was rare enough to be a newsworthy event. Archaeologist Karl Gurcke, in his search for references to brickmaking in the Pacific Northwest, discovered that "by 1864 Idaho had at least three and possibly four brickmakers."[31] Besides Charles May's Boise firm, brickmaking went on in Boise Basin (at Idaho City and vicinity) and in the Owyhee mining camps of Silver City and Ruby City. These were the richest of Idaho's early mining regions and the longest lived of the territorial mining camps, well established enough for the construction of a few "bricks" along the main street.

Erecting brick masonry buildings was limited by a number of logistic problems that were most easily solved in the larger and wealthier settlements: locating suitable clay and lime deposits, then extracting and hauling the material, firing the brick to a suitable hardness, and finding and paying experienced masons. Idaho City had resources for construction of a number of brick buildings to replace frame structures lost in the fires that destroyed parts of the town in 1865, 1867, 1868, and 1871. Fireproofing consisted of metal fire

St. Joseph's Church in Idaho City gives the appearance of a balloon frame building, but under the building's clapboards (horizontal siding) the structure is box construction. The eave returns, moldings, and pedimentlike window heads are references to the Greek Revival style. (ISHS 74-5.56; Henry Griffiths, Jr., photographer.)

doors and shutters freighted to the basin from San Francisco, of an attic floor protected with a layer of brick and a four-inch layer of dirt, and of double-wall brick construction — two common-bond brick walls tied together with headers. The locally fired brick was soft but apparently adequate for its use in bearing walls and facades, as was the adobe mortar — partially protected by a thin lime pointing — used to lay it up. A number of Idaho City's bricks survive to illustrate these details of brick construction: the 1873 Kingsley store (later Boise County Courthouse), the 1867 post office and Pinney's bookstore (now Boise Basin Museum), the 1867 Boise Market (later Idaho World Building), the 1865 Claresy saloon (Miners' Exchange block), and the three buildings that form the Boise Basin Mercantile Company block, built in 1865, 1867, and 1868.[32]

Brick construction did provide merchants with an opportunity to display that they were in step with the architectural styles of the East and the West Coast. The openings of a brick mercantile could be adorned with round relieving arches that created large openings for doors and window displays. In combination with corbeled cornices at the roof line, these large round arches suggested the early Romanesque Revival style of brick blocks in Portland, San Francisco, and St. Louis. This popular style was used for John Claresy's 1865 saloon in Idaho City (the Miners' Exchange Saloon), erected by local carpenter

P. H. Nevins, masons and plasterers Walters and Wallace, and painters Hays and Brothers. The building's fireproof construction withstood two devastating fires, in 1867 and 1871.

By one estimate, 24 of Boise's more than 400 buildings in 1870 were brick.[33] They were probably similar to Cyrus Jacobs' 1864 house, a modest one-and-one-half-story design very much like the Adelmann house, or his 1865 store, a one-story three-bay Romanesque design very much like Idaho City's brick blocks. During the 1870s these were joined by more ambitious brick buildings like the 1874 First Methodist Church, the 1870s Sonna house, and the 1879 C. W. Moore house (also known as the Moore-DeLamar house). The Sonna house was a staid, conservative version of an Italianate double-cell house (two single-cell units without a central hallway). It was identical in design to midwestern town houses of midcentury. However, the Methodist church and Moore's brick mansion both broke with the simple forms that had dominated the 1860s and 1870s. The church contrasted with the boxy frame churches of its era by adopting the complex massing, tall Gothic windows, and corner tower of the English Gothic, ideas available through pattern books like Holly's *Country Seats*.[34] The Moore house had a Mansard roof and precut millwork shipped into Boise.

By the time C. W. Moore was at work on his Boise mansion the essential architectural problems of his era had been solved. Through

The round arches (arches consisting of half circles) of brick commercial buildings like John Claresy's 1865 saloon in Idaho City (left) provided wide openings for doors and windows. Three-bay (tripled) arches were a typical arrangement in these early Romanesque Revival style buildings. The drawing depicts brick veneer laid up in a common bond pattern. (ISHS, HABS Collection, Idaho City, Miners' Exchange.)

A stereopticon view of the Sonna house in Boise (below) picks out the house's raised segmental window arches and under-eave brackets, features of the Italianate style. (ISHS 76-137.1.)

One could hardly exaggerate the dramatic change that occurred in the Idaho landscape between construction of Fort Boise and the C. W. Moore house. Thousands of miners, farmers, soldiers, freighters, and business people had come to the territory, bringing with them the American architectural forms of their day: the Italianate brick mansion, the Gothic or Italianate frame house, the Greek temple-form house, the Gothic frame church, the single-room log cabin, the Greek fraternal building, the Romanesque Revival brick commercial building, and the stone government building.

The landscape they created was not uniform. Even before 1879, regional divisions began to emerge in the territory's architectural tradition. A visitor to a Mormon village would be impressed at the quantity of open space, small folk-plan houses built of log, stone, or adobe, and their inhabitants' conservative architectural taste. All over Idaho Territory architectural styles were conservative, lagging slightly behind their period of national popularity, but in the Mormon villages this tendency was more pronounced, and the Greek Revival style appeared there for housing as late as the mid-1870s.

Traveling to an early mining camp, the visitor would be amused by the shift from order to chaos, from substantial to mixed construction. In the mining town, tents and modest log, box, and balloon frame buildings would contrast with a few fireproof brick commercial

local suppliers and through freighting, Moore was able to acquire all the materials he needed; and Boise had enough skilled craftsmen to accomplish the task. Although he had no architect and apparently acted as his own contractor, Moore did not have to explore for lime and clay or build his own blacksmith shop. His detailed account book for construction of the house shows payment to a number of local bricklayers, brick tenders, laborers, stonemasons, plasterers, and carpenters.

Moore also accounted for the cost of procuring lime, hair, and plaster; specialized carpentry tools; moldings; lumber, shingles, and lath; and hardware and tinware for gutters. He obtained most of his materials from local firms such as Sonna's hardware store, but a portion of the $13,064 cost of the house went to the railway and teamsters for shipping items like doors and a bay window for the drawing room, standard factory millwork available from midwestern firms.[35]

C. W. Moore mustered a corps of masons and carpenters to build his 1879 house in Boise. The house combined Italianate brackets, bay windows, and window arches with a Mansard roof and a cross-wing house plan typical of those found in contemporary pattern books. (ISHS 69-36.)

blocks and a frame church or Odd Fellows' building.

The houses, churches, and government buildings of the supply towns would appear most familiar to the visitor. Through government contracts and proximity to shipping routes, supply towns like Boise and Lewiston and government establishments like Fort Sherman could stay in touch with contemporary trends.

The visitor who happened to have an eye for workmanship would detect evidence of a growing corps of resident carpenters, masons, and other workers, although little sign of trained architects. If the visitor had an eye for materials, regional distinctions would be especially evident. Wood was a basic material everywhere, particularly in northern Idaho where there were abundant pine and cedar stands. In the southwest, Boise sandstone was an important discovery, and adobe was a substitute material for brick. Southeastern Idaho's tuff deposits made stone housing possible there, but it was rare elsewhere.

By 1879, with persistence and resourcefulness, Idaho's early settlers had found the materials and skilled labor that they needed to make a comfortably familiar home in the deserts and mountains of Idaho. They had laid out a pattern of towns and villages, farms and ranches, and forts and agencies that was to see the region through the railroad era and into the twentieth century. Idahoans could look forward to statehood and a period of rapid

turn of the century's development in which Lugenbeel's, or even C. W. Moore's, problems would come to seem old-fashioned.

Notes

1. Epigraph in Maj. Pinckney Lugenbeel to Miss M. Irene Lugenbeel, 27 July 1863, MS161, box 2, file 3, Idaho State Historical Society (hereafter ISHS), Boise.

2. Brig. Gen. Benjamin Alvord to Assistant Adj. Gen., Headquarters Department of the Pacific, San Francisco, California, 18 August 1863, *The War of Rebellion: A Compilation of the Official Records of the Union and Confederate Armies*, series 1, vol. 50, part 2 (Washington D.C.: Government Printing Office, 1897), 579–80; *An Illustrated History of the State of Idaho* (Chicago: The Lewis Publishing Company, 1899), 289–90; and Arthur A. Hart, *Historic Boise: An Introduction to the Architecture of Boise, Idaho, 1863–1938* (Boise: Historic Boise, 1980), 18.

3. C. Aubrey Angelo, "Impressions of the Boise Basin in 1863," *Idaho Yesterdays* 7, no. 1 (Spring 1963):10. Angelo includes descriptions of architecture in his reports of the Boise Basin mining camps, which originally appeared as correspondent reports to the San Francisco *Daily Alta California*, June and July 1863.

4. Mrs. James D. Agnew, "Idaho Pioneer of 1864," *Washington Historical Quarterly* 15 (January 1924):46. For descriptions of Lewiston in 1861 and 1862, see W. A. Goulder, *Reminiscences: Incidents in the Life of a Pioneer in Oregon and Idaho* (Boise: Timothy Regan, 1909; reprint edition Moscow, Idaho: University of Idaho Press, 1990), 178; and Sister M. Alfreda Elsensohn, *Pioneer Days in Idaho County*, 2 vols. (Cottonwood, Idaho: The Idaho Corporation of Benedictine Sisters, 1971), 2:24.

5. Boise, as an example of the early service town, is depicted in two plats and a painting in Hart, *Historic Boise*, 8–11.

6. Farm and ranch location is discussed in Arthur A. Hart, "Farm and Ranch Buildings East of the Cascades,"

in *Space, Style and Structure: Building in Northwest America*, 2 vols., ed. Thomas Vaughan and Virginia Guest Ferriday (Portland, Oregon: Oregon Historical Society, 1974), 1:243. Several early farms and ranches are illustrated in *History of Idaho Territory* (San Francisco: Wallace W. Elliott & Co., 1884). Layout of one early ranch, the Mitchell, Marsh and Ireton ranch, is recorded in the Historic American Buildings Survey (hereafter HABS), ID-35, copies on file at the Library of Congress, Washington, D.C., and ISHS, Boise.

7. The Mormon settlement strategy is outlined in Joel Edward Ricks, *Forms and Methods of Early Mormon Settlement in Utah and the Surrounding Region, 1847 to 1877*, Utah State University Monograph Series, vol. 11, no. 2 (Logan, January 1964). The classic study of the Mormon village is still Lowry Nelson's *The Mormon Village: A Pattern and Technique of Land Settlement* (Salt Lake City: University of Utah Press, 1952). Idaho examples are discussed in Lisa B. Reitzes, *Paris: A Look at Idaho Architecture* (Boise: Idaho State Historic Preservation Office, 1981), 7–14; and Paul L. Anderson, "An Idaho Variation on the City of Zion," in *Chesterfield: Mormon Outpost in Idaho*, ed. Lavina Fielding Anderson (Bancroft, Idaho: The Chesterfield Foundation, 1982), 70–78.

8. Charles Nelson Teeter, "Four Years of My Life, or My Adventures in the Far West (May 14, 1862–December 13, 1865)," in *Thirteenth Biennial Report* (Boise: ISHS, 1932), 93. Reitzes describes makeshift shelters used in Mormon settlement in *Paris*, 20.

9. John L. Campbell, *Six Months in the New Gold-Diggings: Placer Gold Mining in Idaho Territory in 1863* (1864; reprint ed., Fairfield, Washington: Ye Galleon Press, 1979), 44–45.

10. "Number Employed in Idaho in Each Occupation or Industry in Census Years, 1870–1950," comp. Leslie V. Brock, unprocessed MS2, ISHS, Boise.

11. Information about log construction is drawn from Jennifer Eastman Attebery, "The Diffusion of Folk Culture as Demonstrated in the Horizontal Timber Construc-

tion of the Snake River Basin" (Ph.D. diss., Indiana University, 1985). Unless otherwise noted, the buildings mentioned are documented in National Register of Historic Places nomination forms, on file at the Department of the Interior, National Park Service, Washington, D.C., and at ISHS, Boise.

12. Raymond W. Settle and Mary Lund Settle, eds., *Overland Days to Montana in 1865: The Diary of Sarah Raymond and Journal of Dr. Waid Howard* (Glendale, California: The Arthur H. Clark Company, 1971), 213.

13. Junius Wright, MS 334, ISHS, Boise.

14. Ibid.

15. Specifications for the Pierce courthouse are quoted in a Boise *Idaho Statesman* article, "Attic Floor Reveals Rare Old Document," 5 August 1928 (clipping on file at ISHS, Boise). The original document was preserved at the Clearwater County Courthouse, Orofino. See documentation of the building in Thomas B. Renk, "Interim Report: Pierce Courthouse Development Project, 1977"; "Report on Inspection of Pierce Courthouse, Pierce, Idaho" (October 30, 1974); and "Shoshone County Courthouse, Pierce, Idaho: A report on conservation work done in 1978"; all on file at ISHS, Boise.

16. See Hart, *Historic Boise*, 16; and "Architecturally Significant and Historic Buildings of Boise, Idaho," Information Sheet, no. 12 (Boise: ISHS, 1971). At least two other Boise adobes survive in radically altered form: the Tate farmhouse and the Robert Wilson house, both cited in the Idaho Historic Sites Inventory, ISHS, Boise. The building at Walter's Ferry predates 1884; a plate in *History of Idaho Territory* depicts the building as part of Walter and McQuat's Ferry, opposite 74. The ferry was established in 1863 ("Walters Ferry," Reference Series, no. 755 [Boise: ISHS, 1982]). The Walter's Ferry building presents a good example of adobe moisture problems, as revealed in a 1980 examination of the building, field notes on file at ISHS, Boise. A building similar to the Walter's Ferry building has been observed, though not thoroughly documented, in Hailey. The Rich houses are mentioned in

Reitzes, *Paris*, 23.

17. See "Research Report on the Mayor Thomas E. Logan House, Boise, Idaho," and the completion report for restoration work on the Logan house, both on file in the Idaho Historic Sites Inventory, site no. 002628, ISHS, Boise; and Jennifer Eastman Attebery et al., "The Montgomery House: Adobe in Idaho's Folk Architecture," in *Idaho Folklife: Homesteads to Headstones*, ed. Louie W. Attebery (Salt Lake City: University of Utah Press, 1985), 53–54.

18. Hart, *Historic Boise*, 18–19.

19. Donaldson to Cox, 16 October 1869, "Letters Received Relating to the Penitentiary at Boise City; January 14, 1869–November 24, 1890," *Interior Department Territorial Papers, Idaho, 1864–1890*, File Microcopies of Records in the National Archives, no. 191, roll 3 (Washington, D.C.: The National Archives, 1950). This microfilm copy includes other correspondence, a memorial of the territorial assembly, and specifications for the 1871 penitentiary building.

20. The United States assay office in Boise is documented in HABS, ID–10. Copies of the Mullett plans and drawings are on file at ISHS, Boise.

21. See the Pinney and Russell houses in Arthur A. Hart, *The Boiseans: At Home* (Boise: Historic Boise, 1985), 14–15, and 26–27.

22. Even before sawmills were erected, whipsawed lumber was available, although used primarily for the flumes, sluice boxes, and other handmade equipment required for placer mining. In the absence of sawmills, wooden frame buildings could be assembled with hand-split or -hewn timbers. However, few examples have been discovered. Braced-timber frame construction was apparently confined to barn construction (Hart, "Farm and Ranch Buildings," 245.) William Montgomery's house at Middleton (circa 1870) was an intriguing example of post-in-sill construction with adobe brick nogging between its hewn vertical posts, an unbraced construction similar to balloon framing. But the house is something of an oddity

among Idaho buildings; no similar buildings have been identified (Attebery et al., "Montgomery House.")

23. Charles P. Dwyer, *The Immigrant Builder: Or, Practical Hints to Handy-men* (Philadelphia: Claxton, Remsen & Haffelfinger, 1872), 75–78. Dwyer entitles his chapter on box construction, "The Balloon-House"; the construction was called "box" in Oregon and Idaho.

24. Most surveys of Idaho architecture have inspected only the outsides of buildings, and a box constructed building can look very much like a balloon frame building from the exterior. The many board and batten buildings that appear in photographs of the mining camps could have employed vertical plank construction. Recent studies of box construction have shown that it was more common, more prestigious, and more modern than previously supposed and was used into the twentieth century for middle-class housing. See Jan Leo Lewandoski, "The Plank Framed House in Northeastern Vermont," *Vermont History* 53 (1985):104–21; Philip Dole, "Farmhouses and Barns of the Willamette Valley," in *Space, Style and Structure*, 1:98–99; and Steve Mitchell, Donald R. Brown, and Michael L. Swanda, "Board Shanty: Box Construction in White County, Arkansas," *Pioneer America Society Transactions* 10 (1987):9–16. For references to box construction in Idaho see HABS documentation of the Mitchell, Marsh and Ireton ranch; Hart, *Historic Boise*, 16; and Erwin N. Thompson, *Historic Resource Study, Spalding Area: Nez Perce National Historic Park/Idaho* (Denver: U.S. Department of Interior, National Park Service, September 1972), 124, 142, 262. Two early twentieth-century, box constructed buildings have been documented in a Wallace workers' neighborhood by Nancy F. Renk, Idaho Historic Sites Inventory, ISHS, Boise. I am indebted to Frederick L. Walters for sharing with me his observations of the St. Joseph's church.

25. Reitzes discusses the slow development of lumber milling in *Paris*, 21, 25, 29–31. The few early Mormon frame buildings that have been examined reveal the use of adobe nogging between studs.

26. Teeter, "Four Years of My Life," 79.

27. Reitzes, *Paris*, 30–31.

28. Andrew Jackson Downing, *Cottage Residences* (New York, 1842); and Henry Hudson Holly, *Holly's Country Seats* (New York: D. Appleton and Company, 1863). For a discussion of the influence of plan books, see Hart, *Historic Boise*, 24; Hart, *Boiseans*, 14–23, 26–27; and Wallace Kay Huntington, "Victorian Architecture," in *Space, Style and Structure*, 1:267.

29. The Galbraith house is recorded in HABS, ID–7.

Record drawings of the Adelmann house prepared 15 January 1982 by Ronald Thurber and Associates are on file at ISHS, Boise.

30. St. Joseph's is recorded in HABS, ID–12. The remodeling of the Kamiah Presbyterian Church is documented in Allen Morrill and Eleanor Morrill, "Old Church Made New," *Idaho Yesterdays* 16, no. 2 (Summer 1972):19–23.

31. Karl Gurcke, *Bricks and Brickmaking: A Handbook for Historical Archaeology* (Moscow, Idaho: The University of Idaho Press, 1987), 43.

32. Recorded in HABS, ID–9, 11, 13–15.

33. Hart, *Historic Boise*, 20.

34. Holly, *Holly's Country Seats*, 162–67.

35. C. W. Moore account book, MS 2.205, ISHS, Boise. Railway shipping was available to Kelton, Utah, and wagon freighting beyond that junction. See also Arthur A. Hart, "M. A. Disbrow and Company: Catalogue Architecture," *The Palimpsest* 56, no. 4 (July, August 1975):106, 114–15.

3

Streetscapes of the Railroad Era, 1879–1902

What a forbidding place to build a home; . . . my heart sank in a flash of homesickness as I drew out the plans in a great blueprint of the town "to be." There was pictured so enticingly the commercial streets, the residence locations, the parks, the places for churches and schools, the railroad and its switches, the depot and hotel, the wagon roads leading in various directions, and even the shade trees were there, and it all looked so complete that I fairly strained my ears to hear the toot of the engine and the ringing of bells. A lift of the eyelids and the dream vanished, leaving a wide chasm between the dream city on paper and the reality.

In her memoir, *Fifteen Thousand Miles by Stage,* Carrie Adell Strahorn recalled the excitement and discouragement of town building along the Oregon Short Line as it opened southern Idaho to railroad commerce.[1] Strahorn's husband Robert was a public-relations writer for the Oregon Short Line and an officer for the Idaho-Oregon Land Improvement Company. The couple established new communities staged at intervals along the Oregon Short Line, arriving in Idaho Territory amidst the excitement of mining developments in the Wood River drainage. The coincidence of railway and mining expansion caused the Oregon Short Line to construct a spur from Shoshone to Hailey in 1882 before continuing across the Snake River Plain to the sites of Mountain Home, Caldwell, Weiser, and Payette. These towns developed much as Carrie Adell Strahorn imagined them, their residential and commercial streets, parks and institutions modeled after the midwestern towns of Iowa and Nebraska where many of their settlers grew up.

All over the territory similar developments shaped the streetscapes of Idaho between 1879 and 1902. In spite of setbacks during the national panics of 1884 and 1893, Idaho achieved economic expansion over most of this period. In addition to the Oregon Short Line across southern Idaho, the Utah and Northern was built through southeastern Idaho in 1879, bringing settlers from Utah into the towns of Blackfoot, Eagle Rock (Idaho Falls), Rigby, and Rexburg; and the Northern Pacific was built across northern Idaho in 1881, creating Sandpoint, Rathdrum, and other towns. These railroad routes reinforced the territory's emerging regions. With the Utah and Northern the link between southeast Idaho and Utah was strengthened and expanded to include the upper Snake River drainage. The Oregon Short Line strengthened southern Idaho ties to the Midwest and Oregon (and hence to California), while the Northern Pacific, built eastward from Spokane, strengthened northern Idahoans' ties with Washington and with the upper Midwest.

Railroad building dovetailed with new gold discoveries and with the development of quartz mining and silver smelting. Most important were strikes of lead-silver at the Wood River and the Coeur d'Alene mines, but the mining rush also included expanded mining on Yankee Fork, in Boise Basin, and in the Owyhee mines. The new railroads became essential for shipping in the heavy equipment needed for smelting and stamp mills and for shipping out to national markets. Access to markets also affected agricultural expansion. At the same time, white fears of Indian troubles were put to rest by the conclusion of the Bannock War in 1878. With most of Idaho's Indian population living on reservations, white settlers began farming the rich land of the Palouse and began irrigation projects to convert desert lands into agricultural acreage.

Carrie Adell Strahorn and her husband Robert were two of Idaho's town builders in the railroad era. (ISHS 78-15.23/B.)

The town builders did more than create new settlements where none had existed. Construction in the towns platted during the previous two decades was still sparse and sometimes flimsy. Economic expansion during the railroad era filled in the framework of places like Boise and Lewiston with an array of impressive new buildings. Rapid construction of new streetscapes was made possible by several developments. Idaho was suddenly more closely in touch with factory sources for millwork, wrought iron, cast iron, pressed galvanized sheet iron, and steel. Outside sources for shipped materials were contested by the regional development of quarries, brickyards, and lumber mills. Pattern-book plans were widely available, and the territory gained numerous builders who could implement them. The territory also gained a number of professional architects who made up-to-date styles and technology available to the growing number of wealthy individuals, government bodies, and commercial enterprises able to commission building designs.

During this era of Picturesque romanticism, the streetscapes of Idaho blossomed with regional interpretations of the Italianate, Romanesque Revival, Moorish, Gothic Revival, Queen Anne, French Chateau, and Colonial Revival styles. Italianate commercial blocks lined the main streets, bordered by institutional campuses made up of brick or stone buildings designed for use by government agencies or schools. Residential neighborhoods mimicked the pages of popular pattern books. Today we can glimpse these late nineteenth-century streetscapes in scattered survivors, but to the nineteenth-century passerby they presented a playful continuum of variable shapes, textures, colors, and decorative detail. Each type of streetscape — commercial, institutional, and residential — functioned differently and so had its own characteristic motifs and plans.

The commercial streetscape, located in what was thought of as the town center, consisted of mercantiles or cooperatives, office buildings, banks, hotels, stables, lodge halls, a railroad depot, a city hall, and perhaps a fire station. By the turn of the century commercial streets had a full row of business buildings joined by party walls or built closely enough together to create a single block-long facade. Strolling along the boardwalk or sidewalk that separated buildings a few feet from the mostly unpaved roadway, a pedestrian saw the street as a series of cast-iron storefronts framing double doors and large display windows. On the stories above were rows of sash windows with decorative lintels. An ornate, protruding cornice clearly marked the flat rooftop of each building. The surface of the streetscape was broken by oriel windows and turrets and by a variety of textures. Buildings of wood, brick, and stone bordered on each other, and a mixture of these and other materials were used to create surface detail on particular buildings. With its bracketed cornices and segmental or

Wooden frame commercial buildings of the railroad era typically had Italianate false fronts concealing their pointed gable roofs. The Masonic Hall in Murray, built in about 1884, has Italianate brackets and window molding. (ISHS 64-148.3.)

round window openings, the Italianate style came into widespread use for commercial blocks during this period. Its principal rival was the Romanesque Revival style, but commercial clients occasionally preferred French Chateau, Queen Anne, or eclectic designs.

At the beginning of Idaho's railroad era a few commercial buildings continued to be built with a backward look to the trends of the 1860s and 1870s. The Woolley Brothers stone store in Paris, for example, was a gable-front Greek Revival design built in 1883.[2] The Johnson Law Office in Boise (1885) is an-

other 1880s Greek Revival box, but its builders augmented its design with Italianate brick window heads and carved porch posts. Hailey's Watt Building (circa 1889) is a gable-front building without a false front. The Ketchum Greenhow and Rumsey store building (circa 1887) uses the three-arched Romanesque storefront found on commercial buildings a generation earlier in Idaho City, Lewiston, and Boise.

By 1890, however, Italianate was firmly entrenched as the commercial style of choice. Used in Idaho as early as the 1860s for a few

The masons for the 1884 Vollmer Building in Lewiston, shown in the center of this early street scene, used brick to create Italianate features like segmental window arches and a corbeled cornice (a band of decorative outset brick, pictured here above the second story windows). Corbeled cornices were common to Italianate and Romanesque Revival style buildings. (ISHS 712.)

mining-camp and supply-town buildings, the Italianate style came to dominate the commercial architecture of the railroad and mining towns during the 1880s and 1890s. Italianate forms could be rendered simply in wood with a false front attached to a gabled frame building. Typically such a building would have a cornice created by application of a strip of planed molding and a few band-sawed brackets. On a two-story building this cornice treatment could be repeated around the storefront. The Murray Masonic Hall (circa 1884) is a classic example of the Italianate false front building in a town created by the gold rush to the Murray area. Like most fraternal buildings, it was constructed in a commercial area and provided retail space on its first floor, where wooden posts and a bracketed cornice outline the storefront. Wooden window heads on the second story are shaped in imitation of the elaborate stone lintels found during the same period on brick or stone Italianate buildings.

The railroad towns and the new mining camps were rapidly constructed with frame false front buildings, and it is from this era, rather than the preceding mining camp period, that Americans have acquired their Wild West image of main streets. Beside the tracks was the frame depot, usually a simple gabled affair, and a frame building or sometimes a tent serving as a railroad hotel. A block away was the main street. The railroad made lumber widely available, so much so that a street of

Built later in the railroad era than the Lewiston building, Vollmer's building in Genesee (1890s) has an elaborate High Victorian facade of pressed galvanized sheet iron on its second story. The High Victorian architecture of the late nineteenth century became more eclectic (mixing styles) and elaborate with the availability of manufactured materials. (ISHS 78-5.285.)

one-story false front buildings could go up in a day. Strahorn recalls Caldwell before any construction had taken place: "The first enterprise was a pile of lumber, in an impromptu lumber yard, which Pard [Robert Strahorn] had shipped there for building purposes."[3]

Where economic conditions limited builders, the wooden false front continued in use much later than the period of the railroad and mining frontiers, and not always in association with the Italianate style. When they could, though, merchants preferred to build with brick or stone, and town promoters boasted of the construction of their communities' first brick blocks. Obviously, the numerous fires that swept through commercial districts encouraged brick and stone construction. By the 1880s brick was available to the extent that most regional centers had at least a few brick buildings. These displayed the Italianate style with segmental or round-arched windows and brick cornices or through the application of cast iron and pressed galvanized sheet iron, available through railway shipping from foundaries like Mesker Brothers of St. Louis.[4]

The Vollmer blocks of Lewiston and Genesee, built for John P. Vollmer's mercantile business, are examples of the two treatments. In the Lewiston building, dating from 1884, raised brick courses create the building's cornice and outline the segmental second-story windows. The Genesee building, dating from the 1890s, has a facade of pressed galvanized

sheet iron on the second story. This imported facade, with its paired columns, oriel window, and denticulated cornice, brought to the small Idaho town a mass-produced sample of High Victorian eclecticism. Such high-style design in brick or stone would indicate the work of a trained architect.

From the beginning of railroad transport and through the 1890s, cast-iron storefronts and cornices, window heads, and facades of pressed galvanized sheet iron were popular

trappings for Idaho's commercial buildings. Particularly good examples include the iron window heads on the Larson block in Bellevue (1884) and the pressed-iron facade on the Roberts Store in Hagerman (1892). Iron storefronts and cornices were used wherever railways and local freight wagon routes could bring them. One can still see them today on buildings in southeastern Idaho (Oakley, Malad, Franklin), in the south-central mining region (Challis, Ketchum, Hailey, Bellevue), in

Architect James King's design for the Boise City National Bank (1890) was inspired by the Romanesque Revival style buildings of New England architect H. H. Richardson. The building's Richardsonian Romanesque features include rusticated (rough-finished) stone veneer, large round-arched openings that become progressively smaller on each story of the building, horizontal massing, and rounded corners. (ISHS 69-4.24.)

and around the Palouse (Lewiston, Moscow, Genesee), and in the Coeur d'Alene mining region (Wallace). Just as these iron features were themselves created in imitation of the carved stonework one would find on a Renaissance building, their widespread circulation throughout the West inspired wooden features cut to imitate the cast iron. The cornice on a wooden false front building is just such a feature, and there were buildings with wooden window heads in imitation of pressed sheet iron (Pendrey's Drug in Paris, 1890s) and carved posts in imitation of cast iron (Johnson Law Office, Boise, 1885).[5]

Around 1890 a significant change came to commercial streets with the incorporation of a few Richardsonian Romanesque buildings. One of the earliest, the Boise City National Bank (1890; also known as the Simplot Building), was a three-story building designed by Boise architect James King. King had come to Boise from West Virginia to set up an architectural practice in 1888.[6] In his design for the bank building he took advantage of Boise's local sandstone supply and of the bank's corner location to create a round-cornered, rusticated sandstone block reminiscent of H. H. Richardson's Marshall Field Wholesale Store

(1885–1887), completed only three years earlier in Chicago. Richardsonian Romanesque graced the streets of those Idaho cities that were developing into regional commercial centers. By 1902, Pocatello, Lewiston, and Moscow had joined Boise in possessing a few business blocks with a Richardsonian Romanesque character. In Pocatello the 1892 Idaho Furniture Company building made good use of local stone. In Moscow and Lewiston, Richardsonian Romanesque was reinterpreted in brick.

During the 1890s Idaho's commercial streetscapes also became more eclectic. In addition to a few Richardsonian Romanesque buildings, downtowns gained examples of the Queen Anne, French Chateau, and castellated Romanesque Revival commercial styles. These exotics appeared sparingly, marking the corners of major intersections with their turrets, or were used for special buildings such as railroad depots or hotels. The Idanha Hotel in Boise (1900) is a French Chateau design by W. S. Campbell, an architect who practiced in Boise between 1891 and 1904.[7] The turreted hotel of five and one-half stories stood out from the Boise streetscape, as did two other romantic, turreted designs, the city hall and the Columbia Theatre. Both of these were constructed in 1893 and designed by John C. Paulsen of Helena, Montana, whose Boise office produced designs between 1891 and 1893.[8] The city hall was a re-creation of a Rhenish Romanesque castle, but the theater

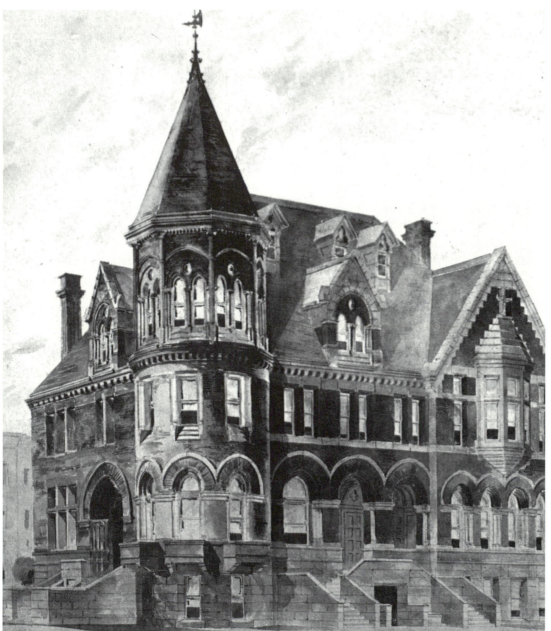

An architect's sketch of the round-towered Boise City Hall emphasized the building's Picturesque features: a steep roof, oriel (outset second-story) and dormer windows, and contrasting colors. (ISHS 442-N.)

was a truly eclectic fantasy. Boise's fanciful, turreted Victorian buildings were among the state's most sophisticated designs of the 1890s, but the new state's regional centers also were touched by these Picturesque Victorian styles. Pocatello had the Seavers Building, an otherwise simple brick block with a crenelated corner tower; Moscow had the Hotel Moscow, an Italianate brick with a Queen Anne corner tower; and Wallace had the turreted Northern Pacific Depot and White-Bender Building.

The 1890s also saw the advent of using structural-steel framing in commercial buildings, a technique that had been perfected in Chicago beginning in the mid–1880s. Boise buildings of the 1880s had steel beams only for support above their wide storefront openings. A building like King's Boise City National Bank of 1890 was structural brick with a sandstone veneer. By 1896 McCaw and Martin of Portland were able to incorporate additional steel beams into the structure of their building for David and Nathan Falk. The Falk-Bloch Mercantile in Boise had steel beams assisting its otherwise standard construction of wooden posts and beams.[9] In style the building looked forward to the plainer, vertically massed buildings of the twentieth century. Its simple flat-headed windows were grouped into threes by pilasters rising the full height of the building. In twentieth-century buildings steel columns and elevators would allow for taller construction and larger window openings. In the Falk Building the use of

McCaw and Martin's design for the Falk-Bloch
Mercantile building had a partially steel-assisted
wooden post and beam structure. Pilasters
between window units unified the building's three
stories. The Boise City Hall is visible on the same
block. (ISHS 83-37.20.)

steel encouraged grouping windows between
vertical piers in a manner that imitated the
much more massive buildings of contemporary cities, like Portland, where McCaw and
Martin's 1892 Romanesque Revival style
Dekum Building was a landmark.

The main street was the center of activity in
most Idaho towns. Town plats, unless they
were Mormon villages, lacked the central
square generally found as part of midwestern
plans. A nineteenth-century pedestrian would
have to walk a block or more from the commercial center to visit a town's institutions.
Grouped on campuses of one or more city
blocks, institutional buildings were clearly

separated from their commercial or residential
surroundings through parklike landscaping
and a deep setback from the street. Courthouses, public schools, private academies,
hospitals, and recreational facilities tended to
maintain this physical and visual separation
from the hubbub of commercial streets. Some
churches, too, were built as part of campuses
when they represented an ecclesiastical unit
larger than a single congregation. The Bear
Lake Tabernacle in Paris (1889), for example,
was constructed in a large block that also
served as the village's central square.

The 1880s and 1890s were decades of institutional building. Many counties, established

in the 1860s, were finally able to finance construction of a brick or frame courthouse. Local school districts replaced their first frame or
log buildings with up-to-date designs. The territorial government established a mental institution in Blackfoot in 1885, and after long
having rented space in Boise, constructed a
capitol in 1886. Expansion of the territorial
penitentiary began with plans drawn up by
James King for the 1893 Richardsonian Romanesque style administration building and
continued with John E. Tourtellotte's 1899
design for cellblocks. Tourtellotte was a
builder-architect who came to Boise in 1890
after garnering design and construction experience in New England, the Midwest, New
Mexico, and Colorado. Based on his plans,
construction at the penitentiary continued
haltingly through the next two decades.[10]

After Idaho achieved statehood in 1890 a
number of state institutions were established.
Southwestern Idaho already had the state
capitol and the penitentiary. In southeastern
Idaho the Albion Normal School (1894) and
the Academy of Idaho at Pocatello (1901)
were created, and in northern Idaho, the state
university at Moscow (1892) and the Lewiston Normal School (1894). Numerous private
institutions also appeared in this period. The
College of Idaho was established in 1891 by
the Presbyterians in Caldwell, and throughout
southeastern Idaho academies for private instruction were established by the Mormons
after they were prevented from serving on

A number of skilled Mormon masons and carpenters devoted their labor to completion of the Bear Lake Tabernacle in Paris's village square. The Romanesque Revival style building features contrasting colors of local stone and a subtly assymetrical facade (front elevation) with unmatched towers. (ISHS 79-5.111/a; Duane Garrett, photographer.)

school boards under the Idaho Test Oath of 1885. One of these, the Bannock Stake Academy at Rexburg, established in 1888, later became Ricks College.

The burgeoning number of state and private institutions provided the state's first major architectural commissions for designers. Some commissions went to out-of-state architects like Elijah E. Myers of Detroit. Myers designed the Richmond, Virginia, city hall and

numerous state capitols and county courthouses throughout the nation. He was chosen as architect for Idaho's 1886 territorial building, which he designed in an eclectic Romanesque style. Some commissions were captured by firms working just over the state borders in Utah, Washington, and Montana. But many commissions attracted architects to the state. This was especially true in Boise, which was growing into a governmental and commercial

center and was farther from Salt Lake City and Spokane than were Pocatello, Moscow, Coeur d'Alene, and the state's other major towns. Paulsen, King, Campbell, Tourtellotte, and Charles F. Hummel came to Boise during this period. Each of them designed a variety of buildings, but institutional designs were the prize commissions that sustained their practices and attracted the attention of potential clients.

Even if its designer lived outside Idaho, an institutional building was erected under the supervision of a local contractor or architect. The Bear Lake County Courthouse in Paris (1884), for example, designed by Salt Lake City architect Truman O. Angell, Jr., was constructed by Woolley Brothers, Paris contractors, with brick and stone masonry by J. H. Brown and Son, Logan, Utah. The Lewiston Normal School's administration building, a design by Preusse and Zittle of Spokane, was completed by local contractor Harry Madgwick in 1896.[11] Because architects were as yet unlicensed and contractors were responsible for the design of many local buildings, collaborations like these were one way that design ideas came into the state. Details such as Italianate brick and stone relieving arches (an arch carrying the load of the wall above an opening) became part of the vocabulary of local masons and appeared on contractor-built houses, commercial buildings, and lodge halls. The G.A.R. Hall, Boise, by contractor William Houtz, and the John

Idaho's territorial capitol, built in 1886, was designed by an out-of-state architect, Elijah E. Myers of Detroit. The eclectic Romanesque building was pictured in a promotional brochure by real estate developer W. E. Pierce. (ISHS 73-98.16.)

Tueller, Sr., house in Paris, by the Tueller family masons, reflect this process.[12] Raised Italianate relieving arches remained popular for vernacular masonry houses in southeast Idaho well into the 1900s.

Institutional facilities required large buildings that provided a public space for foot traffic, reception, or entertainment and smaller spaces for instruction, office work, or housing. The form chosen by most architects included a central mass for the hallway, stairs, reception area, and perhaps a tower, and side wings for classrooms, offices, hospital rooms, dressing rooms, and so forth. This three-part design could be used for a building as simple as the two-story frame schoolhouse at Idaho City (1891), built with very simplified Gothic motifs by local carpenter F. V. Tinker, or it could be rendered in a number of High Victorian styles.[13] Although the Italianate style certainly dominated institutional design in Idaho during the early 1880s, by 1890 design for institutional buildings had become eclectic—more eclectic than commercial design— drawing on features from the Second Empire, Romanesque Revival, French Chateau, Moorish, Colonial Revival, and Beaux Arts styles. The official functions and interior plans of most institutional buildings lent themselves to symmetrical renditions of even the most Picturesque of styles. Paulsen's Boise Natatorium (1892), for example, a fanciful Moorish design, had carefully balanced towers and side wings arcaded with keyhole arches. On otherwise sober buildings the Picturesque age asserted itself in occasional, nearly comic, violations of symmetry. E. E. Myers's design for the territorial capitol (1886) winks at the viewer with a dormer on just one side wing.[14] The Bear Lake Tabernacle, also a Romanesque design, has side towers that are similar but unequal in height. These two buildings demonstrate the subtle assymetries of High Victorian design as influenced by the work of American architects H. H. Richardson and Frank Furness. Parisian William Budge could justly boast of the tabernacle that, although built of "bastard granite" it has a "pleasing effect," being "the finest Church building in Idaho."[15]

Toward the end of this period the classicism of Colonial Revival and Beaux Arts design began to assert itself in Idaho's institutional buildings, as it did nationwide, although some Idaho architects persisted with eclectic Picturesque designs. In 1900, for example, Tourtellotte used the Moorish style for his rebuilding of the Old Soldiers Home in Boise. Much

The Picturesque buildings of the railroad era attempted to convey the charm of painted scenes through their ornate styles and landscaped settings. The Moorish style was one the most fanciful Picturesque styles. Boise's Natatorium featured Moorish keyhole arches in its tall towers and wide side wings. (ISHS 73-2.52.)

more typical of the late 1890s and early 1900s were buildings like the Albion Normal School's administration building designed by W. S. Campbell in 1895 or the Roosevelt School in Coeur d'Alene (1902). The normal-school building combines Picturesque features — rusticated stone arches and an octagonal central tower — with classical columns supporting a front porch and set into the third level of the tower.[16] Roosevelt School mixes features from the Italianate style — a cupola, segmental windows, and a brick cornice — with a porticoed entrance. These designs, similar to numerous schools throughout the state, represent the way in which Victorian forms gave way slowly to twentieth-century classicism.

By contrast, some southeastern Idaho designers and builders were as quick to embrace the new classicism as they were reluctant to discard late Georgian, Federal, and Greek Revival forms. Spori Hall (1899–1903) at Ricks

College in Rexburg displays a pedimented central bay with classical columns set in antis (inset from the exterior wall surface), an early use of a Beaux Arts design motif on an Idaho building. This entry bay departs considerably from Rexburg architect C. W. Speiermann's original plans, which featured a pyramidal-roofed tower.[17]

From the impressive sight of a town's courthouse, college campus, or public school, a nineteenth-century pedestrian could turn to view its residential neighborhoods, usually located around or near institutional campuses. In many Idaho towns, establishing an institution encouraged the development of surrounding land as residential additions. This was the case on Normal Hill in Lewiston, developed around the Lewiston Normal School, and in the southeastern residential neighborhood of Pocatello, developed around the Academy of Idaho. Other neighborhoods came into being along new streetcar lines. This was true of

Hyde Park and other North End additions to Boise that were created between 1891 and 1893 after the Boise Rapid Transit Company was established.[18]

Exclusive neighborhoods like Warms Springs Avenue and Harrison Boulevard in Boise were developed as avenues of large and stylish houses with generous lots for landscaping. Harrison Boulevard in Boise was turned into a tree-lined avenue by realtor W. E. Pierce as part of his North End real estate promotion; his initial planting of trees to line the boulevard was added to in 1904 when property owners created a median strip planted with ornamental bushes and trees.[19] Our film screen image of railroad era neighborhoods, in films like *Meet Me in St. Louis*, is of the boulevard. A pedestrian walking along Harrison or Warm Springs in the 1890s was charmed by views of a succession of Picturesque designs: the crested tower of C. W. Moore's large, brick French Chateau style house (1891); the mixed textures and colors of the Eastmans' brick, stone, and shingle Queen Anne style house (1892); the complex massing, Romanesque arches, and Palladian window of the Northrup house (1893); and the fanciful wooden ornamentation on Italianate houses built in the previous decade.

Even by 1883 Boise's residential neighborhoods presented pleasant vistas. Railroad contractor James H. Kyner visited Boise "after living amid the dust and sagebrush of the desert" and wrote in his reminiscences that Boise

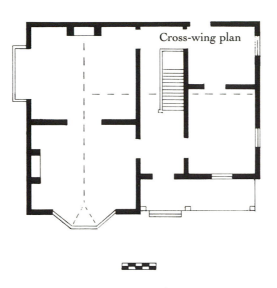

Cross-wing plan

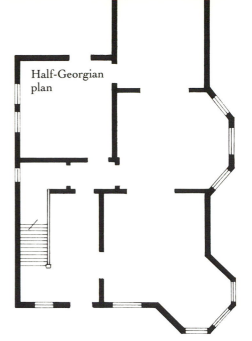

Half-Georgian plan

Cross-wing and half-Georgian house plans (right) came into widespread use with the asymmetrical Picturesque styles of the late nineteenth century. Cross-wing houses featured forward and side gables. The half-Georgian plan had two formal rooms — usually a parlor and a dining room — off of a side hallway. (Drawings by Cheryl Marshall.)

Architect W. S. Campbell's Albion Normal School administration building (below) is typical of institutional design during the 1890s. The building has a central towered section that provides a formal entrance, balanced side wings, and a mixture of Picturesque and classical features. (ISHS 73-221.232.)

was "a beautiful oasis, with fruit trees and beautiful green lawns in profusion" made possible by a network of small irrigation canals and water wheels:

The homes of frame and brick were comfortable and attractive, and the town stands out in my mind as quite the most attractive of any that I ever saw in all that vast expanse from the Missouri to the mountain ranges closest to the coast.[20]

Even if Kyner exaggerated the charms of Boise — he certainly exaggerated the Idaho climate — the town's boulevards did stand out from their contemporaries. For most Ida-

hoans, life was not so fancy. A pedestrian in Sandpoint, Weiser, Rexburg, Lewiston, Murray, or Hailey beheld a sparse residential streetscape with many one-story houses, undeveloped lots between them, and a clear view out to open fields and mountains.[21]

Residential architecture underwent some important shifts in plan and style during this two-decade period. Although many simple, vernacular house plans continued to be built, they generally became more assymetrical and complex. Contractor-built hall and parlor houses like the Adelmann's were among the first frame houses built in the new railroad towns. In Caldwell, Frank Steunenberg, later

to be governor, began his career as a newspaperman, living in just this sort of house.[22] Other simple plans included gable-front houses similar to those found in the 1870s mining camps. Single-room houses also continued to be built of log or frame construction in the Mormon villages, where they served as first homes, sometimes added on to, or were used by poor families.[23]

During the 1880s the central-passage house became common, but its popularity was soon eclipsed by the more complex cross-wing and half-Georgian house plans. The latter two plans owed their popularity to the new style of the age, the Queen Anne, which called for complex massing, and to published distribution of plans through the popular press. Cross-wing houses were used as company housing in railroad towns like Pocatello, where the residential section was restricted to an avenue between the tracks and the main street:

Each house of Battle Creek Row had four rooms and a pantry, same design. No tree was in Pocatello at that time, nor green lawn. These Company houses were fenced and supplied with a company water system from City Creek but water for other houses was still obtained from the Portneuf river and bought at 50c a barrel.[24]

By the 1890s Victorian plans like the cross-wing house and the half-Georgian plan were relegated to use in urban streetscapes,

Some late nineteenth-century architects designed houses in which the formal hall was open to the front parlor. The plan of the Standrod house in Pocatello illustrates this open plan: (A) entry hall, (B) library, (C) parlor, (D) dining room, and (E) kitchen. (Drawing by Cheryl Marshall.)

whereas the single-room, hall and parlor, and central-passage houses were generally more common in the Mormon villages and the rural countryside.

Late in the railroad era there were further changes in house plans that reflected new ideas about the function of the hallway. New England architects William Ralph Emerson and H. H. Richardson experimented with plans that opened the house's entry hall to the front parlor, creating one large—and often awkward—space out of the two rooms. The resulting open plan was accepted in a limited way across the country. Although most pattern-book houses clung to the smaller, private rooms of the cross-wing and half-Georgian plans, some local architects put the new open plan to use. Such a plan was used in the Standrod house, built in Pocatello in 1901 for one of the city's more eminent families. For southeastern Idaho the building was unusual not only for its plan but also for its size and elegance. (Its style, in fact, is unusual statewide, for it is one of the state's few French Chateau buildings.) The house's parqueted and paneled entry, containing a stairway, opens directly onto a front parlor that is divided by pocket doors (doors that slide into a partition wall) from a dining room. The house has been attributed to Marcus Grundfor, a Pocatello builder-architect.[25]

This age saw a marked improvement in the availability of materials for house building. In the railroad towns lumber came into wide use

for housing, and brick and stone were increasingly available beginning in the 1880s. Planed, lathed, and band-sawed woodwork was available from local mills like the Paris Cooperative mill (later Robert Price's mill), from local retailers who carried factory millwork, or through the catalogs of midwestern factories like M. A. Disbrow and Company of Lyons, Iowa.[26]

In the mining towns and Mormon villages log construction was a continuous practice, rivaling frame, brick, and stone construction in its extensive use.[27] Adobe brick also continued to be used in some places. Two Oakley houses of this period, for example, have been found to have walls built with a combination of adobe and fired brick, the fired brick used on the exterior of the wall. "Hasty" McMurray's contemporary log hall-and-parlor house, also in Oakley, is a good example of the continuity of log construction in Idaho's Mormon villages.[28]

Architects employed ornamental materials that had to be shipped for patrons who could afford the extra expense. The Standrod house was built with local stone, but its electric light fixtures were shipped by railroad from the Gibson Gas Fixture Works in Philadelphia. For the 1900 Galloway house in Weiser, a showplace costing rancher Thomas C. Galloway $5,000, the staircase and china closet were factory-made and installed by the contractor. Episcopal Bishop Funsten's house in Boise, a 1901 remodeling by J. E. Tourtel-

lotte, used mostly local materials, including millwork. For his oak and redwood mantels, fireplace tiles, and beveled and plate glass, though, Funsten traded with out-of-state firms in Tennessee and Minneapolis, paying for railway shipping and drayage from the Boise depot. Like many people undertaking buildings in this era, Funsten acted as his own contractor, paying Tourtellotte $250 for his architectural services.[29]

The general stylistic trends of the era, usually grouped under the term *Picturesque*, emphasized verticality, complex massing, and variety in surface texture and color. The Italianate style continued in use through the 1880s, but the dominant style of the period was Queen Anne. In its early Stick phase, the Queen Anne style emphasized the wooden framework of a house through the application of ornamental wood to the wall surface and numerous protruding wings, bays, and towers. In its later Shingle phase, Queen Anne presented a more unified appearance through the use of classical motifs, a shingled wall surface, rusticated stone foundations or first stories, and a more compact massing.

Queen Anne was a natural culmination of the Picturesque age, but even at its height there were conservative builders who held to classical tastes. Some mining-town houses of the 1880s harked back to the Greek Revival style, then long outmoded nationally and in most of the territory. A house known as the McNary house in Bellevue (circa 1881) and

The 1889 Cornwall house in Moscow retained features of the Italianate style in a period when the Queen Anne style was nearing the peak of its popularity. The house imitates the texture of stone with scored stucco veneer and metal under-eave brackets. (ISHS 80-5.154.)

the Feehan house in Murray (1884) both have three-bay gable fronts with Greek Revival style window heads. Greek Revival also persisted in some Mormon villages. The Spencer house in Paris (1880), for example, is a brick temple-form house that suggests its Picturesque era origins only through segmental relieving arches and a roof pitch somewhat steeper than that found on Greek Revival period buildings.

By the mid–1880s the Italianate style was waning in residential architecture, although houses were built throughout the 1890s and even later with Italianate window heads, bay windows, and porch trim. The bracketed porch and dropped window heads of the 1896 Whitney house in Payette are good examples of such latter-day nods to a lingering taste for Italianate. The Mason Cornwall house in Moscow, completed in 1889, is among the state's last Italianate houses. The house was contractor-built in a two-story cross-wing plan, with an octagonal forward bay. Its brick walls are covered with a stucco veneer scored to imitate stone. The cross-wing plan, quoining, metal under-eave brackets, and round relieving arches over the first-story windows make the house a good example of contractor-designed Italianate.[30] Moscow's 1886 McConnell house and the 1887 Christiana Price house in Paris are other late examples. Whereas the Price house uses thin, lathed millwork from Robert Price's Paris lumber yard, William J. McConnell's house displays

the thicker Eastlake ornamentation of late Italianate design.

Queen Anne made its appearance in Idaho in 1881, when Henry Miller, owner of the Minnie Moore Mine, had an elaborate frame house built in Bellevue, one of the growing Wood River mining supply centers. Stick style versions of Queen Anne were beginning to wane in popularity nationwide, just when Idaho's best example was going up. Typical of the Stick mode, the wooden framework of the Miller house is emphasized through dimensional lumber and milled trim applied to the

surface of the building. Interest in the complexities of Queen Anne grew slowly throughout the 1880s, but during the 1890s references to the style became ubiquitous. Near the McConnell and Cornwall houses in Moscow numerous Queen Anne houses went up during the 1890s; in Boise Tourtellotte became known for his fanciful, turreted residential designs; in Silver City, lumberman J. W. Stoddard remodeled his house in the Queen Anne style (circa 1895); and mercantile owner J. R. Shepherd built Paris's first Queen Anne house in the same decade.[31]

The 1881 Henry Miller house in Bellevue (left) is one of Idaho's best examples of the Stick mode. The building's wooden frame structure is emphasized by plain lengths of wood applied to the wall surface. (ISHS 78-5.7/B.)

Frank and Irene Coffin's house in Boise (below) was a stylish Queen Anne with a complex asymmetrical plan, corner tower, variety of wall claddings, large wraparound porch, and turned porch trim. (ISHS 70-169.3.)

housing of Mormon Utah. This tradition combined skilled craftsmanship in various materials, a few standard house plans, and an essentially classical taste for symmetry and simple massing. The Mormons were not unresponsive to popular design, however, and the Queen Anne style was as prevalent in southeast Idaho as elsewhere. The earlier Italianate style, for example, could be used to dress up a folk plan like the central-passage house by applying exterior ornament without meddling

The Queen Anne style and its related floor plans were widely disseminated in several formats. Drawings of Victorian houses set amid graceful landscaping, published with their plans in newspapers and magazines, whetted the public desire for Picturesque residential streetscapes. Pattern books like Henry Hudson Holly's *Modern Dwellings*[32] published plans and elevation drawings for houses ideal for the middle class. Local architects designed Queen Anne houses for the elite, adding to the style's prestige. In the capital city, for example, W. S. Campbell and James King designed two of the state's most sophisticated renderings of Queen Anne for Frank and Irene Coffin and Mary and Will Ridenbaugh.[33] With these sources at hand, local builders soon added Queen Anne's asymmetrical plans and decorative porches to their repertoire.

In southeast Idaho a strong vernacular design tradition had emerged during the first decades of settlement, based on the traditional

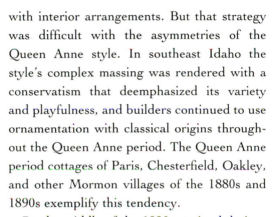

In southeast Idaho masons and carpenters used classical features like pedimented gables and Italianate window arches on otherwise Queen Anne style houses. These vernacular buildings had a formal appearance even during the height of the Picturesque era. (ISHS 72-100.32; Arthur A. Hart, photographer.)

with interior arrangements. But that strategy was difficult with the asymmetries of the Queen Anne style. In southeast Idaho the style's complex massing was rendered with a conservatism that deemphasized its variety and playfulness, and builders continued to use ornamentation with classical origins throughout the Queen Anne period. The Queen Anne period cottages of Paris, Chesterfield, Oakley, and other Mormon villages of the 1880s and 1890s exemplify this tendency.

By the middle of the 1890s, trained designers began to express the Queen Anne in much the same way that the folk builders of southeast Idaho always had. In contrast to the Stick mode, these new houses were contained and symmetrical, and used unified ornamentation drawn from classical forms: the arch, the column, the entablature, the Palladian window, and so forth. It was not in southeast Idaho, however, that this later phase of Queen Anne — called the Shingle style — was most popular. The Shingle style was in vogue in southwest Idaho, where Boise sandstone could be used for the style's rugged first stories and where designers aware of the latest eastern trends had set up practice. The style also became popular in northern Idaho, where it was interpreted entirely in wood. In Lewiston and Moscow, many late Queen Anne houses were built with compact massing, classical ornamentation, and shingled and jettied second stories. Their first stories, however, were typically clapboard rather than stone. A

rental house in Lewiston (1899) designed for W. F. Kettenbach by LaGrande, Oregon, architect W. J. Bennett is a good example of the Shingle mode in northern Idaho.[34]

James King's design for the 1896 Kingsbury house in Boise is one of the first Idaho houses to exhibit the influence of Shingle style as it was being developed by William Ralph Emerson, H. H. Richardson, and other New England architects. The two-and-one-half-story house is unified by a single gable that

shelters house and porch in one unit. The exterior walls are rusticated Boise sandstone, and the large, jettied gable spaces of the half-story are shingled. The porch columns are classically massed. The house demonstrates full-blown the Shingle characteristics only hinted at in King's earlier Watlington house in Weiser (1890).[35]

Another southwestern Idaho architect who preferred the Shingle mode was Charles F. Hummel. As historians Wright and Reitzes

The New England Shingle mode had an impact on Idaho housing beginning with the S. B. Kingsbury house in Boise, a design by James King. The house's Picturesque features are unified by an all-encompassing gable roof. Classical columns support the front porch. (ISHS 78-5.152; Duane Garrett, photographer.)

point out in their monograph about Tourtellotte and Hummel, there was an essential difference in the tastes of Hummel and his partner Tourtellotte. While Tourtellotte was designing many-turreted mansions with complex massing, Hummel created a number of well-unified sandstone and frame houses for clients in Boise and Weiser. Tourtellotte's Bishop Funsten house remodeling (1901) and his Pierce-Borah house (1897) contrast with Hummel's Van Sicklin house (1899) and Elwell house (1900), both in Weiser.[36]

By the time King's Kingsbury house was built, pattern books like Holly's had made some principles of the Shingle mode popular, such as using classical motifs and cladding a jettied upper story in shingles. The Moses Alexander house, built in Boise in 1897, uses these forms without displaying the compact massing more appropriate to Shingle style. Attributed to plans published in a local newspaper, the house is typical of the many late Queen Anne style houses designed by builders that only alluded to the Shingle mode.[37]

The Shingle style reinforced the taste for classicism that some Idaho contractors had never entirely discarded; and concurrent with the construction of Shingle-influenced Queen Anne houses with Doric-columned porches, there began to appear a few Colonial Revival designs that expressed classicism in their symmetrical massing and full-Georgian plans as well as through ornamentation. In Boise, architect W. S. Campbell was responsible for an

The Shingle mode influenced pattern-book versions of Queen Anne houses by introducing shingled upper stories and classical motifs. The Alexander house in Boise is ornamented with carved garlands, classical porch columns, and shingled sections on the upper walls. (ISHS 77-39.1.)

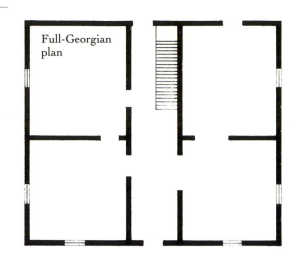

Full-Georgian plan

Classical motifs and full-Georgian house plans became popular at the turn of the century with the Colonial Revival style. R. M. Davidson's house in Boise, a 1901 design by W. S. Campbell, has a balanced facade, doubled classical columns, and a hipped roof with pedimented dormers. The house imitated the Georgian houses of America's colonial period. (ISHS 78-5.151; drawing by Cheryl Marshall.)

early Colonial Revival design in the Davidson house (1901), which imitates the Georgian houses of colonial New England. The Davidson house was foreshadowed, though, by an earlier Campbell design, the 1892 Logan house, which presents classical forms in a slightly assymmetrical plan.[38]

In northern Idaho Colonial Revival plans were imported from the upper Midwest. In Moscow an early Colonial Revival design, built in 1902–1903, is attributed to plans brought from Wisconsin by its owner, Charles L. Butterfield. Similarly, the Smith house of

Lewiston's fashionable Prospect Avenue has a pedimented portico based on the design of the Smiths' previous home in Minnesota.[39] Colonial Revival designs like the Davidson and Butterfield houses were to become standard during the state's next building boom of 1902–1910, but in their day they were dramatic departures from the complexities of Queen Anne.

An integral part of the residential streetscape of the 1880s and 1890s was the small church. Designed in a compatible Picturesque style, these modest houses of worship blended

with their surroundings in size, massing, materials, setback from the street, and landscaping. Many new congregations formed during the late nineteenth century, and they were responsible for a burst of church building as they grew beyond meeting in members' homes or rented halls.

Highly organized faiths like Mormonism, Episcopalianism, or Catholicism provided leadership for church building through their clergy or hierarchy. Such organized efforts eventually resulted in institutional campuses like that centered around St. John's Cathedral in Boise (1904–1921), the seat of the Boise Catholic diocese. In this period, though, the ecclesiastical campus was represented only by the Paris Tabernacle, which was truly a monument to the success of nineteenth-century Mormon cooperative settlement.

Nineteenth-century church building by the Catholics, Episcopalians, and Mormons generally was limited to small buildings, and their organizational abilities can be judged in the impressive number of buildings constructed for small communities. When Catholic Bishop Alphonse J. Glorieux arrived in Boise in 1885 he "found as his cathedral a small, plain chapel,"[40] but he set as his highest priority obtaining pastors and buildings for the small congregations of Catholics scattered throughout the vast territory he administered. As a result, construction of a suitable cathedral was greatly delayed, but Glorieux oversaw construction of thirty-three churches and eleven

Temple Beth Israel is one of Boise's distinctive Moorish style buildings of the railroad era. The style is expressed on the interior with keyhole arches that spring from classical columns. (*Idaho Statesman*, Boise.)

parish schools, hospitals, and academies between 1885 and 1902.[41] Similarly, small Mormon communities all over southeastern Idaho built ward meetinghouses under the direction of a lay clergy and through the volunteer efforts of skilled craftsmen who had been selected to help in the cooperative settlements.

The Methodists, Baptists, Presbyterians, Congregationalists, and other low-church Protestant faiths, built their churches through grass-roots efforts, as did the Boise Jewish congregation that constructed Temple Beth Israel (1896). Congregations began meeting in homes, then rented the use of a hall or the church building of another group, and finally gathered enough money for construction of their own building on donated land, sometimes with the additional support of a grant or loan from their national church board.

Women's groups were usually the instigators in establishing local Protestant churches and financing building projects. Many such groups enlisted energetic ministers who helped bring their plans to fruition. In Weiser, Reverend Edward A. Paddock is said to have "dug the basement, laid the foundation and [begun construction of] the building"[42] for the Congregationalist group that he served. In Caldwell the Presbyterian Building Society was formed in 1885, began construction of a church building in 1887, and then attracted a minister, William Judson Boone, to the town. Carrie Adell Strahorn described the women's protracted campaign for completion of the

building in her remarks at the building's dedication:

Nine ladies of Caldwell met at the residence of Mrs. J. E. Meacham to formulate some plans for raising money to build this First Presbyterian church. The project was discussed in its various phases as only women can do, and one of our best workers remarked that she did not want to go around the rest of her life with a church on her shoulders. . . . It was decided in September 1887, to begin the building and simply go as far as our means would allow.[43]

The construction of Temple Beth Israel in Boise was an exception to the pattern of wom-

en's involvement. Men played the major role in the organization of Congregation Beth Israel in Boise and in the efforts to construct a temple for the group, completed in 1896. Meetings of the organization were attended by prominent Jewish businessmen like Moses Alexander and David and Nathan Falk. With that support, the Moorish style building, designed by Boise architects Chesney and Schroeder, was financed with considerable dispatch.[44]

The struggle to gather money for construction of a church made its design a secondary consideration, and many churches of this period used standard plans in the Gothic Revival

Simple wooden frame church buildings in the Gothic Revival style were typical of the 1880s and 1890s (left). The original section of St. Paul's Episcopal Church in Blackfoot (on left) has Gothic (pointed) arches and a pierced apron decorating the peak of the main gable. (ISHS 79-5.22.)

St. Michael's Episcopal Cathedral in Boise (below) is a sandstone rendition of the Gothic Revival style. (ISHS 69-4.37.)

designs Tourtellotte and Hummel employed doubled columns and a round arch in the entry porch, a subtle reference to the Palladian motifs of Beaux Arts classicism.

By the end of this period, church groups were able to build more ambitious buildings that reflected their religious commitments. In Boise, for example, the Episcopalians built a cathedral (1902) designed by Henry M. Cogdon of New York and constructed under the supervision of J. E. Tourtellotte and Company. The cross-plan building, built of Boise sandstone, re-created a Gothic style Anglican country church.[46]

Gothic was clearly the choice of Catholic

style. Some were provided by church organizations. The Methodist Episcopal Church in Post Falls, built 1890, was based on a Methodist church plan provided by the Board of Church Extension. Others were recycled plans by local architects. Two identical Episcopal churches in Blackfoot and Weiser in Gothic Revival style are attributed to C. W. C. VanWinkle of Hailey. Tourtellotte and Hummel's church designs in Mackay, Shoshone, and St. Anthony, commissioned by Episcopalian Bishop Funsten in 1902, are nearly identical Gothic Revival designs.[45] These buildings are simple rectangular boxes with outset entry porches on one gable wall and bell towers centered above the entry. Gothic design is expressed through their steep roof pitch, pointed windows, and carpenter Gothic ornamentation. For their Episcopalian

Mormon ward buildings like this one in Rexburg's second ward frequently combined pointed and round openings and continued to use Greek Revival features like returned eaves. Substantial brick or stone construction was used to construct these churches. (ISHS 63-211.233.)

and Episcopal congregations in this period, and the style also dominated the architecture of most of the Protestant groups. A few groups departed from this standard style to experiment with the Queen Anne style, as in the Weiser and Eagle Rock (Idaho Falls) Baptist churches (both 1885), or to persist in using the Greek Revival style, as in the Payette Church of the Brethren (circa 1900).[47] Perhaps the most clearly distinct group of churches are those constructed by the Mormons. In plan they differ only slightly from the Protestant meetinghouses, but in ornamentation their combination of pointed and round arches, wall buttresses, stone or brick construction, and retention of Greek Revival forms belie the Enlightenment origins of Mormonism; underline the religion's debt to Masonic symbolism; and reflect the influence of the group's most famous building, the Temple at Salt Lake City and its precursors at Kirkland, Ohio, and Nauvoo, Illinois. The second-ward building in Rexburg, a rusticated stone building with a pedimented gable, Romanesque and Gothic arched openings, and a semicircular window was a good example of the form many of the eclectic late-nineteenth-century ward buildings took.[48]

When Idaho achieved statehood in 1890 much of Carrie Adell Strahorn's imaginary streetscape had been achieved. Railroad shipping had made Mesker Brothers ironwork and Disbrow woodwork more easily and economically obtainable. The number of brick manufacturers active in the 1880s and 1890s tripled over those active in the previous two decades, and brick construction became a realistic alternative for builders. Quarries in Boise provided sandstone for numerous Boise, Payette, and Weiser valley structures, and volcanic stone was quarried in several locations throughout southeastern Idaho. Sawmills became ubiquitous, and many had the capability to produce lathed and planed woodwork to compete with the catalog trade in millwork.[49]

The railroad era created capital, much of which left the state, but some of which was used for the construction of impressive architect-designed buildings. Idaho had at least 180 firms active in the building trades during the late nineteenth century, and about 50 architectural firms were active in the state. A few commissions were designed by out-of-state

The Idaho building at the Chicago Columbian Exposition of 1893 was a Swiss chalet constructed of materials indigenous to the state. The photograph shows the building during dismantling after the exposition had closed. (ISHS 64-2.3.)

architects located in Spokane, Portland, Salt Lake City, and even farther afield, but the majority of architect-designed buildings were the work of local firms.[50] By 1902 Idaho architecture lagged only slightly behind the national trends for architectural plans, materials, and styles.

In view of how much Idaho architecture had advanced during the 1880s and 1890s, it is ironic that the state chose to represent itself at the Chicago Columbian Exposition of 1893

with a rustic chalet designed by a Spokane architect. K. K. Cutter's Idaho building displayed native construction materials in the rough, including walls of unpeeled pine logs. Otherwise it was representative neither of the state's designed architecture nor of its vernacular buildings. Better representatives could be found in the state's southwestern sandstone Shingle style houses and several Moorish style institutions, in its southeastern tradition of vernacular classicism and eclectic religious

buildings, or in its northern use of local wood and brick to interpret styles and plans popular in the upper Midwest.

According to historian Don Hibbard, the Columbian building did provide "Idahoans . . . with an opportunity to discover the richness and diversity of their land," and it "contributed to the creation of a distinctive statewide identity."[51] That rustic identity bears little resemblance to the dreams and accomplishments of Idaho's railroad era town builders.

Notes

1. Epigraph in Carrie Adell Strahorn, *Fifteen Thousand Miles by Stage*, vol. 2, *1880–1898* (1911; reprint ed., 1 vol. in 2, Lincoln, Nebraska: University of Nebraska Press, 1988), p. 123.

2. Lisa B. Reitzes, *Paris: A Look at Idaho Architecture* (Boise: Idaho State Historic Preservation Office, 1981), 39. Unless otherwise indicated, the buildings described in this chapter are documented in National Register of Historic Places nomination forms on file at the Idaho State Historical Society (hereafter ISHS), Boise, and at the Department of the Interior, Washington, D.C.

3. Strahorn, *Fifteen Thousand Miles*, 126.

4. Arthur A. Hart, "Notes on Sources of Architectural Iron in the West," in *Festschrift: A Collection of Essays on Architectural History*, ed. Elizabeth Walton Potter (Salem, Oregon: Northern Pacific Coast Chapter, Society of Architectural Historians, 1978), 41–46.

5. I am indebted to Lisa B. Reitzes (*Paris*, 66) and Arthur A. Hart (*Historic Boise* [Boise, Idaho: Historic Boise, Inc., 1980], 34–35) for their observations of these two buildings.

6. Hart, *Historic Boise*, 36.

7. Ibid., 42.

8. Ibid., 40. See plans for Paulsen's Boise City Hall, on file at ISHS, Boise.

9. See Historic American Buildings Survey (hereafter HABS) documentation of the Boise City National Bank (ID-23) and the Falk-Bloch Mercantile Co. (ID-18), on file at the Idaho State Historical Society, Boise, Idaho, and at the Library of Congress, Washington, D.C. See also plans for "Alterations and Additions to Building of Falk Mercantile Co." (n.d.) on file in the private collection of Hummel LaMarche Hunsucker Architects PA, Boise.

10. Patricia Wright and Lisa B. Reitzes, *Tourtellotte & Hummel of Idaho: The Standard Practice of Architecture* (Logan, Utah: Utah State University Press, 1987), 3; Hart, *Historic Boise*, 56; and Arthur A. Hart, "Money Lack Stalled Cells," *The* (Boise) *Idaho Statesman*, 17 September 1973, 6.

The 1886 territorial capitol is discussed by Hart in *Historic Boise*, 32–33.

11. See Reitzes, *Paris*, 34–35; and Don Hibbard, *Normal Hill* (Lewiston, Idaho: Luna House Historical Society, 1978), 23. Angell designed the Mormon temple at Logan, Utah, an eclectic Romanesque building whose tower suggests a federal cupola. The Bear Lake Courthouse was a simpler, straightforwardly Italianate design before later Colonial Revival additions.

12. Hart, *Historic Boise*, 50; and Reitzes, *Paris*, 76.

13. The Idaho City Schoolhouse is documented in HABS, ID-6.

14. Hart, *Historic Boise*, 32–33, 38–39.

15. Budge wrote his remarks in an 1888 description of the Bear Lake settlements addressed to Gov. E. A. Stevenson; reprinted as "Footnotes to History," *Idaho Yesterdays* 7, no. 3 (Fall 1963):21.

16. Campbell's plans for the normal-school building are on file at ISHS, Boise.

17. Paul W. Jensen, "An Architectural Documentary of the Jacob Spori Administration Building," Report 67, Idaho Historic Sites Inventory, ISHS, Boise. Thomas Carter and Peter Goss note late examples of Georgian, Federal, and Greek Revival buildings in *Utah's Historic Architecture, 1847–1940* (Salt Lake City: University of Utah Press, 1988), 95–101.

18. Planmakers, "Hyde Park Commerce District History," Report 38, Idaho Historic Sites Inventory, ISHS, Boise, 1.

19. Ibid., 2; and Todd Shallat and David Kennedy, eds., *Harrison Boulevard: Preserving the Past in Boise's North End* (Boise: School of Social Sciences and Public Affairs, Boise State University, 1989), 11.

20. James H. Kyner, *End of Track* (Caldwell: Caxton Printers, 1937), 139.

21. General photographic views of residential neighborhoods are rather rare, but one can visualize this era's neighborhoods by looking at Sanborn Fire Insurance Maps, in which sparse development is readily apparent.

22. Jennifer Eastman Attebery, "Domestic and Commercial Architecture in Caldwell," *Idaho Yesterdays* 23, no. 4 (Winter 1980):4.

23. Jennifer Eastman Attebery, "The Square Cabin: A Folk House Type in Idaho," *Idaho Yesterdays* 26, no. 3 (Fall 1982):25–31.

24. Minnie F. Howard, *Early Life and Times of the First Congregational Church of Pocatello* (Pocatello, Idaho, 1928), 12. According to Howard, these cross-wing houses were built in 1886 in Omaha, Nebraska, of Michigan pine and transported from there by rail.

25. The history of the Standrod house is clouded by numerous unverifiable anecdotes that are good examples of the sort of legendry that grow up around a town's largest and fanciest Victorian house. Bobbi Rahder has completed the most thorough research to date about the house in her "Report to the Historic Preservation Commission and the City of Pocatello on the Standrod House Research" (August 17, 1988), on file at the Community Development and Research Department, City of Pocatello, Idaho.

26. Arthur A. Hart, "M. A. Disbrow and Company: Catalogue Architecture," *The Palimpsest* 56, no. 4 (July/August 1975):98–119.

27. Photographs of log buildings from this period can be found in the many local histories of southeastern Idaho communities. Two studies especially useful for architectural studies are Lavina Fielding Anderson, ed., *Chesterfield: Mormon Outpost in Idaho* (Bancroft, Idaho: The Chesterfield Foundation, 1982); and Newell Hart, ed., *Hometown Album* (Preston, Idaho: Cache Valley Newsletter Publishing Co., 1973). See also Jennifer Eastman Attebery, "The Diffusion of Folk Culture as Demonstrated in the Horizontal Timber Construction of the Snake River Basin" (Ph.D. diss., Indiana University, 1985), 86–87.

28. See documentation of these Oakley houses by Tom and Nancy Renk, on file in the Idaho Historic Sites Inventory, ISHS, Boise, sites 007718, 007719, and 007721.

29. For the Standrod house materials, see photocopies

of bill for hauling stone, receipt for fixtures, and bill of lading for railroad shipment in Rahder, "Report." The Galloway house is discussed in Don Hibbard, *Weiser: A Look at Idaho Architecture* (Boise: Idaho State Historic Preservation Office, 1978), 50; and "Specifications: For the Finishing and Completion Of A Two Story Residence for Thos. C. Gallaway, Weiser, Idaho," are on file at ISHS, Boise, MS 2.110. The "Episcopal church account book for building the Bishop's House" is on file at ISHS, Boise, MS 2.99.

30. For the Cornwall and McConnell houses, see Lillian Woodworth Otness, *A Great Good Country: A Guide to Historic Moscow and Latah County, Idaho*, Local History Paper, no. 8 (Moscow, Idaho: Latah County Historical Society, 1983), 81–82, 94–95. For the Price house, see Reitzes, *Paris*, 52–53.

31. William P. Statham presents research about the Stoddard house in "Historic Structure Report for the J. W. Stoddard House in Silver City, Idaho," Report 79, Idaho Historic Sites Inventory, ISHS, Boise. The Pierce-Borah house (1897), Boise, is a prime example of Tourtellotte's Queen Anne houses, in Wright and Reitzes, *Tourtellotte and Hummel of Idaho*, 22–23; plans and elevation drawings on file at ISHS, Boise. Shepherd's house is illustrated in Reitzes, *Paris*, 59.

32. Henry Hudson Holly, *Modern Dwellings in Town and Country* (New York, 1878).

33. Arthur A. Hart, *The Boiseans: At Home* (Boise: Historic Boise, 1985), 48–49, 52–53.

34. Hibbard, *Normal Hill*, 39–40.

35. See the Kingsbury house in Hart, *Historic Boise*, 38–39; and the Watlington house in Hibbard, *Weiser*, 10–11. Many architectural historians treat the Shingle mode as a separate style rather than as a phase of the Queen Anne style. I do not do so here because in Idaho architecture Shingle characteristics appear chiefly in buildings whose overall style is best described as Queen Anne.

36. See Wright and Reitzes, *Tourtellotte and Hummel*, 22–23, 34–35.

37. See drawings of the Alexander house by David A. Cooper, in the HABS collection, ID–22.

38. Hart, *Boiseans*, 54–55.

39. The Butterfield house is discussed in Otness, *Great Good Country*, 87; the Smith house, in Hibbard, *Normal Hill*, 36.

40. Cyprian Bradley and Edward J. Kelly, *History of the Diocese of Boise, 1863–1952*, 2 vols. (Boise, 1953), 1:207.

41. Ibid., 207–14.

42. "A Brief History of the Congregational Churches in Southern Idaho, Written in 1932 by Mrs. Phelps," 5. Manuscript on file in the Intermountain West Collection, Eli M. Oboler Library, Idaho State University, Pocatello, Idaho.

43. Carrie Adell Strahorn, "History of the Ladies Presbyterian Building Society," quoted in H. H. Hayman, *That Man Boone: Frontiersman of Idaho* (Caldwell, Idaho: College of Idaho, 1948), 73.

44. Congregation Beth Israel minute book, MS 2.19, ISHS, Boise.

45. See David Osterberg, "Religious Events and Church Buildings in Kootenai County, Idaho," Report 90, Idaho Historic Sites Inventory, ISHS, Boise; Hibbard, *Weiser*, 48; and Wright and Reitzes, *Tourtellotte and Hummel*, 28.

46. Hart, *Historic Boise*, 58–59.

47. Hibbard, *Weiser*, 55; Roger Edwin Sappington, *The Brethren along the Snake River: A History of the Church of the Brethren in Idaho and Western Montana* (Elgin, Illinois: The Brethren Press, 1966), 28; and Howard, *Early Life and Times of the First Congregational Church*, 24 (for the Eagle Rock church).

48. Pictured in David L. Crowder, *Rexburg, Idaho: The First One Hundred Years* (Caldwell, Idaho: Caxton Printers, 1983), following p. 85. Other Mormon ward buildings are depicted in J. Meredith Neil, *Saints and Oddfellows: A Bicentennial Sampler of Idaho Architecture* (Boise, Idaho: Boise Gallery of Art Association, 1976); and Anderson, *Chesterfield*, figures 1–4 and 1–5. The New England and Masonic origins of this distinctive Mormon church architecture are discussed in Allen D. Roberts, "Religious Architecture of the LDS Church: Influences and Changes since 1847," *Utah Historical Quarterly* 43, no. 3 (Summer 1975):301–27; Robert Winter, "Architecture on the Frontier: The Mormon Experiment," *Pacific Historical Review* 43 (February 1974):50–60; and Laurel B. Andrew, *The Early Temples of the Mormons: The Architecture of the Millennial Kingdom in the American West* (Albany, New York: State University of New York Press, 1978), 41–43, 83–85, 112.

49. Mills capable of manufacturing lathed, planed, and band-sawed millwork are listed in the *Oregon, Washington and Idaho Gazetteer and Business Directory* (Portland, Oregon: R. L. Polk & Co., 1888), 1,223–24, 1,246, 1,248–49. I am indebted to Kathleen Watt for sharing with me her compilation of early Idaho brickmaking firms.

50. The number of people active in architectural design and the building trades is estimated from a compilation of newspaper references to building construction during this period. Those references are on file at ISHS, Boise.

51. Don Hibbard, "Chicago 1893: Idaho at the World's Columbian Exposition," *Idaho Yesterdays* 24, no. 2 (Summer 1980):29.

4

Classicism in a Progressive Age,
1902–1920

Idaho conceived the idea in 1905 to build a Capitol, which should stand as a monument before the world truly representing the spirit of her commonwealth. She chose for the purpose of working out her conception a Capitol Commission of representative wise men of various occupations, who have with the co-operation of the architects, architectural draftsmen and builders, created a design and worked it out in stone with this object in view. . . .

Her deep foundations rest on river gravel fifteen feet below the surface of the ground. . . . The construction throughout is fire proof, with marble floors and side walls in the rotunda and with marble wainscoting and marble floors throughout the balance of the public space in the building. . . . The atmosphere is pure, bright, healthful and is supplied mechanically. . . . Idaho's Capitol on the interior is flooded with light. Its rotunda, corridors and interior as a whole is nearer perfect in this respect than any building of its kind perhaps in the world. Does it represent the people of her commonwealth? . . . If the people are well balanced in their ideals and understand that a commonwealth, like the individual, to be worth while and endure, must have a soul; that the great white light of conscience must be allowed to shine and by its interior illumination make clear the path of duty and in the clarity of that vision that they must act and go forward with courage, to perfect the outward form by the developing and conserving of her resources; encouraging legitimate enterprise and industry, and by embracing and perfecting all that tends to the upbuilding of the moral, intellectual and physical needs of her people; if the people of Idaho hold these ideals and are striving to make them real, then this Capitol truly represents the Commonwealth of Idaho.

Completion of the state capitol (1905–1919) provided formally arranged space for the deliberations of Idaho's legislature. Here, classical columns with Corinthian (leafed) and Ionic (scrolled) capitals lend the house chamber a sense of decorum. (ISHS 60-65.67.)

John E. Tourtellotte's *Souvenir Booklet*[1] for the newly completed Idaho capitol described the building in ornate prose and depicted its marble halls in an album of full-page photographs. But Tourtellotte's booklet was more than a souvenir. Writing in 1913 at the height of Progressivism in Idaho, the architect articulated a number of that movement's ideals as they were reflected in the classical architecture of his age. In the capitol Tourtellotte saw architecture expressing the ideals of a democratic commonwealth whose representatives worked cooperatively toward a perfect society.

The notion of perfecting society through social reforms produced a number of changes in Idaho during this era. Women had already won the vote in an earlier Populist age, but the Progressives can claim other major reforms: a school system centralized under a state board of education; highway and public utilities commissions; the city commission form of government; and provisions for initiatives, referendums, recalls, and direct primaries.

However, many of the reforms linked to Progressivism elsewhere in the nation came late to Idaho. The first state architectural licensing law was passed in Illinois in 1897; Idaho's law came in 1917. The 1903 legislature passed a bill requiring fire escapes on public buildings, and a 1911 act required that public buildings be built with exit doors that opened outward, but further safety and health codes remained a local matter until the state adopted the Uniform Building Code in 1972, in an act regulating factory-built housing, and the Idaho Building Code Advisory Act in 1975.

Local planning and model housing, promoted elsewhere by adherents of the Progressive City Beautiful movement, were pursued informally in Idaho, without the official sanction of law or ordinance. Enabling legislation for local planning by cities was established in 1967; and a Local Planning Act making planning mandatory was adopted in 1975. In the Progressive era, though, local groups, especially women's clubs, saw the need for beautification and improved services, especially for free libraries. In this era most of Idaho's major population centers gained Carnegie public libraries through the initiative of local women's groups whose concerns were twofold: public education and temperance (the library was seen as an alternative to the saloon). Other groups addressed local-planning and public-service issues, most of which were left unresolved until much later. In Caldwell, for example, the Village Improvement Society set forth an ambitious program in 1904 that included parks, art exhibitions, free libraries, lectures, concerts, museums, literary societies, kindergartens, and adult education. President Eleanor Steavenson cited precedents for the group's programs in cities across the country. Although many of its plans came to fruition years later, if at all, the society was successful with its city park project. Similar neighborhood beautification projects were underway in Boise during this same period.[2]

The new towns that were built so rapidly during this era might have provided a testing ground for model towns, but few localities took that direction. Farmers at New Plymouth had tried out a model cooperative village planned in a horseshoe shape in 1895–1901. After the group disbanded, through fiscal and organizational difficulties, the town's odd plan continued in use, but without its original utopian aspects. The company town of Potlatch, built by the Potlatch Lumber Company beginning in 1906, was the work of one architect, C. Ferris White of Spokane. However, White's designs for workers' houses—essentially variations on a few three- to seven-room house plans—reflect little intention to create a set of model homes. The town itself benefited from the Potlatch company's desire to attract and retain workers with families. The company offered a number of public services from the town's beginning, with the exception that there were no indoor toilets in the workers' section of town.[3]

In most towns a standard grid plan and a traditional sense of neighborhoods and commercial areas guided development. It was possible for commercial clubs and city councils to speak of their towns as "model" when promoting services and improvements that are now considered basic, such as waterworks, sewage, bridges, paving and curbing, parks, and fountains. Blocks for institutions or commerce were sometimes reserved around a town park. At Rupert, a reclamation town established in 1905, a city park was planned as the center of the business district. In Twin Falls a city park was planned by the Twin Falls Land and Water Company as a centerpiece for churches, a high school, and the county courthouse.[4]

The civic planning-and-building reform programs of Progressivism were somewhat irrevelant to westerners because they lived in a rapidly expanding economy. The first two decades of the twentieth century were a prosperous time for the western states, where projects begun under the Carey and Newlands Reclamation acts created thousands of acres of new irrigated farmland and where the lumber industry, transplanted from the upper Midwest, established a new economic base. Now that three interstate railroads ran through the Northwest, the new farms and lumber mills had access to national markets. Railroad development also continued with the building of branch lines and intrastate lines.

During this era Idaho's population approximately tripled, and the new population generated myriad architectural commissions for new residential neighborhoods, new schools, courthouses for newly created counties, and whole new towns. The arable tracts brought under irrigation by the Twin Falls and Minidoka projects of south-central Idaho created the towns of Jerome, Twin Falls, Buhl, and many smaller burgs. Those agricultural communities, railroad towns like Montour, and lumber company towns like Potlatch were swiftly created with designs from pattern books or by local or regional architects.

Although the City Beautiful reforms had little impact in Idaho, the notion of perfectability did affect architecture in a number of ways. One can see Progressivism in the pervasive taste for classicism; in experimentation with stronger, practical materials; and in the establishment of standards for professional architects. This was an era of new professionalism in architectural practice.

The decorum and dignity imparted by correctly proportioned classical forms and motifs was important to the architecture of the 1900s and 1910s. In domestic architecture the Colonial Revival achieved ascendancy over the Queen Anne. In commercial architecture the Chicago School and Sullivanesque styles perfected by Chicago architects for the design of tall buildings drew on the balanced proportions and the vocabulary of classicism. Monumental institutional buildings expressed classicism outright in designs that mimicked classical and Renaissance buildings. One can even detect classicism in the way that Greek and Roman motifs were applied to vernacular houses of this era.

Classicism was a reaction to the excesses of Picturesque architecture, just as Progressivism can be seen as a reaction to the excesses of the railroad era. The turn to classical forms in architecture was accompanied by a complementary counter-movement, the Arts and Crafts school. Cherishing natural materials and vernacular forms from the Orient, Europe, and Great Britain, the styles that drew upon the Arts and Crafts movement — Frank Lloyd Wright's organic Prairie School designs, the Art Nouveau style, and the bungalow — belong to a design tradition that challenged the dominance of classicism during the Progressive era while acknowledging a debt to classical forms in their use of symmetry. Because classicism and Arts and Crafts styles were often practiced by the same architects, the two movements can be seen as alternative but equally reform-minded reactions to the Picturesque.

The proper use of classical proportions and motifs was not a simple matter of copybook work. Before a building like the state capitol could be designed and built in Idaho, several things had to happen. Building monuments required not just an expanding economy, but also appropriate new materials and trained talent. In the first two decades of this century all three ingredients came together. At the same time that Idaho experienced unprecedented growth, a number of new materials became available to accommodate the new styles. And most important, the state acquired a new generation of experienced craftsmen and trained architects.

The aesthetics of classicism put new demands on architectural materials. Red brick, a standard material during the 1890s, was too

Steel framing was used in Idaho's new capitol, shown here in 1906 or 1907 as the first story and rotunda were going up. (ISHS 80-163.21/a.)

colorful; rusticated stone offered too much texture. Classicism required the substantial appearance and smooth pale surface of large blocks of ashlar stone and the sculptural quality of carved stone ornamentation. Contractors needed materials for domed institutions and tall commercial blocks; they needed to bridge wide window openings. Idaho architects and builders put several new materials to use to achieve these effects: pressed brick, terra-cotta, steel, cast stone, and poured concrete.

The number of local brickyards continued to multipy during this period. The activities of twenty-two brickyards can be documented during the 1880s and 1890s, but during the next two decades at least eighty-six yards were in business. By this time a few brickyards were advertising the manufacture of pressed brick, although their product may actually have been repressed brick, which is brick that is molded, partially sun dried, and then machine pressed. True pressed brick could be manufactured in colors other than conventional brick red and therefore offered new aesthetic opportunities.[5] In Pocatello, contractor J. F. Murray made what he called pressed brick in 1902. According to *The Pocatello Tribune*, it was "said to closely resemble . . . the famous golden pressed brick of Denver,"[6] a material that was imported for many Idaho buildings. In Salmon, F. M. Pollard ordered a molding machine for his brickworks in 1906, and in 1909 was considering purchase

Nisbet and Paradice's Empire Building in Boise has a three-part design. At the base are storefronts and formal entrances. A middle section of office windows is unified by outset brick-veneered piers that rise to be capped by the third element, a large outset cornice. (ISHS 62-20.01; Harold Sigler, photographer.)

of a dry-press machine. Pollard's aim was to use a deposit of white clay for his pressed bricks, which, according to the *Lemhi Herald,* would rival those shipped in from Omaha.[7] Sand-lime brick, white bricks made of calcium silicate rather than conventional clay, also came into use in this period, and its local manufacture was contemplated in 1906, when the Intermountain Building Material Company was planning construction of its Boise sand-lime brick plant. Sand-lime bricks from Boise were available by 1909, when they were used for the veneer of the Twin Falls Methodist Church.[8]

Another new material that offered superior durability and the light color of stone was concrete block. When it was cast in molds that gave the block a carved or rusticated stone appearance, this material was commonly called cast stone. Its manufacture in Idaho began in most localities between 1906 and 1910, and its novelty drew attention. In Salmon an early concrete molding machine evoked the *Lemhi Herald* editor to comment,

> Wm. Anderson has been busy this week molding the concrete blocks for the water table to grace the foundation of his residence. It is a new industry in Salmon to see this stuff put up into building stones of perfect mold, and many persons went around to rubber[neck].[9]

Cast stone appeared at about the same time throughout the state as local manufacturers

purchased and began experimentation with the newly available molding machines. In Moscow, Wylie A. Lauder, a contractor and brickmaker, began manufacturing concrete blocks in about 1910. In 1906 Caldwell contractors Lem Harding and George Williams began constructing houses and commercial buildings with blocks from their Miles machine, capable of making "any sized or shaped block" with "that fine rich veneered facing."[10] When the Twin Falls Northside Investment Company began development of Jerome in 1907, concrete block manufactured by contractor Paul Kartzke was used for many of the early commercial buildings.[11] In addition to being used for building block, cast stone was used for ornamentation on brick buildings. Cast-stone lintels, sills, coping, cornices, and cornice and coping ornaments could be used in much the same manner as terra-cotta ornamentation, and at less expense.

Poured concrete could also be used to mimic stone masonry, though not so convincingly as the cast blocks. The campus of the Intermountain Institute at Weiser is made up of five concrete buildings built between 1907 and 1930. The exterior of the reinforced concrete walls are scored to give the appearance of an ashlar stone veneer.[12]

Steel, like concrete, had had some limited uses in Idaho buildings during the late nineteenth century, but became more widespread in Idaho during the 1900s. A building like the capitol uses the compressive and tensile

strength of steel to support its tall dome as well as in the structure throughout. Steel for the capitol was manufactured according to the architects' plans by the American Bridge Company, New York, and the Minneapolis Steel and Machinery Company. Among the earliest Idaho buildings to use a steel structure is the Federal Building in Boise, a design by U. S. Treasury Department architect James Knox Taylor. Steel for that building was obtained from Paxton and Vierling Iron Works of Chicago after considerable difficulty regarding the drawing and interpretation of setting plans. Even though the use of steel involved the potential complications of long-distance ordering and inspection, steel-assisted construction was fairly common by the 1910s for large institutional and commercial commissions. C. Harvey Smith's Twin Falls Bank and Trust Company building in Twin Falls (1909–1910) was said to have a steel structure that could support an additional two or three stories. In a building like the Valentine block (First National Bank) in Pocatello (1915–1916), a remodeling designed by Pocatello architect Frank H. Paradice, Jr., the wall structure combined steel with concrete and brick, the whole hidden behind a classical terra-cotta facade.

Steel framework made it possible to build taller buildings and to group windows together. Idaho could hardly claim to have any skyscrapers, but a number of Boise and Pocatello buildings in this period used the three-

Terra-cotta, a glazed and fired ceramic material, was used to decorate early twentieth-century commercial and institutional buildings. Frank H. Paradice's design for the Valentine Building in Pocatello included drawings from which molds for the terra-cotta cladding could be cast. (Photograph by Cuzzin's Photos, Pocatello, reproduction courtesy of Wallace-Hudson and Associates, Pocatello.)

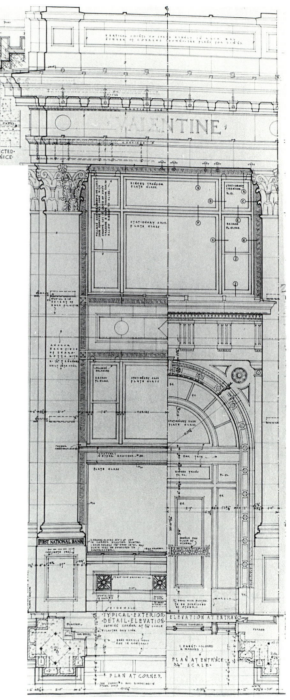

part design (base of storefronts, column of piers and office windows, and an exaggerated cornice) that Louis Sullivan had made popular for the tall buildings of midwestern cities. Nisbet and Paradice's Empire Building in Boise and the Idaho Building in Boise, a design by Chicago architect Henry J. Schlacks, are two of the state's best examples of the tall commercial building. Paradice, who moved from Boise to Pocatello in 1914, went on to design several other Sullivanesque commercial buildings of a smaller scale.[13]

Terra-cotta, a glazed and fired ceramic material, was never used on Idaho buildings to the extent that it was found on commercial buildings in West Coast cities. When terra-cotta was employed, it was generally limited to cornice or window and entryway ornamentation designed to give the appearance of carved stone. Available from more than one western manufacturer, terra-cotta was used for ornamentation as early as 1902, when the Boise Federal Building incorporated terra-cotta detailing cast by a Spokane manufacturer. Gladding, McBean and Company of Lincoln, California, manufactured terra-cotta for the state capitol and for several Idaho buildings constructed in the 1930s. In southeast Idaho, Frank H. Paradice designed the majority of his commissions with terra-cotta ornamentation, probably from the Denver Terra Cotta Company.[14]

The Boise Federal Building, designed by James Knox Taylor, and Campbell and Way-

land's 1902 First National Bank of Idaho Building in Boise were regarded as advanced in their artistry, partly because of their early use of terra-cotta. Generally, though, terra-cotta appeared much later than 1902. Paradice's claim that his Franklin Building (1915) was Pocatello's "first real terra-cotta job" was probably accurate.[15] During the same year, Paradice designed one of the state's first terra-cotta-clad Renaissance Revival buildings, the remodeling of the Valentine Building in Pocatello, completed in 1916. Buildings like it are rare in Idaho and always have been. Similarly veneered buildings appeared in Twin Falls in 1917 (the Twin Falls Title and Abstract Company building by Burton E. Morse), in Jerome in 1921 (the Jerome National Bank), and in Boise in 1924 (the Alexander's Store building by Tourtellotte and Hummel). According to a local newspaper account, Moses Alexander traveled to New York to bring back the latest in architectural ideas to his Boise architects for his Alexander's Store building.[16] In fact, since extensive provincialism no longer existed in Idaho architecture, Alexander had only to travel to Twin Falls or Pocatello to see the use of terra-cotta veneer, and the junior architects at Tourtellotte and Hummel, trained at the University of Pennsylvania, were undoubtedly aware of both terra-cotta veneer and the Renaissance Revival style.

It was an architect's role to be careful of the quality of these new materials. For large and

important commissions, most architects ordered from proven out-of-state sources. Pressed brick from Denver or Omaha was a common facing material. Terra-cotta came from Spokane, California, or Denver; steel, from foundries in Minneapolis, Chicago, or

The Twin Falls Title and Abstract Company building by architect Burton E. Morse used classical motifs cast in terra-cotta. They include columns and pilasters framing the entrance and windows, the triangular pediment above the entrance, and an entablature that unifies the entire facade. (ISHS 77-5.78.)

other industrial cities in the East. These last two materials required special attention, and architects traveled to inspect the quality of a terra-cotta casting made from their drawings and had steel inspected by eastern laboratories.

Construction of the Boise Federal Building, among the most complex Idaho commissions of the era, illustrates the exacting role of the architect in regard to materials. The building was a long-distance collaboration between W. S. Campbell and Company, Boise, acting as contractor for the building, and the supervising architect of the U. S. Treasury Department, James Knox Taylor. Campbell had to

obtain clearance for materials from Taylor and permission for any changes from specifications. Material samples had to be sent to Washington, D.C., sometimes in duplicate. Taylor's office tested varnish, common brick from Thomas Finnegan's Boise brickyard, and sandstone from the Jellison quarry in the Boise foothills. Steel manufactured by a Chicago foundry had to be inspected by a Pittsburg laboratory specified by the Treasury Department. Government supervisors also oversaw such details as brick bonding patterns and the color of the building's decorative terra-cotta. Campbell's search for a nonstaining cement prompted his suppliers to consult

other regional firms, one of whom replied with some exasperation:

> The matter of non-staining Cement seems to be a fad of some Government inspectors, which comes up once in every five years or so.
>
> We would state that there is only *one* brand of Cement we know anything [of] that is non-stainless [non-staining], and that is a French Cement unobtainable West of Chicago. We have never known of its being used here [Portland], as as soon as the Government finds out how expensive it is, they use the regular brands.[17]

Changes in the architectural profession went far beyond the handling of new materials. Architecture was becoming a complex occupation in which the time spent on creative design was overshadowed by calculating engineering loads, writing specifications, corresponding with suppliers and contractors, and negotiating contracts. In many respects this era saw the beginning of modern architectural practice in Idaho. As numbers of trained architects came to the state to set up practice, joining the few from the turn of the century who had stayed, they brought with them new ideas about the role of the architect. Their presence led to official recognition of the profession in a licensing law, in professional organizations, and eventually in creation of an in-state degree program.

Licensing was established by state law in

1917. In the act, passed March 15, the Idaho legislature created a State Board of Examiners of Architects and set forth its duties and the qualifications for licensing. The five-member board consisted of a member of the architectural or engineering department at the University of Idaho (although an architectural program did not yet exist at the university), "a person whose views on sanitation shall meet the approval of the State Board of Health,"[18] and resident architects who had practiced in Idaho for five years or more. In order to apply for an architectural license, an individual had to be an adult citizen (or had to declare an intention of naturalizing) of good character and had to provide proof of schooling: a high school diploma, two years' college study in mathematics or English, and at least three years' experience in an architect's office. Licenses were granted by examination, by presentation of a diploma or certificate from an architectural school (and three years' experience), or through reciprocity with other states whose licensing qualifications were equivalent to Idaho's. A grandfather clause in the law provided that those practicing architecture in Idaho when the law was passed could obtain licenses without meeting these requirements. Thus, the builder-architects working in the state before 1917 could continue their practice as architects. And, contractors could continue to design buildings, so long as they did not advertise as architects. Section 19 of the new law provided that "nothing . . . shall be con-

strued to prevent [anyone] from making plans . . . for . . . any building that is to be constructed by himself."[19]

The board of examiners began its work, conducting much of its business by correspondence. Eventually bylaws were established, regular meetings and testing dates declared, and tests adopted that met the standards of the National Council of Architectural Registration Boards. All licenses were granted by waiver under the grandfather clause or by reciprocity until 1919, when the first license was granted by examination. Although the law did not require it, Idaho's governors maintained a regional balance in board membership. Representatives were generally drawn from the University of Idaho at Moscow and from firms in Boise and Idaho Falls. From the University of Idaho, Ivan C. Crawford of the engineering department served during the 1920s and early 1930s, and Theodore J. Prichard of the art and architecture department served a long term beginning in the 1940s. From Boise, Tourtellotte and Hummel and Wayland and Fennell, and their successor firms, have had members on the board continuously. Frederick C. Hummel served the board for forty-one years, until his retirement in 1962. During his chairmanship formal regulations were drawn up that were the basis for a 1965 document pulling together the board's rules, regulations, and forms in response to the 1965 Administrative Procedures Act. From Idaho Falls, Clinton A. Sundberg served on the board contin-

uously from 1921 until his death in 1967.[20]

At the same time Idaho gained an architectural board of examiners to provide protection and standards for professional architects, the community of architects formed a statewide organization. On 26 July 1916, architects met in Pocatello to form the Idaho Society of Architects. Officers were elected; and with Jesse B. Boyer of Pocatello serving as the group's first president, the group appointed constitutional and judiciary committees and a third committee "to formulate plans so that the state association may become a branch organization of the American Institute of Architects."[21] At its fall meeting the next year, the society voted to protect the practices of architects serving in World War I by carrying on their commissions in their absence. They also arranged a public exhibition of drawings and discussed Idaho building legislation.[22] An Idaho chapter of the American Institute of Architects was formed much later, in 1951, when an unincorporated chapter, with Ernest H. Gates as its first president, was recognized by the A.I.A. Until establishment of the Idaho chapter, Idaho architects maintained individual membership in the national organization, and many southern Idaho architects also joined its Utah chapter.[23]

The 1917 licensing law provided that excess monies from licensing fees should assist the University of Idaho in establishing an architectural degree program. It was another several years before that program was formed.

The university faculty and regents recognized a new architecture curriculum in 1923–1924, and a schedule of classes was announced in the university's 1924–1925 annual catalog, "making it possible for students to take work not heretofore available to young men and women in this state."[24] The new department of architecture was directed by the university architect until 1929, when Prichard became head of a combined art and architecture department.

Before the Moscow department was underway, all of Idaho's formally trained architects were educated abroad or in the eastern United States (or, in one case, California). Among the few nineteenth-century designers with architectural schooling were C. W. Speiermann of Rexburg and Charles F. Hummel and John C. Paulsen in Boise. Speiermann learned masonry in Utah before obtaining degrees in civil engineering and architecture from Scranton College, Pennsylvania, and Hummel and Paulsen were trained in Germany.[25] Most of the turn-of-the-century architects were men with enough formal architectural training or self-taught experience to call themselves architects before licensing began. They were concentrated in the state's largest and oldest cities—Lewiston and Boise—but a few were active in smaller or more isolated locations. For example, Genesee had J. H. Dutton and Company, Weiser had O. M. Harvey, Paris had Will Hurst, Wallace had H. K. Helborstad, and Salmon had Ed Sealander.

With the exception of Tourtellotte and Hummel, the architects who had had a tremendous impact on Boise architecture during the 1890s—King, Paulsen, and Campbell—had departed or were no longer active by 1904. The architects of the new generation were born in the last quarter of the nineteenth century, and many of them received academic training at American schools, where their instructors were graduates of the École des Beaux Arts in Paris. The École was considered the finest school of architecture, and its principles, including the use of classical forms and axial planning, dominated architectural training in America during this period. B. Morgan Nisbet and Hummel's sons, Frederick C. and Frank K., studied at the University of Pennsylvania, where Paul Philippe Cret, a graduate of the École des Beaux Arts, prepared students in the principles of classical form. Ralph Loring studied at the Massachusetts Institute of Technology; Ernest Gates, at the University of Iowa; and Frank H. Paradice, Jr., at the Chicago Art Institute and Armour Institute of Technology's joint architecture program, established by another École des Beaux Arts student, Louis Millet.[26]

The profession grew in numbers as well as preparation. The 1880 census for Idaho lists no architects. By 1902 there were at least eleven working in the state, and many more had been active in the interim and departed. During the first two decades of the twentieth century at least ninety-seven architects had of-

fices in Idaho, some briefly and some over the entire period. After the 1917 licensing act was passed, thirty-two Idaho architects obtained licenses between 1917 and 1920. In addition to the resident architects, fifty-five out-of-state architects were licensed in Idaho during the first three years of the act. Half of them practiced in the neighboring cities of Spokane (seventeen) and Salt Lake City (ten). In spite of their numbers, the out-of-state architects worked on only a few projects each. Their presence just over the border made Idaho architecture a more competitive business than it otherwise might have been, but most of Idaho's designed buildings remained the work of architects living within the state.[27]

The number of early twentieth-century architects was relatively small in comparison to the number of projects going up during this prosperous period. In each region of the state a few resident firms designed the major buildings as well as many smaller commissions. As a result, the design philosophy of the architect and the taste of his community of clients had considerable influence on the architecture of the area where he practiced.

The reciprocal relationship between architect and client as cocreators was probably most evident in residential design. As Frederick C. Hummel noted in an interview after his retirement, architects of his generation were expected to be able to provide their residential clients with the choice of a number of styles.[28] The manner of client-architect negotiations

Julia and Xavier Servel's Colonial Revival style house in Pocatello was designed by architect Palmer Rogers with collaboration from Julia Servel. The building is veneered with white glazed brick. Its large round-arched first-story, dormer, and gable windows and formal columned entry link the house with the architecture of America's Federal period. (ISHS 77-5.145.)

undoubtedly varied, but Frank H. Paradice's correspondence with his clients is illustrative of how very genial such dealings could be. Before coming to Boise, Paradice had a practice in Denver in which he designed some buildings for out-of-state clients. To a client in Alamogordo, New Mexico, he wrote,

As I am not able to determine at this time what style Mr. Jackson wants I will get up a sketch . . . I think would suit and if it does not hit the spot the first time I will make another. I would like to know the size of a standard adobe brick as used in Alamogordo before starting the finished plans also, the kind of stone he wants to use.[29]

Other, more specific negotiations suggest that

clients tended to be more concerned with cost and interior arrangements than with exterior style. Negotiations with a Milwaukee client hinged on the cost of drawing up new plans. "I could make a few small changes such as changing windows without any trouble but to change [the] bath upstairs would mean a new set of plans."[30]

Women frequently took a hand in the arrangement and decoration of the interiors of houses designed for their families. In Potlatch, C. Ferris White designed the houses of Nob Hill in consultation with Potlatch company managers and their wives. Anna Laird, for example, participated in both exterior and interior design of the house she and her family would inhabit. Similarly, Ora B. Miller of

Caldwell was credited as designer of her bungalow style house in that town. In Pocatello, Julia Servel was the principal decision maker for the details of the Colonial Revival style house that Palmer Rogers designed for her and her husband Xavier in 1917. The house was closely modeled on Federal period residences. Julia Servel worked with Rogers to chose its materials from manufacturers' catalogs, including the white glazed brick used for an exterior veneer, mantelpieces, and ceramic floor tile for the kitchen. The house was appointed with two modern conveniences, a built-in cooler and a central vacuum system.[31]

The taste of architects and their communities of clients further distinguished Idaho's already well established regions. In the architecture of northern Idaho during this period one can detect more enthusiasm for the Arts and Crafts movement than in any other part of the state. The most active northern Idaho architects were George Williams of Coeur d'Alene and James H. Nave and Ralph S. Loring of Lewiston. Nave and Loring produced a number of Arts and Crafts designs. The popularity of Arts and Crafts styles was augmented by the work of Kirtland K. Cutter of Spokane, who designed several Idaho buildings.

In southwest Idaho, the firms of Tourtellotte and Hummel and Wayland and Fennell captured the major commissions in the capital city and its region. Both firms designed in many styles, but Beaux Arts classicism and and the Second Renaissance Revival style un-

George T. Williams of Coeur d'Alene designed a number of institutional buildings in northern Idaho with motifs from Beaux Arts classicism, many of them featuring large, round arches. In this construction photograph of the Coeur d'Alene City Hall the bracing is still in place for the building's arched entry. (ISHS 78-208.73.)

derlay much of their work. In south-central Idaho, a number of architects practiced out of Twin Falls, and Frank H. Paradice, Jr., Pocatello, was a purveyor of taste in southeastern Idaho. These two regions share a predilection for the Renaissance Revival, for the use of terra-cotta, and for Sullivanesque ornamentation on commercial buildings.

Southern Idaho was not without examples of the Arts and Crafts styles. But whereas Cutter and the northern Idaho architects favored Tudoresque and Swiss Chalet designs, southwestern Idaho architects, influenced by California trends, favored bungalow and Spanish Colonial designs. Southeastern Idaho designers, influenced by Utah, produced houses, schools, and apartment buildings with a Prairie style flavor. South-central Idaho shared in the tastes of the regions to east and west. There one can find, for example, Spanish Colonial style hotels built to promote the Carey and Newlands Reclamation acts towns and Prairie style houses.

Typical of immigrants to northern Idaho, Williams, Nave, and Loring were from the northern states. George T. Williams was born in Kewanee, Illinois, in 1861. He set up an architectural practice in Coeur d'Alene and worked on Idaho buildings from 1903 to 1912. His work extended as far afield as Sandpoint, St. Maries, Spirit Lake, and even Blackfoot, where he produced a design for the 1911 high school. Less is known of Williams's work than of Nave's and Loring's. Among his finest

buildings are three classical monuments: the Coeur d'Alene City Hall (1907), the Bonner County Courthouse (1907), and the Coeur d'Alene Masonic Temple (1909), whose ornate Corinthian-columned facade draws on Beaux Arts classicism.[32]

James H. Nave was born in Fort Wayne, Indiana, in 1864, and lived in Kansas before coming to Lewiston to set up an architectural practice in 1903. He maintained his Idaho license until 1933, when he abandoned design work to manage the quarry he owned at Clarkston, Washington. Most of his work

dates from 1903 to 1921. During 1903 and 1904 Nave established his Lewiston practice with a few major commissions. In 1903 he designed the Bollinger Hotel; in 1904, the St. Stanislaus Church and several houses in the exclusive Blanchard Heights neighborhood, a development on Normal Hill that restricted house construction to investments of $2,000 or more. By 1906 Nave had expanded his work to other Clearwater Valley towns and to the communities of Camas Prairie. He designed houses, schools, churches, and commercial buildings in Orofino, Grangeville,

Regional stone appears in many of James Nave's designs. His Grangeville Savings and Trust Bank building is trimmed with rusticated sandstone. (ISHS 78-5.1.)

Lapwai, Kendrick, Juliaetta, and many other northern Idaho towns. Nave also captured a few out-of-state commissions, including commercial buildings at Asotin, Washington; Eugene, Oregon; and Glendale, Arizona.[33]

Nave's work is marked by a fondness for stonework and for his fragmented use of classical motifs. His use of stone is hardly surprising in view of his owning a quarry at Clarkston. In the St. Stanislaus Church in Lewiston, he used lava rock to create a sturdy Gothic design dominated by an octagonal entry tower with a domed roof. The stone is dark basalt laid up with a light mortar that emphasizes the stone's rugged texture, dark color, and coursed rubble bond. In the 1906 H. C. Kettenbach Building, Lewiston, and the

Grangeville Savings and Trust Bank (1909) Nave used a golden sandstone, perhaps from his own quarry, to trim two otherwise conventional brick business blocks with corner piers, string courses, and relieving arches. The Grangeville building has an unusual feature in a corner arch that is supported in part by a chunky granite column. Other stone buildings by Nave exhibit an Arts and Crafts influence: his 1904 Hurlbut house in Lewiston, a Tudoresque design; his 1914 Nave Apartments, designed in the Swiss Chalet style; and his 1912 Stone house, which drew on Spanish Colonial and bungalow characteristics.

Historian Don Hibbard describes the many houses designed by Nave as large, conventional late Queen Anne–early Colonial Revival

designs.[34] However, one can see a persistent taste for the Picturesque in Nave's work that led him to isolate classical motifs, when he used them, as eclectic decoration. He was not essentially a classicist. The 1910 Baptist church in Lewiston offers a fine example. The Palladian motif appears throughout, not just to surround the large end-wall windows on the two cross-wings but also at the entry and in the tower gablets.

Ralph S. Loring, born in Boston in 1879, graduated from the Massachusetts Institute of Technology in 1901. He worked for the Army Corps of Engineers in the Southwest, then came to Boise as a U. S. War Department architect at Fort Boise. His association with the Boise firm of J. E. Tourtellotte and Company began in 1905, and from 1906 to 1910 he managed the firm's new Lewiston branch office. At the end of 1910 that office was closed, and Loring established his own office in Lewiston. His practice extended throughout north-central Idaho and eastern Washington. Licensed until 1926 to practice in Idaho, he produced designs for Idaho buildings at least through 1922, moving to California in the early 1920s.[35]

Loring has been credited with a "playful and unpredictable use of the classical vocabulary."[36] However, this tendency, although somewhat akin to Nave's use of classical motifs as ornament, is moderated by the way Loring assembled classical motifs within contained, balanced forms like the two-bay facade

Arts and Crafts styles appear in the work of many north Idaho and Spokane architects. In his Nave Apartments in Lewiston, James Nave created an Arts and Crafts effect through rustic materials and Swiss chalet style balconies and gables. (ISHS 78-203.90.)

In his design for the Thompson Apartments in Lewiston, Ralph Loring used Tudoresque balconies and half-timbering (dimensional lumber applied to the wall surface to imitate the appearance of braced-timber construction). (ISHS 78-5.238.)

of the Lewiston Commercial Trust Bank (1906) or the templelike front wall of the Clarkston Public Library (1906). (Perhaps coincidentally, Nave and Loring both used oddly placed classical columns in the Grangeville bank and the Kamiah State Bank, otherwise quite different buildings.) When he was not designing classical institutions or commercial blocks, Loring was busy with numerous residential designs for Lewiston's wealthiest families. His houses show the influence of the Arts and Crafts movement as it was reflected in Frank Lloyd Wright's Prairie style and in the Tudoresque style. His design for the Thompson Apartments (1920) draws on the Tudoresque style; his designs for the Kettenbach and Beach houses reflect Prairie style ideas and Spanish Colonial Revival style motifs; and the Crapo house (1909) and his own house in Lewiston (1912) use Prairie style massing and detailing like Art Nouveau stained glass. In his house he experimented with the new concrete block, designing what

was locally claimed to be the state's first fireproof building.

Williams, Loring, and Nave were joined by a number of less prolific northern architects. James S. Arnot moved from Spokane to Lewiston to practice there with Nave for only a year, 1905 to 1906. I. J. Galbraith practiced in Lewiston from 1901 to 1904 after having worked as the South Dakota state architect and having designed the Montana building for the 1893 Columbian Exposition. Moving to Spokane in 1904, he continued to do Idaho designs from across the border. His major commissions included St. Joseph's Academy and Hospital, several residences, a Nez Perce school, and the Moscow Elks building.[37]

Spokane architects gave these designers considerable competition. Probably best known was Kirtland K. Cutter, who designed numerous Spokane-area houses in Arts and Crafts styles. Cutter, born in Cleveland, Ohio, in 1860, studied at the New York Art Student's League and traveled extensively

throughout Europe before settling in Spokane, where he had a long career beginning in 1889. He maintained a hand in Idaho architecture beginning with the design of Idaho's Columbian Exposition building and ending in the early 1920s with two Boise residences. His several Arts and Crafts designs for Idaho clients undoubtedly had an influence on the popularity of that movement in northern Idaho.

After completing Idaho's Columbian Exposition building, Cutter was hired by Coeur d'Alene mining entrepreneur John Finch to design an Arts and Crafts style resort home on Hayden Lake (1903); by the Hayden Lake Improvement Company for the Chalet style design of the Bozanta Tavern, a resort on Hayden Lake (1907); and by John and Stella Gray to design a Tudoresque lakeside residence in Coeur d'Alene (1913). A number of other Idaho commissions are attributed to Cutter, including designs for a few buildings in the Lewiston and Coeur d'Alene areas and the Holy Trinity Episcopal Church in Wallace (1910, with his partner Malmgren). In the early 1920s, with his regional reputation well established, he designed the Leo J. Falk and C. C. Anderson houses in Boise (completed 1922 and 1925), and the Lewis and Clark Hotel in Lewiston (1920–1922) is also attributed to him. Cutter kept his Idaho license, obtained through reciprocity with Washington, current from 1920 through 1924, when he completed plans for the Anderson house from his new

Architect K. K. Cutter of Spokane was commissioned by a number of wealthy Idahoans to design recreational houses or large houses in town. His design for John and Stella Gray's house in Coeur d'Alene created Tudoresque styling with narrow windows, half-timbering, and a complex roof line. (ISHS 78-5.201/A.)

home in Long Beach, California.[38]

Preusse and Zittel, a firm based in Spokane, also produced a few major designs in northern Idaho, including the 1894 State Normal School building at Lewiston and Zittel's 1925 Kootenai County Courthouse. Julius A. Zittel was a German immigrant whose contributions to Idaho architecture spanned at least four decades. It was not uncommon for a community to favor an out-of-state bidder for a large commission such as a courthouse. The Shoshone County Courthouse (1905) was the design of Lewis R. Stritesky and Francis P. Rooney, Spokane architects who also de-

signed the Coeur d'Alene St. Thomas Church (1912) and buildings in Wallace and Kellogg.

J. E. Tourtellotte and Company, later Tourtellotte and Hummel, and Wayland and Fennell were the preeminent Boise firms. Perhaps more than any other firms in the state, their practice deserves to be called statewide or regional rather than local, since they were successful in capturing commissions all over the state as well as out of state. Both firms also have a claim on shaping an Idaho design tradition. The state's first few Idaho-reared and native-born architects were members of the Hummel and Wayland families, and both

firms have experienced the continuity that comes with overlapping personnel with long tenures. Members of the two firms have played important roles in the formation of the Idaho chapter of the American Institute of Architects and the State Board of Examiners of Architects. If Idaho has an indigenous high-style design tradition, it lies in the work of these two firms.

John E. Tourtellotte and Charles F. Hummel practiced architecture separately in Boise and Weiser before forming a partnership under the name J. E. Tourtellotte and Company in 1900. In 1910 the firm's name was changed to Tourtellotte and Hummel. Even though Tourtellotte moved to Portland in 1913 and the two partners died in 1939, the name Tourtellotte and Hummel continued in use until 1942 when the firm closed for the duration of World War II. After the war the firm reopened as Hummel, Hummel, and Jones.

The senior member of the firm, Tourtellotte, was born in East Thompson, Connecticut, in 1869. His training was typical of the many self-taught builder-architects of his day. He completed high school at Webster, Massachusetts; was tutored in architectural drawing by Albert A. Barker, a Worcester architect; apprenticed to Webster contractors Cutting and Bishop; and later completed a correspondence course in architecture. He came to Idaho in 1890, having worked for a year as a builder in Chicago, Kansas City,

A taste for the Picturesque lingered in some of Boise architects Tourtellotte and Hummel's early twentieth-century work. Their Knights of Pythias Hall turned a lodge hall facade into a rusticated sandstone castle. (ISHS 78-56.1.)

Albuquerque, and Pueblo, Colorado. In Boise he engaged in both designing and contracting, but in 1894 he had enough work to devote his practice entirely to architectural design. As noted in chapter 3, his taste for the Picturesque is apparent in the few Queen Anne houses that can be attributed to him alone and in the remodeling of the Moorish style Idaho Soldier's Home. Although Tourtellotte moved to Oregon in 1913 to establish and manage the firm's Portland-based office, he maintained an Idaho license until his death in 1939.[39]

Charles F. Hummel was born in Germany in 1857 and, like many immigrant architects of his day, received formal academic training in architecture before coming to the United States, in his case in a technical college at Stuttgart. Hummel graduated in 1879, worked in Freiburg as a draftsman, and immigrated to the United States in 1885. He worked in Chicago and St. Paul as a carpenter, and moved to Tacoma in 1888, where he worked as an architect and builder in the Puget Sound area before moving to Boise in 1895 during a national recession. There he had no difficulty finding design and construction work, and his commissions before joining up with Tourtellotte included houses and commercial buildings in Boise and Weiser. As noted in chapter 3, Hummel's taste for classicism, perhaps a result of his academic training, contrasted with Tourtellotte's pattern-book Picturesque inclinations. According to Wright and Reitzes, Hummel's training was

By 1904 classicism was apparent in much of Tourtellotte and Hummel's work. Their Boise Carnegie Public Library has a central pedimented entry with carefully proportioned wings. Two-story pilasters and a continuous cornice molding unify the building into a balanced composition. (ISHS 3767.)

critical to the success of the firm's major commissions. They write that "it seems improbable that Tourtellotte could have designed such complex buildings as St. John's Cathedral or the capitol without [Hummel]."[40]

Tourtellotte and Hummel employed Hummel's two sons, Frederick C. and Frank K., in 1909 and 1916. This was the first generation of Idaho-bred architects. Although they were born out of state, Frederick in Germany in 1884 and Frank in Everett, Washington, in 1892, both spent their childhood years in

Boise. The brothers studied architecture at the University of Pennsylvania, and both returned to their home state to work for, and eventually join, the family firm.[41]

Tourtellotte and Hummel was responsible for over four decades of Idaho design, and the successor firm headed by Frederick's son Charles F. Hummel is still a major regional firm. The most renowned examples of the firm's work from the first two decades of this century include two Beaux Arts monuments in the capital city: the state capitol and Boise

High School. The firm also produced a number of Boise-area schools and institutional buildings between 1902 and 1909 that reflect a continuing Picturesque aesthetic. The Knights of Pythias Hall in Weiser, a Rhenish Romanesque style building with a sandstone exterior, is the most fanciful of these designs. More typical were the 1903 St. Theresa's Academy in Boise and the University of Idaho's gymnasium of the same year, both in a style that Wright and Reitzes call "Italian-esque eclectic"[42] for its mixture of Italian

Campbell and Wayland's First National Bank of Idaho building in Boise clearly drew upon the Second Renaissance Revival style for its separate treatment of first and second stories, its wide first-story windows, and its terra-cotta cornice. (ISHS 69-4.27.)

campaniles with chateauesque features. By 1904, with their design for the Boise Carnegie Public Library, Tourtellotte and Hummel were showing a strong classical bent that continued with Colonial Revival houses, Second Renaissance Revival business blocks, and Beaux Arts institutions.

Wayland and Fennell were Tourtellotte and Hummel's chief competitors for building projects in southern Idaho. Charles W. Wayland, born in Boston in 1873, completed his school-

ing in Duluth, Minnesota, where his father was a lumberman. In Duluth, Wayland received some tutoring in architectural design and served as a draftsman. In 1900 he came to Boise and did drafting for W. S. Campbell. The young man must have shown promise, for Campbell made him a partner only two years later. Wayland worked with Campbell until 1904, when his senior partner left Boise.[43]

James A. Fennell was a westerner, born in Linden, California, in 1872. Fennell studied

architecture in California and worked as a draftsman for San Francisco architect Alexander F. Oakley. Moving to Butte, Montana, in 1897, he was employed with J. W. White as a draftsman, then practiced architecture with his partner, George B. Cove. The partnership of Fennell and Cove designed buildings throughout Montana. Fennell's association with the Campbell and Wayland partnership began in 1902, and later he and Wayland formed a successor firm. In Boise, Fennell was active in the Civic Art League and the Boise Art Club.[44]

The designs of Wayland and Fennell span at least four decades, and the successor firm is still active in Boise. Wayland's son Charles V., born in Boise in 1902, was one of the first Idaho natives to practice architecture in Idaho. He attended the University of Washington and the University of Idaho, and obtained his Idaho license in 1931. In the 1950s, Charles V. joined with Glenn E. Cline in the first of many successor firms, Wayland and Cline. Both men were presidents of the Idaho chapter of the A.I.A., and both served on the architectural licensing board.[45]

A fondness for classicism and Renaissance design can be seen in Campbell and Wayland's 1902 First National Bank of Idaho building, Boise. The bank was one of the city's first Second Renaissance Revival buildings, a style apparent in the building's differentiation of stories (a rusticated-sandstone first floor and pressed-brick second and third stories),

A shallow dome and doubled columns are Beaux Arts motifs used by Wayland and Fennell in their Fremont County Courthouse, depicted here on a tinted picture postcard. (ISHS 64-120.5.)

its wide first-story window openings, and its prominent cornice with terra-cotta ornament.[46] Classicism can be traced through much of the firm's work. Wayland and Fennell went on to design a classical exposition building to represent Idaho at the 1914 Panama-Pacific Exposition at San Francisco. Among their numerous Boise business blocks, institutional buildings, and residences are two Colonial Revival style buildings that draw upon Georgian motifs: the 1916 Davidson house and the 1910 Idaho Statesman Building. The latter building is an unusual design, Colonial Revival style commercial buildings being rare in Idaho.

Wayland and Fennell's work took them east to Albion, St. Anthony, Dubois, and to the Shoshone Indian Agency in Wyoming, and west to Vale and Baker City, Oregon. The 1909 Fremont County Courthouse in St. Anthony, with its shallow dome and columned entryway, is one of the firm's finest Beaux Arts designs. Wayland and Fennell designed dormitories for the Albion Normal School and the State Industrial School at St. Anthony; Carnegie libraries for Idaho Falls and Baker City, Oregon; and schools and churches for communities throughout southern Idaho, from Carey to Weiser. A large part of their practice in the period 1904 to 1912 was de-

voted to schools, churches, and hotels in the new towns of south-central Idaho. In 1908 the firm produced designs for hotels in Burley, Richfield, and Jerome, and for an addition to the Perrine Hotel in Twin Falls. Their school buildings include Twin Falls High School, built 1910–1911. The building was constructed with a shallow dome and outset central bay reminiscent of the Fremont County Courthouse. However, the high school lacks the courthouse's dramatic full-height columns, and its grouped rows of double-hung sash windows and large cast-stone cornice ornaments link the building stylistically with the many Prairie-influenced schools of south-central and southeast Idaho.

A number of architects maintained local practices in Boise and the smaller towns of Boise and Payette valleys. John W. Smith of Boise designed commercial buildings and houses in Boise and school buildings scattered across southwest Idaho. He may have been the only Idaho architect to publish his plans. In a weekly column of the *Evening Capital News* during 1909, Smith presented drawings of houses, commercial buildings, and institutions accompanied by essays regarding the importance of hiring architects.

Herbert W. Bond of Weiser had a practice there from 1905 until World War I. Born in East Dedham, Massachusetts, in 1869, Bond entered architectural practice at the rather late age of thirty-six after a varied career that included learning carpentry from his father in

County Court House, St. Anthony, Idaho.

LUDLOW PHOTO.

When the south-central Idaho architects drew upon Arts and Crafts styles, they favored Spanish Colonial Revival or Prairie style motifs. The Spanish Colonial style appears in B. Morgan Nisbet's Buhl City Hall: stucco veneer, curvilinear parapets, and round-arched openings. (ISHS 77-5.49.)

Boston, cowboying in Owyhee County, managing a planing mill in California, doing carpentry in Boise, and constructing the Kelley planing mill in Weiser. His architectural knowledge was acquired through self-study. In Weiser, Bond formed a partnership with George A. Smith, a Missourian. The firm of H. W. Bond and Company designed houses and a few churches, schools, and commercial buildings. Bond's practice extended to nearby Payette, Parma, Council, New Meadows, and Vale, Oregon.[47]

No mountains or canyons divide southwest from southeast Idaho, but the two regions were sufficiently separated by distance and by their different settlement histories to have developed identifiably distinct architectural traditions. The area between—arid south-central Idaho—developed later than the regions to the west and east and so provided a further barrier between them. It was natural for the Boise architects to look eastward when the irrigation projects began opening up south-central Idaho to settlement in 1904. The Wayland and Fennell firm was particularly successful at tapping that new design market. But the south-central region also acquired a few resident architects of its own. B. Morgan Nisbet was one. Born in Pittsburg in 1873, Nisbet graduated from the University of Pennsylvania's architecture program in 1898. He worked as an architect in Pittsburg before coming to Boise to work in the Boise office of J. E. Tourtellotte and Company from 1903 until

1909. In that year he joined Frank H. Paradice, Jr., in a partnership based in Boise. After five years' work with Paradice, Nisbet established an office in Twin Falls in 1914, at the same time that Paradice moved to Pocatello. Nisbet and Paradice's Empire Building in Boise remains the city's best example of a Sullivanesque commercial building. Among the few Twin Falls County buildings that can be attributed to Nisbet are the 1916 Methodist church addition in Twin Falls, a Tudor Gothic design that employed Boise sandstone veneer, and several buildings in Buhl, including the 1919 city hall, a Spanish Colonial Revival design, and the 1920 high school.[48]

The work of the south-central Idaho architects produced a number of elegant renditions

of the Second Renaissance Revival style, many of them employing terra-cotta or cast stone for coping, cornices, string courses, window surrounds, or other ornamentation. One of the most striking Renaissance Revival buildings is the terra-cotta-ornamented St. Edward's Catholic Church in Twin Falls. Its architect, Ernest H. Gates, modeled the building after the Renaissance churches of northern Italy, with twin towers designed after campaniles. Gates was born in 1880 in Hornell, New York, graduated from the University of Iowa, practiced architecture in California and Idaho, and then worked for the Federal Housing Administration until 1949. Gates was active in the Idaho Society of Architects, serving as secretary in 1917. When

In his twin-towered Renaissance Revival design for St. Edward's Catholic Church, Twin Falls architect Ernest H. Gates used terra-cotta ornamentation for a dramatic recreation of Italian Renaissance architecture. (ISHS 77-5.71/A.)

Idaho architects formed their own chapter of the American Institute of Architects, Gates served as the chapter's first president. His Idaho design work also included the Twin Falls hospital (circa 1918) and nurses' home (1919–1920).[49]

C. Harvey Smith came to Twin Falls from Spokane in 1908 and quickly established a successful practice with commissions for the Twin Falls County Courthouse, the Twin Falls Bank and Trust Company, and other Twin Falls and Kimberly commercial blocks. Even in small buildings like his own one-and-one-half-story house Smith employed monumental classicism. His courthouse is one of Idaho's most impressive big little buildings. The two-story building manages to give the viewer a feeling of monumental height, the result of a two-story portico whose double columns rest on bases that are level with a tall, raised basement story.[50]

Burton E. Morse was one of the most prominent Twin Falls architects. Born in Farmington, Illinois, in 1867, Morse came to Twin Falls from Chicago. He was a founding member of the Idaho Society of Architects, serving as first vice-president in 1916 and president in 1917. His many Renaissance and Colonial Revival designs include his own home of 1908, the Maxwell and Sweeley houses (1909 and 1910), a 1916 school for the Twin Falls School District, the 1917 Twin Falls Title and Abstract and Herriott Auto buildings, the 1918 Rex Arms, and the 1920 Twin Falls high

Architect C. Harvey Smith gave the Beaux Arts portico of Twin Falls County Courthouse a sense of monumental height by raising its paired columns on heavy one-story bases. (ISHS 73-221.440/b; Clarence Bisbee, photographer.)

During the Progressive era James Knox Taylor, architect for the U.S. Treasury Department, was responsible for six new federal buildings in Idaho. Masons for the Moscow Federal Building posed for this photograph while laying ornamental brickwork and terra-cotta for the building's third story. (Latah County Historical Society.)

school and intermediate school. The title and abstract building is one of his best works, an ornate terra-cotta-veneered Renaissance Revival design.[51]

The preeminent Pocatello architect of this era was Frank H. Paradice, Jr., who was responsible for most of that city's major commercial and institutional buildings. Paradice's fondness for using terra-cotta on buildings with Sullivanesque proportions and decoration may be an outgrowth of his Chicago background. As mentioned before, he studied at the Chicago Art Institute and Armour In-

stitute of Technology, schools that offered a joint architecture program with a Beaux Arts orientation. Paradice was born in Ontario, Canada. He worked in Denver and Portland before moving to Idaho. After moving to Pocatello, Paradice worked alone for some time, then formed a partnership with Ray S. Hunter. After Paradice's death in 1952, Hunter and Grant C. Brower formed a successor firm that still has a Pocatello practice. In addition to the Boise Empire Building, Paradice's major commissions include the Franklin Building (1915), the Fargo Building

(1916), and the Valentine Building (1916), all in Pocatello. The terra-cotta facade of the Valentine Building is a classical design with full two-story pilasters. Paradice was a fine draftsman who did much of his own drawing, including plans prepared to guide manufacturers in casting terra-cotta ornament.[52]

Other local architects in southeast Idaho included builder-architect Marcus Grundfor, born in Denmark in 1869, who designed several Pocatello buildings, including the Sonnenkalb and Dietrich buildings (1915 and 1916). Jesse B. Boyer of Pocatello, born in LaFayette County, Missouri, designed buildings in Malad, Montpelier, and Pocatello. His partner from 1915 to 1917 was Palmer Rogers, who had as one of his major Pocatello commissions the design of the Servels' Colonial Revival style house (1917–1918), described earlier. Charles B. Onderdonk also practiced architecture in Pocatello, designing the Kane Building (1914), a Renaissance design in cream-colored pressed brick with a terra-cotta cornice and parapet. Fisher and Aitken were the principals of an early Idaho Falls firm responsible for the design of the Bonneville County Courthouse (1919–1921), an Aberdeen school (1914) and the Williams store in Shelley (1920). Lionel E. Fisher was born in Fremont, Illinois, and his partner, Charles Aitken, was born in Scotland. Their courthouse building for Bonneville County was a simplified classical design built in concrete with a brick veneer.

The largest towns of southeastern Idaho are much farther from Salt Lake City than northern Idaho is from Spokane, but cultural and economic ties with Utah through railroad links, family, and religion have always been strong. Thus, Salt Lake City architects looked northward for major commissions and had some success in bids on the region's important work. Hyrum Pope of Pope and Burton, a Salt Lake firm, obtained an Idaho license through reciprocity with Utah and maintained it until 1939. The firm designed the monumental 1918 Mormon Tabernacle at Montpelier, an eclectic building that combines a semicircular plan with simplified Georgian motifs. (They later adapted the same plan for a tabernacle in Blackfoot.)

Although it was unusual for an Idaho client to seek architects outside of the Idaho, Utah, or Washington markets, a few buildings were designed by Montana architects and an occasional building was designed by architects from cities on the East and West coasts. These commissions tended to be specialized projects for organizations or firms that had a multistate basis or for the federal government. They included an occasional commission for a federal building, church, bank, or theater. In addition to the Boise Federal Building, for example, Renaissance Revival style federal buildings designed by the office of James Knox Taylor were constructed in Moscow, Pocatello, Idaho Falls, Lewiston, and Twin Falls.

Idaho architects' main rivals, though, were not from out of state. Alongside the high-style tradition of twentieth-century classicism was a strong vernacular tradition that belonged to carpenters and masons, farmers and ranchers. In spite of Tourtellotte's glorification of the architect-designed monument, and in spite of John W. Smith's homilies on the need to hire architects, most of Idaho's buildings were not architect-designed. Instead, as becomes apparent in chapter 5, they were the work of vernacular builders who built small and modestly styled buildings laid out according to folk or pattern-book plans and often constructed with indigenous materials. Even so, Idaho architects achieved much during the Progressive era toward their goal of legitimizing and codifying architecture as one of the professions. Through their training, travel, and reading, architects had become a chief source of new architectural ideas. Their Beaux Arts training brought decorum to Idaho streetscapes of the Progressive age.

Notes

1. Epigraph from Tourtellotte and Hummel, *Souvenir Booklet: Capitol of Idaho at Boise* (Boise: Overland Publishing Co., 1913).

2. Eleanor Steavenson, "Plans for Beautifying Caldwell," *The Caldwell Tribune*, 16 April 1904, 1. For Boise beautification, see Todd Shallat and David Kennedy, eds., *Harrison Boulevard: Preserving the Past in Boise's North End* (Boise: School of Social Sciences and Public Affairs, Boise State University, 1989), 14–16.

3. Information about New Plymouth is in Steven Dotterer, "Cities and Towns," in *Space, Style and Structure: Building in Northwest America*, 2 vols., ed. Thomas Vaughan and Virginia Guest Ferriday (Portland, Oregon: Oregon Historical Society, 1974), 1:199–205. Information about White and his Potlatch designs is available in Keith C. Petersen, *Company Town: Potlatch, Idaho, and the Potlatch Lumber Company* (Pullman, Washington: Washington State University Press, 1987), 88–93. As Petersen notes, the records of the Potlatch Lumber Company in the University of Idaho Library Special Collections include correspondence, plans, and drawings pertaining to the town's architecture. Unless otherwise indicated, the buildings described in this chapter are documented in National Register of Historic Places nomination forms, on file at Idaho State Historical Society (hereafter ISHS), Boise, and at the Department of the Interior, Washington, D.C.

4. Patricia Wright, *Twin Falls Country: A Look at Idaho Architecture* (Boise: Idaho State Historical Society, 1979), 13.

5. I am indebted to Kathleen Watt for sharing with me her compilation of early Idaho brick manufacturers. For pressed and repressed brick in the Pacific Northwest, see Karl Gurcke, *Bricks and Brickmaking: A Handbook for Historical Archaeology* (Moscow, Idaho: The University of Idaho Press, 1987), 88–95. According to Gurcke, a dry-press machine was in use at Weiser as early as 1890. However, those 1890s Weiser and Boise buildings that have been surveyed show no use of pressed brick.

6. *The Pocatello Tribune*, 2 May 1902, 1.

7. For the Salmon brickyards, see *The* (Salmon) *Idaho Recorder*, 21 June 1906, 8; and *The* (Salmon) *Lemhi Herald*, 9 September 1909, 3.

8. *The* (Boise) *Idaho Daily Statesman*, 17 March 1906, 5; and Wright, *Twin Falls Country*, 26.

9. *The* (Salmon) *Lemhi Herald*, 3 June 1909, 3.

10. *Caldwell Tribune*, 28 April 1906, 1. For Lauder's activities in Moscow, see Lillian Woodworth Otness, *A Great Good Country: A Guide to Historic Moscow and Latah County, Idaho*, Local History Paper, no. 8 (Moscow, Idaho: Latah County Historical Society, 1983), 80.

11. "A Walking Tour of Downtown Jerome" [Jerome Certified Local Government, 1989].

12. Don Hibbard, *Weiser: A Look at Idaho Architecture* (Boise: Idaho State Historic Preservation Office, 1978), 36–41.

13. For steel in the capitol, see "Second Biennial Report of the Capitol Building Commission . . . State of Idaho" (Boise: Syms-York Company, [1909]), 2–3. For the Boise Federal Building, see John M. Bailey to W. S. Campbell and Company, 1 November 1901; W. S. Campbell to James K. Taylor, 31 March 1902; Campbell to Taylor, 24 April 1902; Taylor to Campbell, 5 May 1902; Paxton and Vierling Iron Works to Taylor, 21 June 1902; and Taylor to Paxton and Vierling Iron Works, 26 June 1902; all in MS 168, ISHS, Boise. Similar complications arose over many other matters during construction of the Boise Federal Building. For the Twin Falls Bank and Trust Company building, see Wright, *Twin Falls Country*, 33. Plans and elevation drawings for the Valentine block and other Paradice designs are on file in the private collection of Wallace-Hudson and Associates, Pocatello, Idaho. The Empire and Idaho buildings are discussed in Arthur A. Hart, *Historic Boise* (Boise: Historic Boise, 1980), 54–55, 62–63.

14. For the Federal Building, see Campbell to Taylor, 31 March 1902, MS 168, ISHS, Boise. For evidence of terra-cotta manufacturers, see "Job Order Listing Sheets of Gladding, McBean & Co., Inc.," Bancroft Library, University of California, Berkeley. Unfortunately, most of Paradice's papers have not yet surfaced, but a promotional desk ornament manufactured by the Denver Terra Cotta Company survives at Wallace-Hudson and Associates, Pocatello, to suggest that Paradice had some dealings with the firm.

15. This statement of Paradice's, which may be apocryphal, is quoted in "Designing Paradice," a pamphlet prepared by the Pocatello Historic Preservation Commission, City of Pocatello (n.d.).

16. Patricia Wright and Lisa B. Reitzes, *Tourtellotte &*

Hummel of Idaho: The Standard Practice of Architecture (Logan, Utah: Utah State University Press, 1987), 66.

17. Balfour, Guthrie & Co. to Fletcher Steen Co., 18 April 1902, in MS 168, ISHS, Boise.

18. *General Laws of the State of Idaho Passed at the Fourteenth Session of the State Legislature* (Boise: Capital News Publishing, 1917), chap. 116, sec. 1.

19. Ibid., sec. 19.

20. See file cards for architectural license applicants and the Board of Examiners of Architects' minute book for 1926 through 1966, on file at the Bureau of Occupational Licenses, State of Idaho, Boise. I am indebted to bureau chief Marvin D. Gregersen for his explanation of these files.

21. "Architects Perfect a State Body," *The Pocatello Tribune*, 26 July 1916, 1.

22. "Architects Show Their Patriotism," *Twin Falls Times* 1 November 1917, 1.

23. "Past Presidents; Idaho Chapter AIA" [1985]; and bylaws of The Idaho Chapter, The American Institute of Architects, 1 January 1964; both on file at the Idaho chapter office, Boise. I am indebted to Boise architect Charles F. Hummel for discussing the history of the Idaho chapter with me.

24. *The University of Idaho Bulletin* 20, no. 15 (April 1925):122. See also *The University of Idaho Bulletin* 19, no. 7 (April 1924):57–58; 20, no. 1 (January 1925):15; 23, no. 21a (September 1928):10; and "The University of Idaho Dedicates a New Art and Architecture Building" [1966]; all on file at the Idaho State Library, Boise.

25. Paul W. Jensen, "An Architectural Documentary of the Jacob Spori Administration Building," Report 67, Idaho Historic Sites Inventory, ISHS, Boise, 8–9; Hart, *Historic Boise*, 38; and Wright and Reitzes, *Tourtellotte and Hummel*, 5.

26. Hiram T. French, *History of Idaho*, 3 vols. (Chicago: Lewis Publishing Company, 1914), 1:722; Wright and Reitzes, *Tourtellotte and Hummel*, x, 2; Frederick C. Hummel, interviewed by Arthur A. Hart, 18 May 1974,

OH498B, ISHS, Boise; obituary for Ernest H. Gates, 5 October 1958, clipping on file at Bureau of Occupational Licenses; and Hart, *Historic Boise*, 62.

27. Figures for architects practicing in Idaho are compiled from newspaper indexing, on file at the ISHS, Boise, and from the files of the Bureau of Occupational Licenses.

28. Frederick C. Hummel, interviewed by Arthur A. Hart, 4 May 1974, OH498A, ISHS, Boise.

29. Frank H. Paradice, Jr., to A. J. King, 12 January 1904, in MS 2.210, ISHS, Boise.

30. Paradice to Chas. T. Lange, 2 March 1904, in MS 2.210, ISHS, Boise.

31. Petersen, *Company Town*, 91; and David T. Armstrong, "The Servel Home," on file in the Intermountain West Collection, Eli M. Oboler Library, Idaho State University, Pocatello.

32. In addition to the sources credited in the following notes, information about architects and their work is from newspaper indexing and the blueprint collection at ISHS, Boise, and from files at the Bureau of Occupational Licenses.

33. Don Hibbard, *Normal Hill: An Historic and Pictorial Guide* (Lewiston: Luna House Historical Society, 1978), 5–7.

34. Ibid., 7.

35. Ibid., 7–8; and Wright and Reitzes, *Tourtellotte and Hummel*, 2, 17, 52–53.

36. Wright and Reitzes, *Tourtellotte and Hummel*, 52.

37. Hibbard, *Normal Hill*, 5, 8.

38. Hart, *Historic Boise*, 48, 78–79; and Sally B. Woodbridge and Roger Montgomery, *A Guide to Architecture in Washington State* (Seattle: University of Washington Press, 1980), 14–15.

39. Wright and Reitzes, *Tourtellotte and Hummel*, x, 2–5; Frederick C. Hummel, interview with Arthur A. Hart, 18 May 1974, OH498B, ISHS, Boise; and French, *History of Idaho*, 2:658–60.

40. Wright and Reitzes, *Tourtellotte and Hummel*, 5. See also Frederick C. Hummel, interview with Annabelle Al-

exander and Nona Dobberpfuhl, 25 November 1969, OH49, ISHS, Boise; and French, *History of Idaho*, 2:641.

41. Wright and Reitzes, *Tourtellotte and Hummel*, x, 5–6.

42. Ibid., 24.

43. French, *History of Idaho*, 2:641–42.

44. Ibid., 718–19.

45. George S. Koyl, ed. *American Architects Directory* (New York: R. R. Bowker, 2d ed., 1962), 123, 742; and Colleen Birch-Maile, "Partners in Progress," *in* Merle W. Wells, *Boise: An Illustrated History* (Woodland Hills, California: Windsor Publications, 1982), 164.

46. "Architecturally Significant and Historic Buildings of Boise," Idaho State Historical Society Information Sheet, no. 6 (Boise, 1970).

47. Hibbard, *Weiser*, 4, 6; and French, *History of Idaho*, 2:813–14.

48. French, *History of Idaho*, 2:722.

49. For St. Edward's, see Wright, *Twin Falls Country*, 20–21. For Gates' career, see his obituary, 5 October 1958, clipping on file at the Bureau of Occupational Licenses; "Architects Show Their Patriotism," 1; and "Past Presidents, Idaho Chapter AIA" [1985], on file at the Idaho chapter office, Boise. I am indebted to Elizabeth Egleston for sharing with me her research on the Twin Falls Hospital and nurses' home.

50. Wright, *Twin Falls Country*, 14–15, 33, 45.

51. Ibid., 27, 29, 46–48, 60, 74; "Architects Show Their Patriotism," *Twin Falls Times*, 1 November 1916, 1; and "Architects Perfect a State Body," *The Pocatello Tribune*, 26 July 1916, 1.

52. Hart, *Historic Boise*, 62; plans and elevation drawings on file in the private collection of Wallace-Hudson and Associates, Pocatello, Idaho; and John F. Gane, ed., *American Architects Directory* (New York: R. R. Bowker Company, 3d ed., 1970), 108.

5

The Rural Landscape,
1880–1920

Sunday, May 21st. [*1939*]

In camp on the Snake on the Oregon side, above Salt Creek. Got up early. Came to a charming, small ranch house. Was asked in to see Mrs. Johnson. Had coffee with her. They have 20 square miles, 3000 sheep. An old log cabin ranch house, very nicely fixed. Garden, grape vine arbour, flowers, electric light, frigidaire, strawberries. Electric light made by wind apparatus and batteries.

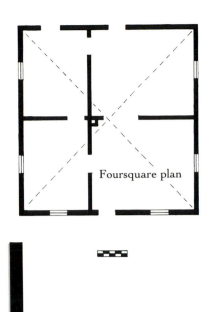

Foursquare plan

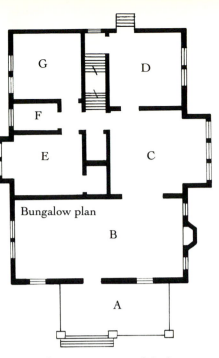

Bungalow plan

This ranch (facing page) on the Salmon River near the town of Whitebird is typical of the many ranches dotted along the Snake and Salmon river canyons. (ISHS 74-5.43/b.)

Foursquare houses (left) and bungalows (right) were pattern-book plans commonly used for farm housing after the turn of the century. The foursquare plan had a four-room arrangement under a pyramidal roof. Bungalows retained the large living rooms (B) and dining rooms (C) of earlier Georgian and half-Georgian houses but introduced the idea of a hall, bathroom, and bedroom wing (E,F,G). The first floor of this bungalow plan also includes an open front porch (A) and a kitchen (D). (Drawings by Cheryl Marshall.)

In 1939, when Edith Clegg made her remarkable journey up the Snake River by boat, much of the rural landscape of Idaho and eastern Oregon was made up of log cabins, central-passage houses, and timber-frame barns.[1] These basic forms and others were still in use, and in the most remote places still were being built. But it would be a gross misrepresentation to say that the Idaho countryside was static.

Idaho's farms, ranches, and isolated mines yield a complex story of adaptation and tenacious holding to tradition. Of the traditional forms that can be traced to early exploration and settlement, some were still used into the 1920s. Traditional log construction in Idaho dates as early as the Spaldings' 1838 mission house at Lapwai and at least as late as Polly Bemis's house on the Salmon River, built in 1923. Construction with logs is probably the most widespread and enduring of traditional constructions. Farmhouses built from 1880 to 1920, however, show a successive displacement of the hall and parlor house by the central-passage house, the central-passage house by the cross-wing house, and the cross-wing house by foursquare houses and pattern-book bungalows. Clearly it is not correct to think of rural forms as unchanging, as though they existed separate from the effects of environment, transportation, architectural publishing, and the parallel tradition of architect-designed buildings.

The single most accurate statement to be made about rural architecture in Idaho is that much less is known about it than about urban architecture. For that reason the generalizations in this chapter are at best suggestions of the ways in which rural architecture of the period 1880 to 1920 is distinct from that of the state's urban centers. First of all, rural architecture is primarily vernacular; that is, it is designed and constructed by owners and builders without the involvement of trained architects. In the countryside, architects were employed primarily for institutional buildings—rural schools and churches—and only very occasionally for a farmhouse or barn. Second, although rural architecture does follow certain basic patterns throughout the state, it is also highly regionalized; and that regionalization is more obviously keyed to local materials and environment than are the regions of urban architecture. Anyone who takes a drive from the center of Lewiston south to Camas Prairie or from Idaho Falls to the farms of New Sweden experiences the obvious differences between the style-conscious urban streetscape and the pragmatic rural landscape. Those differences can be clarified by asking, first, who were the rural builders? And, second, what did they build?

The Idaho legislature recognized the importance of vernacular architecture when it established architectural licensing in 1917. Beyond the reach of the licensing law were buildings designed by their builders. This provision, a standard one in licensing laws throughout the United States, was codified more specifically in a 1961 revision of the law. This version singled out, as exempt from licensing, the design of farmhouses and related outbuildings and of residences of two stories or less. The law recognized what had always been the case: small houses, farms, and ranches were traditionally the province of builders working within a popular or folk tradition. These small buildings were not just beyond the reach of architects; they were generally beyond their interest as well.

By 1880 numerous builders had immigrated to Idaho.[2] The federal census for that year lists 513 Idaho residents who were making their living in the building trades, which at that time included carpentry, brick and stone masonry, and a few specialized crafts such as plastering, roofing, and making shakes, doors, sash, and moldings. The census also included a few contractors and civil engineers, who sometimes engaged in building design, but they were generally located in mining towns or associated with irrigation projects. An interesting example is Arthur and Mary Foote's 1885 house in the Boise canyon, designed and built by Arthur, who engineered irrigation projects on the Boise and Snake rivers that were built years after his time in Boise Valley. With the help of his project workers, Arthur fashioned the house of basalt, plaster, and cement from sources at the house site.[3]

It is difficult to determine the extent to which rural areas benefited from the work of

In rural areas, buildings were sometimes designed and erected by engineers. Arthur Foote, an irrigation project engineer, designed and built this house in Boise canyon for his family in 1885. He used basalt from the canyon and mixed plaster and concrete from nearby materials. (ISHS 2505-A.)

Finnish log construction (right) features carefully scribed and cut long grooves that allow one log to fit snugly over the one below it and a variety of tight notches. The notch pictured is one of the most complicated, a keyed notch that locks the logs in place. (Drawing by Cheryl Marshall.)

hired carpenters and masons. The census shows that most builders of the 1880s were located in areas where there were concentrations of people and commerce: the most prosperous mining towns, the urban centers of Lewiston and Boise, and the Mormon villages. Newspaper reports of builders' activities during the 1880s and 1890s emanated from those centers. However, carpenters, contractors, and builders listed in the *Oregon, Washington and Idaho Gazetteer and Business Directory* of 1888 include a few working in towns so small that their business must have reached out into the countryside.[4] It appears that, although the rural house of the 1880s and 1890s was typically built by its owner or a group of neighbors with varying degrees of skill, it is possible that by the late 1880s some rural con-

struction was undertaken by professional carpenters and masons. Certainly by the mid–1900s, professional stone masons were building numerous south-central and southeastern Idaho farmhouses and outbuildings. In the 1920s and even later, though, many rural buildings continued to be erected by owners.

Construction by farmers and isolated miners is well documented in their reminiscences, letters, and journals; and the frequency with which house construction is mentioned bespeaks its importance as a personal event. Foster Steele noted with pride his "father's skill as an axeman and a builder," at his family's 1888 farm in Rudy (Jefferson County).[5] Edward Swenson remembered the construction of his family's 1891 homestead in the Norwegian settlement at Park Valley (Latah

County), during which "several neighbors would get together and they knew how to fit the logs together."[6]

Many writers convey the impression that a rural house was never entirely finished, that its owner-builders, who knew both the building's design and how well it functioned, were tinkerers making frequent adjustments and additions. The journal of Lou G. Caswell records construction of a number of cabins in the Big Creek region between 1895 and 1900, when the Caswell brothers were prospecting and placer mining there. As the brothers set up new camps and moved between camps in the fall and spring, cabin building and repair became seasonal activities, taking substantial time from equally important spring and fall labors, such as setting up placer boxes, planting gardens, washing clothes, hunting, and cooking. Caswell's entries for March 28 through 30, 1898, are representative:

> 28 Dan and I cut a lot of fir poles and joice. Peeled them, cut out a door. Mended clothes, Wes made gloves.
> 29 Dan and I worked on cabin and put on some shakes. Wes tanned a buckskin. Tom and Ben played solitary.
> 30 Dan and I snaked logs in forenoon. Wrote 2 letters and worked on cabin in afternoon. Wes baked[7]

Barns and other outbuildings were also the result of continued adjustments and additions. Farmers explain the intentions of neighbor

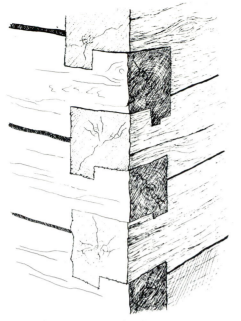

builders who constructed a lean-to, expecting to add a gabled section and another lean-to to produce a full-sized barn. Many barns were the result of neighborhood work parties, but a truly owner-built barn was the work of months or years. At his subsistence farmstead in Washington County, Cartter Hilliard spent three years constructing a three-level, forty-by-seventy-foot pole-frame barn. In 1979, about four decades after having begun the building, Hilliard still regarded the hay door and hood as unfinished.[8]

Owner modifications also included moving buildings. Log buildings could be disassembled and rebuilt at a site many miles away. Small, box or frame houses, such as those built for homestead entries, could be moved with a team of horses, as was done with the box-constructed J. L. Colson house (1909), built on a homestead near Kuna. Frame houses could be labeled, dismantled, and rebuilt, as the William and Jennie Bower family did with their frame house, purchased in Elk River and reassembled on their farm near Deary in 1936. Family stories also include accounts of two buildings being moved together to form a larger farmhouse, as was the case on the Isaac and Ruby Lazelle farm (1884) near Viola.[9]

The skill of owner-builders varied considerably. Nordic settlers in the northern Idaho panhandle and in Long Valley near McCall produced tightly fitted log buildings on homesteads taken up during the 1890s through the

1920s. As Alice Koskela comments in her study of the Finnish builders of Long Valley, "one can usually determine with a glance if a log building is the work of a Finnish craftsman"[10] by observing details like keyed notching and long-groove construction (a groove cut in the bottom of a log to fit the curve of the log just below it). Then there were builders who admitted to their complete lack of prior experience. A story in the Lawrence family of Grand View tells of Samuel Harrison Lawrence's inexperience in constructing a homestead house for his family in 1892:

Sam was a railroad man, not a carpenter, and accidentally put the longer roof boards on the sides of the house. When it came time to put on the roof, the only pieces left were too short but were used anyway.[11]

The evidence suggests that it was when a settler desired a building larger than one or two rooms that outside design or construction assistance was sometimes used. Community assistance was undoubtedly the first resort. Barn-building parties receive frequent attention in pioneer reminiscences, but houses also could be joint projects. On American Ridge near Kendrick, three houses, one of them on the Frank May farm, were built by the community from similar plans.[12]

Pattern books and state agricultural publications also offered design ideas. Plan books

for houses had been available since the beginning of the nineteenth century and had become widely available in Andrew Jackson Downing's and Henry Hudson Holly's books. Plans for barns, hog houses, and other outbuildings were available beginning in the 1890s and became increasingly more prevalent in the 1910s. The University of Idaho's Agricultural Experiment Station, for example, began including farm-building plans in its bulletins in 1909, when it issued *Better Dairy Methods*. That bulletin and subsequent ones about raising hogs, poultry, and potatoes included drawings and floor plans for dairy barns, hog houses, chicken houses, turkey pens, and potato cellars. To a certain extent these publications merely adapted plans from vernacular construction already present on Idaho farms. The 1919 bulletin providing advice on potato storage, for example, stated that "the most satisfactory storage cellars found in Idaho are those typically of western or arid country origin and development"[13] and proceeded to offer plans based on traditional potato cellar construction.

There was a middle ground between owner or neighborhood construction and construction by professional builders. Buildings could be erected by bartering skilled work. In exchange for their work, craftsmen received a comparable amount of labor from the home or barn owner. In the Minaloosa Valley of the Idaho panhandle, a log barn was built for the Roberts family "with exchange labor" in 1914:

Rural construction was often dependent on community work parties and bartered labor. Here a group erects a log house on the upper Salmon River. (ISHS 60-72.43.)

Fir trees, straight and tall and even-sized, had to be cut, dragged to the site, peeled, rolled up inclined skids to their position in the wall, and their ends notched to interlock with the end walls. Irregularities had to be sawed off to permit tighter joints and keep in the warmth. Ours was a big barn for that time and place. It had an extended lean-to area for four horses, with saddles and harnesses hanging behind them. It had a loft for hay, and under the loft were four stalls for milk cows.

Almost seventy years later, I can picture the construction scene, with skids leaning in position for the next log to be rolled up and two men sitting astride the top log of each of the end walls, chopping the notches. The logs would fit tightly when the next log was rolled into place. The men were artists with saws and axes. When they finished the building, it stood plumb, square, and solid as a monument for twenty years until it was burned down by a forest fire.[14]

There are enough gaps in our knowledge to make it difficult to estimate how many rural buildings were built by professionals as early as the 1880s. Who built the large horse barn (late 1880s) on the Mitchell, Marsh, and Ireton ranch near Montour? The barn, an impressive timber-frame building constructed with hewn timbers joined with pegged mortise-and-tenon joints, suggests the work of experienced craftsmen.[15] Who built the

Twenty-one Ranch house for Frank and Mary Goddard in 1886? The Queen Anne style house south of Lewiston exhibits unusual fashionability for its setting and early date, combining hewn porch columns with Queen Anne windows and millwork.

Certainly, architect-designed farmhouses and barns—like the farm buildings near Weiser that Tourtellotte and Hummel designed for engineer Archie Larson in 1910—were exceptional occurrences.[16] But by the 1900s the work of professional carpenters, masons, and contractors was making a mark on the countryside. Some of these skilled

Builder Henry Schick built a number of large timber-frame and concrete barns in the dairy farming area near Buhl. Pictured is his barn for the Art and Frieda Maxwell farm. The tall gambrel roof and pointed hay door hood allowed hay storage in an upper loft. (ISHS 80-5.109.)

builders were farmers first and craftsmen second. Jacob Thunborg, for example, combined farming his homestead at Hayden Lake with work as a mason and seasonal harvest laborer in the Palouse. His skill as a carpenter, probably acquired as a young man in northern Sweden, can be seen in the closely fit logs and dovetail corners of his own farmhouse.

Rural professional builders were at work in south-central Idaho while that region was undergoing rapid settlement with the development of the Twin Falls and North Side ir-

rigation projects just after the turn of the century. Two studies of rural architecture in south-central Idaho have turned up evidence about professional barn building and basalt masonry during the 1900s and 1910s. In the Buhl area, builder Henry Schick was responsible for several large, timber-frame and concrete dairy barns. Schick came to Buhl in the early 1900s after obtaining experience in construction, cement work, and ironwork in Chicago. He eventually purchased a farm of his own and combined dairy farming with con-

struction work. His Buhl barns date from 1912 through 1915. According to Madeline Buckendorf's analysis of the barns, Schick began his barn building using a braced post-and-lintel framing system and shifted to using a truss system that would accommodate the gambrel roofs becoming popular at the time.[17]

Basalt construction (known locally as lava rock) was used a great deal in south-central Idaho, and the same masons who constructed stone buildings in the new irrigation-project towns also built many barns, well houses and other outbuildings, and farmhouses that show the influence of the Colonial Revival and bungalow styles. Marian J. Posey's study of basalt buildings in south-central Idaho differentiates the work of skilled masons from that of farmers and builders who were locally known as mud-masons, self-taught masons who worked for pay. Farmers and mud-masons typically built rubble or coursed rubble walls with a sand-and-soil mortar and cement pointing. Skilled masons also did rubble and coursed rubble work, but at least one mason split the basalt to produce courses of dressed stone. Skilled work was also marked by the use of stones of consistent color and size, beaded joints, cast concrete lintels, watercourses, and quoining. Among the skilled masons were immigrants who had received their training in the Basque region of Spain, in Germany, and in Wales.[18]

As with many vernacular building crafts, the skills of the south-central Idaho masons

Basalt, or lava rock, construction was used by skilled masons and self-taught mud-masons for farmhouses, barns, and other outbuildings. This outbuilding on the Lucky J Ranch near Jerome was constructed with rubble (uncoursed) walls and beaded mortar joints. (ISHS 77-5.90/B.)

The Rocky Mountain Cabin (right) was a gable-front house identical in plan to the Anglo-western house, with the addition of a front roof extension that created an outdoor work area or porch. Builders created the roof extension by using long purlins (log roof supports running the full length of the building with their ends resting on the log gables). (Drawing by Cheryl Marshall.)

western states like New York and Illinois and—the single largest sector of the 1880 population—Chinese miners. (No solid evidence has been discovered to suggest that the Chinese did much construction or that, if they did, it was in any way Chinese.) In central Idaho, dominated by the boom economy of gold and silver rushes, miners came from China, Ireland, and eastern states like New York, Ohio, and Pennsylvania. Farmers came into southwest Idaho from Missouri, Illinois, New York, and Ohio, whereas the farmers of southeast Idaho were mostly foreign-born Mormon converts, from England, Wales, and Denmark. Those from the United States shared a common Missouri and Illinois heritage with the southwestern Idaho farmers.

In 1880 builders with British, Celtic, western European, or Nordic backgrounds made up about 28 percent of the carpenters, masons, and other construction workers in north and central Idaho. In the southwest, that percentage was 20; in southeast Idaho, 54. The substantial number of foreign-born builders was increased with new waves of immigration in the 1890s through the 1920s. By the late 1890s, many new Nordic immigrants had come into north and central Idaho from the upper Midwest or directly from the Nordic countries. By the 1890s the southern population had also been enriched by Iowa and Nebraska farmers, who came to southwest Idaho, and by natives of Utah, who moved into the upper Snake River valley. Southeast

were not passed on to a second generation of builders. This is one of the reasons that the contributions of immigrant builders from Great Britain, western Europe, and the Nordic countries are generally forgotten as the names of the builders fade from living memory. Even in 1880, before much of the Nordic immigration and before the second wave of immigrant Mormons came to the upper Snake River Valley, British, Celtic, western European, and Nordic immigrants made

up a disproportionate part (one and one-half times the proportion of United States natives) of those working in the building trades in southern Idaho. (In northern and central Idaho the presence of a higher percentage of builders from the northeastern United States made that ratio about one to one.)

The rural population varied considerably throughout the state in 1880. In northern Idaho, a mixed farming and mining economy attracted farmers with roots in eastern or mid-

Idaho continued to receive many English and Nordic immigrants during this period, including a number of non-Mormon Swedes.

The rural landscape that the farmers, ranchers, isolated miners, and a few professional builders created followed certain consistent patterns based on a common background of nineteenth-century Anglo-European traditions and on American patterns that had been perfected in the Midwest. Farmsteads were isolated from one another; they generally had two main sections, domestic and barnyard, which were separated by a lane or simply by a few yards' distance. Farmhouses were built first as small, one-or-two-room cabins or shacks, then replaced or added onto; buildings were plain and functional. Field systems, although they made some compromises with topography, generally conformed to section divisions based on the rectilinear federal land survey. The whole farm, including house and barn, generally conformed to this same orientation, with houses facing a section road, for example.

Regional diversity can be seen in certain forms that arose out of special conditions like climate, regional crops, or materials. On the landscape, the network of irrigation canals throughout southern Idaho is the most obvious example. But one can also define a few types of buildings that have distinctly regional distributions. In northern and central Idaho there are large barns with hay hoods as well as Nordic log buildings; in central Idaho, a house type known as the Rocky Mountain Cabin; in southwest Idaho, willow-and-mud ranch buildings; in southeast Idaho, small English barns and farmhouses built of tuff; throughout southern Idaho, potato cellars (locally known as spud cellars); and in south-central Idaho, bungalows, well houses, and outbuildings built with basalt.[19]

Whatever region of the state they came to, farmers and ranchers were drawn here by various federal laws that linked land acquisition to working and living on the land. "Government land is so cheap, and homesteads, pre-emptions, timber culture claims can be taken and held on terms so easy, that every family, however poor, can have a home,"[20] wrote an Oregonian to *The West Shore* in 1880. The Homestead Act of 1862, the Desert Land Act of 1877, the Timber and Stone Act of 1878, and the Forest Homestead Act of 1906 encouraged many immigrants to Idaho to take up farming, whether they had prior experience or not. Some of these acts could be used in tandem to capture more than the 160 acres of the Homestead Act.

One of the prescriptions of the Homestead Act was construction of a house, and the first farm and ranch houses — on many unsuccessful farms the only house — tended to be small, frequently the traditional Anglo-American single-cell house of about sixteen feet on each side. These single-room buildings were indistinguishable in plan from the many one-room cabins of isolated mines dotted throughout the state's central mountains during this same period.

The one-room homestead, ranch, or mining house was built in at least three versions: the lateral-front single-cell house and two sorts of gable-front buildings: the Anglo-western house and the Rocky Mountain Cabin. Anglo-western houses, single-room houses with the door on a gable wall, were named for their presence in the prairie states. In the Rocky Mountain states the form appears to have developed during the 1880s into a gable-front house with a front roof extension, a type which archaeologist Mary Wilson has named the Rocky Mountain Cabin.[21] Rocky Mountain Cabins are common to mining and agricultural settlements in mountainous central Idaho. By the 1900s, the type began to be constructed with motifs drawn from the Rustic style. The log homestead house constructed for Elsie Watkins Pfeil in the Clearwater drainage near Clarkia was just such a blend of folk forms with high-style ornamentation. Pfeil's niece Carol Ryrie Brink described the cabin as

built of large logs chinked with mud. On the inside the logs were roughly hewn, but on the outside they still had their bark. A little rustic porch was on the front of the cabin, and only one large room inside it. There were two windows in the room, two large built-in beds, a cookstove, and some home-made chairs and tables.[22]

Fashionable farm and ranch houses appear in conjunction with periods of rural affluence. This Bungalow style house (right) was built for D. E. Burley's ranch near Buhl. The ranch also had a large gambrel-roofed barn. Beside the open haystack is a hay derrick, used for stacking loose hay. (ISHS 73-221.28; Clarence Bisbee, photographer.)

The first expedient shelter on a homestead was often a box-constructed shack with a small single-cell plan. This homestead shack was located in the Kuna area. (ISHS 60-77.5.)

The rustic porch was embellished with criss-crossed branches filling in the front railing and with upright poles supporting the roof purlins.

Many farm, ranch, and mine houses of the 1880s and 1890s were log rather than stone, frame, or box-constructed, but examples of all these constructions can be found from the period 1880 through 1920. Outside of southeast Idaho, where tuff was used for farmhouses into the 1910s, stone construction was unusual for small houses, but it was used where workable stone was locally available and timber was scarce. The Louise Trealor cabin (circa 1899) near Custer was a one-room basalt masonry building with adobe mortar and sand-lime pointing. Basalt was similarly exploited for one- and two-room houses in Owyhee County at the Cove, or Halverson Bar, built during the 1890s by miners.[23] Log construction was widespread geographically, chronologically, and ethnically, ranging from homestead-ranches in Sawtooth Valley during the 1910s to Nez Perce farms during the 1880s, from the farms of the 1880s established by Mormons on the upper Snake to Finnish farmsteads in Long Valley during the 1920s. As practiced by Finns and Swedes, log construction produced substantial buildings like Pfiel's cabin.[24]

These two substantial constructions—stone and log—occupied a somewhat higher place in the mind of settlers than what they termed "shacks," probably box-constructed buildings.

Settlers expected to replace the first board building on a homestead, built to satisfy the Homestead Act. The Colson house (1909) near Kuna is representative of these quickly built shelters. The building is constructed of vertical one-by-twelves with one-by-fours nailed over the gaps between them. The vertical-lumber walls, attached to sills and plates, provide the building's structure without the benefit of corner posts. Its original twelve-by-fourteen single room was later supplemented by a rear lean-to.[25]

Farmers started small, with a one-room house, built their barn, added to the house, and when they achieved a certain comfortable level of affluence—which some did within just

a few years — they built a larger farmhouse. At this point many farmers and ranchers left simplicity behind for the social standing that a stylish house could signal, and the most affluent period of a particular farm region in Idaho can be assessed partly on the basis of architectural styles. A few farmhouses were built in the Queen Anne style, for example, in areas of southeast Idaho. Colonial Revival style houses are found on the Palouse, and bungalow style houses in south-central Idaho. For their second homes farmers also adopted the popular house plans of the day, whether supplied by tradition, pattern books, lumberyards, or local builders. During the 1880s and early 1890s hall and parlor and central-passage houses were constructed; during the 1890s and early 1900s, cross-wing houses; during the 1910s, foursquare houses and bungalows. Although

rural homeowners showed their interest in the current styles, they usually kept to standard plans even in the Picturesque period, expressing Picturesque assymmetry in applied ornamentation more often than outset bays, oriels, and wings.

As folklorist Louie Attebery notes in *Idaho Folklife*, there are farmers who neither left their homesteads in defeat nor became wealthy. Subsistence farming-ranching has always been a force running counter to stylistic changes. Through some periods and in some remote parts of the state, subsistence farms were a significant settlement form. In 1909 the Coeur d'Alene Indian reservation was opened up for settlement by whites, producing a number of late homesteads. Settlement of the Salmon River region has continued well into the twentieth century. The years of the agri-

cultural depression encouraged a return to the marginal lands of Idaho's mountain meadows, where subsistence farming helped families through the hard times. Similarly, an exodus from the center of Boise to five-, ten-, and twenty-acre farms at the edge of the city occurred during the first two decades of the twentieth century and accelerated during the depression years. As Attebery's Washington County fieldwork has shown, on the most isolated of the subsistence farms and late homesteads, house forms like the single-cell house or Rocky Mountain Cabin remained in use.[26]

In contrast to rural housing, barns and outbuildings are somewhat more difficult to analyze for changes in style, type, or construction. On the basis of barn surveys completed in the Palouse, Boise Valley, the Buhl vicinity, Bear Lake Valley, and Long Valley, it appears

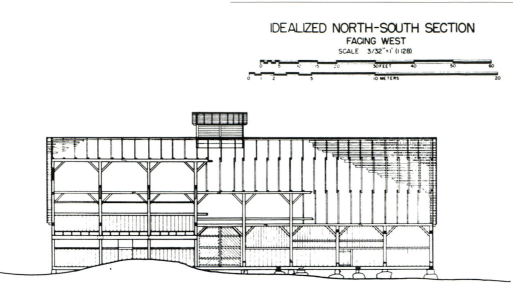

IDEALIZED NORTH-SOUTH SECTION
FACING WEST
SCALE 3/32"=1' (1:128)

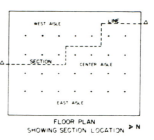

FLOOR PLAN
SHOWING SECTION LOCATION ▶ N

Basilica-plan barns have a central aisle for traffic and side aisles that are usually partitioned into stalls. The drawings depict the basilica-plan horse barn at the Mitchell, Marsh, and Ireton ranch near Emmett. The cross section shows the barn's braced-timber frame construction. The floor plan depicts the position of structural posts and the location of aisles. (ISHS, HABS Collection, Mitchell, Marsh, and Ireton ranch.)

that both regional climate and agricultural innovations had an impact on barn development.[27] The arid climate of southern Idaho contrasts with the relatively humid panhandle and central region of the state. In south Idaho loose hay was stacked outside the barn using a hayfork attached to a derrick. This device, apparently a Great Basin invention, spread into Idaho with the in-migration of Utahns.[28] Consequently, the barns of southeast Idaho's Mormon villages and farms tend to be small gable-roofed shelters with an English barn plan—the principal entry on the long side of the building. Frequently they were built with log construction. In the Buhl vicinity and in Boise Valley, larger barns with a basilica plan and an upper loft appeared in connection with the dairy and cattle industries, but these frequently had no hood to shelter their hay door. In southwest Idaho the so-called western barn, a basilica plan with a low, central gabled section and lean-tos over the two side aisles, dates as early as the late 1880s, when the Mitchell, Marsh, and Ireton barn was built, and continued in use well into the twentieth century. In north Idaho, large basilica-plan cow or horse barns built for dairy or wheat farms frequently had hay hoods.

The basilica plan, the upper loft, and the mechanical hayfork were convenient for feeding cattle or horses. In about 1900 they were joined by a major barn innovation, the gambrel roof, which allowed greater headroom and storage room in the hayloft. The gambrel

roof never became the dominant type in southeastern Idaho, but it was an important secondary roof type in southwestern, central, and northern Idaho. Later, by about 1915, rounded roofs became popular.[29]

Barn construction similarly reveals the effects of region and invention. In the period 1880 to about 1915 braced-timber frame or pole-frame construction, secured by mortise and tenon joints, gradually gave way to balloon or platform framing with machine-made nails and dimensional lumber. At the same time, however, regional constructions persisted. In southern Idaho a construction called crib construction on Sanborn Fire Insurance maps, and perhaps in local dialect as well, was used for granaries and silos. Crib construction was done with dimensional lumber—usually two-by-fours—laid flat in even tiers to create a smooth, tight wall. This construction is associated with Mormon areas in Idaho and also appears in Utah. In southwest Idaho a willow and mud construction was used for buildings on at least two Owyhee County ranches of the 1900s and 1910s. The construction is similar but not identical to mud-wall buildings on central Nevada ranches.[30] In Long Valley, Finnish settlers built distinctive log barns with steep gambrel roofs having a very high break. Evidence about these regional types is spotty, but still suggestive of the powerful influences of climate, available materials, and ethnic heritage.

By 1920 the main patterns of the rural land-

scape had been laid down, and significant changes in settlement patterns would wait until after World War II, when pump irrigation systems created entirely new ways of dealing with the land. After that time, fields and farms became larger, and new farmsteads were created with ranch style houses built on a rise and looking out upon circular drives, metal sheds, coniferous windbreaks, and distant mountains. Fields became large and unfenced, and in irrigated areas sprinkler irrigation lines dictated the configuration of fields, some of them circular. Amidst grain or potato crops, farmers preserved traces of the older settlements by carefully plowing around abandoned farmhouses and outbuildings. Today the rural landscape is made up of settlement patterns from periods of prosperity and decline, overlaid to create a rich and complex fabric for historians and folklorists to unravel.[31]

Born of a common Anglo-European heritage and diverse environmental conditions, the rural landscape reveals the operation of a few basic principles that put a high value on land ownership and self-sufficiency. Among them are starting small, conserving materials, building for the climate, improving the farmyard first, and subsisting on the land. However damaging many farming, ranching, and mining practices have been, the patterns of rural settlement reflect a general respect for natural surroundings that has eventually resulted in support for legislation that forced compromises in land use, such as the Taylor Grazing

Act of 1934. This vernacular land ethic,[32] originally based in practicalities like crop rotation and materials salvage, became the basis of considerable nostalgia over things rural and rustic among second-generation city dwellers of the early twentieth century. Their return to the land for recreation, one of the topics of the next chapter, was a major force in architecture of the 1920s and 1930s.

Notes

1. Epigraph from Edith Clegg and Cort Conley, "Rattlesnakes and Rapids: A Woman's Journey Against the Current in 1939," *Idaho Yesterdays* 28, no. 3 (Fall 1984):17.

2. The data used in this study relating to Idaho's population in 1880 were supplied in partially proofed form by the Idaho Population Project which bears no responsibility for the interpretations expressed herein. I am indebted to Ron Hatzenbuehler for his able and patient assistance in assembling this data.

3. Julia Longenecker, Darby Stapp, and Mary Ellen Walsh, "Mary Hallock Foote Stone House in the Cañon: Archaeological Investigation," University of Idaho, 1987, 3. Unless otherwise noted, the buildings mentioned in this chapter are documented in National Register of Historic Places nomination forms, on file at the Idaho State Historical Society (hereafter ISHS), Boise, and the Department of the Interior, Washington, D.C.

4. *Oregon, Washington and Idaho Gazetteer and Business Directory* (Portland, Oregon: R. L. Polk & Company, 1888), 1,076–82. Newspaper references to the activities of contractors are indexed at ISHS, Boise.

5. "The Old Rudy, Idaho Homestead" [Christmas card], MS 2.277, ISHS, Boise.

6. Sam Schrager, ed., *Homesteading in the Valley of Park as Told by Edward Swenson* (Moscow, Idaho: Latah County Museum Society, 1975), 5.

7. "L. G. Caswell Diaries," MS 2.437, ISHS, Boise, 25.

8. Louie W. Attebery, "A Contextual Survey of Selected Homestead Sites in Washington County," in *Idaho Folklife: Homesteads to Headstones*, ed. Louie W. Attebery (Salt Lake City: University of Utah Press, 1985), 134–35.

9. For moving log buildings, see Jennifer Eastman Attebery, "The Diffusion of Folk Culture as Demonstrated in the Horizontal Timber Construction of the Snake River Basin" (Ph.D. diss., Indiana University, 1985), 123–24; for moving the Colson house, see [Joe Toluse], "J. L. Colson House," Report 55, Idaho Historic Sites Inventory, ISHS, Boise, 1; for moving the Bower and Lazelle houses, see "Century/Historic Farms Project Report" (Latah County Historical Society, June 1988), Report 115, Idaho Historic Sites Inventory, ISHS, Boise.

10. Alice Koskela, "Finnish Log Homestead Buildings in Long Valley," in *Idaho Folklife: Homesteads to Headstones*, ed. Louie W. Attebery (Salt Lake City: University of Utah Press, 1985), 30.

11. Charles Sherwood Lawrence and Nancy Lawrence Rodriguez, "The Unlikely Homesteaders," in *Owyhee Outpost* 19 (May 1988):51.

12. "Century/Historic Farms Project Report."

13. E. R. Bennett, "Growing the Idaho Potato," University of Idaho, Extension Division Bulletin, no. 29 (Moscow, Idaho, September 1919), 24. See also in the same series, Pren Moore, "Poultry Husbandry in Idaho," no. 30 (November 1919), 7–9. In the University of Idaho, Agricultural Experiment Station Bulletin series, see J. H. Frandson, "Better Dairy Methods," no. 67 (May 1909), 19–25; W. L. Carlyle and E. J. Iddings, "Hog Raising for the Idaho Farmer," no. 74 (August 1912), 22–25; and O. E. McConnell, "Swine Management in Idaho," no. 116 (March 1919), 13–16. The effects of agricultural publications are discussed in Madeline Buckendorf, "Early Dairy Barns of Buhl," in *Idaho Folklife: Homesteads to Headstones*, ed. Louie W. Attebery (Salt Lake City: University of Utah Press, 1985), 156–57; and Marvin Moore, "Palouse

Hills Farmstead Architecture, 1890–1915," University of Idaho Museum, Palouse Hills Farm Museum Project (Moscow, Idaho, May 28, 1980).

14. J. Russell Roberts, "Growing Up on the Last Frontier: A Minaloosa Valley Boyhood," *Idaho Yesterdays* 26, no. 2 (Summer 1982):4–5.

15. The barn is documented in the Historic American Building Survey (hereafter HABS), ID–35, copies on file at ISHS, Boise, and the Library of Congress, Washington, D.C.

16. Don Hibbard, *Weiser: A Look at Idaho Architecture* (Boise, Idaho: Idaho State Historic Preservation Office, 1978), 58.

17. Buckendorf, "Early Dairy Barns," 157–58.

18. Marian P. Anderson [Marian J. Posey], "Lava Masonry Structures in Jerome County, Idaho" [1978], Report 56, Idaho Historic Sites Inventory, ISHS, Boise.

19. In addition to the sources already cited, I am basing these generalizations on my own survey of rural landscapes, "Agricultural Landscapes Survey" (1987), Survey 104; Madeline Buckendorf, "Ada County Farmstead Survey Report" (draft, August 1989); and Nancy F. Renk, "Priest Lake Planning Unit" (July 1988), Report 118; all in the Idaho Historic Sites Inventory, ISHS, Boise.

20. G. H. Atkinson, "The Choice of a Home by Settlers in Oregon or Washington or Idaho," *The West Shore* 6 (February 1880):38.

21. Mary Wilson, *Log Cabin Studies*, Cultural Resource Report, no. 9 (Ogden, Utah: United States Forest Service, Intermountain Region, 1984). Wilson considers the possibility that the Rocky Mountain Cabin was a regional innovation, among several possible origins for the house type. Terry G. Jordan and Matti Kaups believe that the Rocky Mountain Cabin is instead a vestige of the Finnish origins of American log construction in their *The American Backwoods Frontier: An Ethnic and Ecological Interpretation* (Baltimore: The Johns Hopkins University Press, 1989). Further study of specific buildings — and their builders, dates of construction, and original features and loca-

tions—will be necessary before a reasonably valid determination can be made about the origins of this house type.

22. Carol Ryrie Brink, *Four Girls on a Homestead*, Local History Paper, no. 3 (Moscow, Idaho: Latah County Museum Society, 1977), 14.

23. [Fred Walters], Ronald Thurber and Associates, "Historic Structures Report: Trealor Cabin, Custer, Idaho," Report 95, Idaho Historic Sites Inventory; and, for Halverson Bar, see Sharon Brown, "The Built Environment," in *Prospects: Land-Use in the Snake River Birds of Prey Area, 1860–1987*, ed. Todd Shallat, Social Sciences Monograph, no. 1 (Boise, Idaho: Boise State University, 1987), 63–83.

24. For log construction, see Jennifer Eastman Attebery, "Diffusion of Folk Culture"; Jennifer Eastman Attebery, "Log Construction in the Sawtooth Valley of Idaho," *Pioneer America* 8, no. 1 (January 1976):36–46; Jennifer Eastman Attebery, "'A Dry and Comfortable Habitation': Popular Attitude and the Role of Log Construction in the West" (Paper delivered at the Building the West Conference, Reno, Nevada, 21 September 1989); Koskela, "Finnish Log Homestead Buildings"; and Wilson, *Log Cabin Studies*.

25. Toluse, "J. L. Colson House," 1–2.

26. Louie W. Attebery, "A Contextual Survey," 129, 142; and Buckendorf, "Ada County Farmstead," 6–8. Numerous subsistence farm-ranches in the Salmon River drainage are described in Johnny Carrey and Cort Conley's two books, *River of No Return* (Cambridge, Idaho: Backeddy Books, 1978) and *A Guide to the Middle Fork and the Sheepeater War* (Cambridge, Idaho: Backeddy Books, 1977); John Hartung, "Documentation of the Historical Resources in the Idaho Primitive Area, Big Creek Drainage" (Master's thesis, University of Idaho, 1978); and S. J. Rebillet, "Final Report on the South Fork of the Salmon River: The Place and the People," Report 114, Idaho Historic Sites Inventory, ISHS, Boise.

27. Studies and surveys of Idaho barns and outbuildings include Arthur A. Hart, "Farm and Ranch Buildings East of the Cascades," in *Space, Style and Structure: Building in Northwest America*, ed. Thomas Vaughan and Virginia Guest Ferriday, 2 vols. (Portland, Oregon: Oregon Historical Society, 1974), 2:241–54; Moore, "Palouse Farmsteads Architecture"; Buckendorf, "Early Dairy Barns"; Lisa B. Reitzes, *Paris: A Look at Idaho Architecture* (Boise, Idaho: Idaho State Historic Preservation Office, 1981), 50; Koskela, "Finnish Log Homestead Buildings," 33–34; and Donnaclaire Blankinship, "Boise Valley Barns,"

[1979], IFA 83/21, ISHS, Boise.

28. For a discussion of hay derricks, see Austin E. Fife and James M. Fife, "Hay Derricks of the Great Basin and Upper Snake River Valley," in *Idaho Folklife: Homesteads to Headstones*, ed. Louie W. Attebery (Salt Lake City: University of Utah Press, 1985), 2–11.

29. Hart, "Farm and Ranch Buildings," 246.

30. Mud houses superficially similar to those in Owyhee County have been identified in Nevada by Blanton Owen. See his "The Great Basin 'Mud' House: Preliminary Findings," abstract in *Perspectives in Vernacular Architecture, III*, ed. Thomas Carter and Bernard L. Herman (Columbia: University of Missouri Press, 1989), 245–46.

31. Leonard J. Arrington discusses the impact of pump and sprinkler irrigation systems in "Irrigation in the Snake River Valley; An Historical Overview," *Idaho Yesterdays* 30, no. 1–2 (Spring/Summer 1986):8–9; and Arthur Hart describes modern trends on the rural landscape in "Farm and Ranch Buildings," 249–52.

32. For a discussion of a vernacular land ethic among Idaho farmers and ranchers, see Brian Attebery, "Land Use Attitudes and Ethics in Idaho Folklore," in *Idaho Folklife: Homesteads to Headstones*, ed. Louie W. Attebery (Salt Lake City: University of Utah Press, 1985), 223–29.

6

Standard Plans and Romantic Styles in the Depression Era, 1920–1945

6/20/22 . . .

Left Idaho Falls, 9:00 AM. Mother feeling pretty bum. Everybody else in fair shape. . . .

St. Anthony, 40 mi. Drove thru grounds of Idaho State Industrial School.

Ashton, Ida. 12:10 PM, 17 mi.

Good roads, very few signs. Necessary to guess at the way. Bum tourist camp at Ashton so went on to Marysville and stopped along the road for lunch.

On the way again at 1 PM. Struck the pines about 2 PM. Nicest sight we have seen since leaving home. Road very bad after first few miles, being worked and nearly a foot deep [dust]. No signs on new road. Ripley's Ranch along Henry's Fork. Out on good road at last, 4:10 P.

Puncture, 5:30 PM., on the road at 5:50 P with some very poor tires and nothing to fix with.

First sight of snow about 5:30 PM.

West Yellowstone, 70 mi. 6:30 PM.

Mosquitoes are arriving in flocks.

Stayed at Madison Hotel. Very rustic and clever. Had a dandy dinner next door. $3.00

ENJOYING LIFE IN A BUICK.
BISBEE PHOTO - 793.

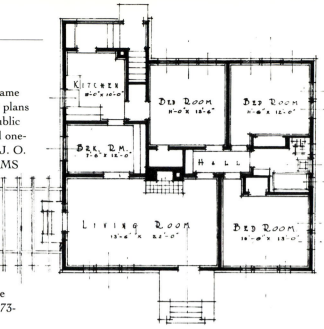

Houses built during the depression years became smaller than those of previous eras, and their plans made a clear distinction between blocks of public and private rooms. This 1923 plan for a small one-story house was drawn by Boise contractors J. O. Jordan and Son. (ISHS, Jordan Collection, MS 535.)

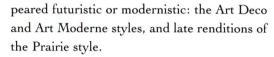

A motoring party enjoys the view of Shoshone Falls (left) in their Buick touring car. (ISHS 73-221.26; Clarence Bisbee, photographer.)

In 1922 the Anketell family left Nampa, Idaho, in a 1919 Studebaker, and Harriet Anketell recorded the trip in a diary that details mileage, meals and accommodations, and an average of one mechanical breakdown or flat tire per day.[1] The Anketells' journey east seems slow and frustrating to us today. But their perspective on the Idaho landscape was novel and exciting. That perspective — a series of glances through automobile windows — represented a new way of life that wrought changes in American architecture during an era of hard times, new mobility, and standardization.

The two trends that dominated the architecture of 1920 through 1945 would appear contradictory except for the fact that they found expression in the same buildings. The first — standardization — had had its beginning much earlier than the twentieth century. Standardization in American architecture can be traced to colonial regulation of brick sizes, nineteenth-century pattern books, and other early means of enforcing or encouraging conformity in building plans, styles, or construction.

In the 1920s, though, standardization became a widespread means for getting buildings constructed. In Idaho architecture a tendency toward model plans and homogenious styles can be seen in most of the spheres of life where any capital was available for construction. In fact, standardization was a means of producing numbers of buildings in an era when capital was scarce and construction di-

minished dramatically. Standard plans were employed by government agencies to insure quality construction and to improve living conditions. Standard plans and styles also came to be used as signs of reliability to the passing motorist. Art Moderne became associated with gasoline stations; the Rustic style, with tourist camps and mountain lodges.

The second trend was a continuation of the romanticism that builders of earlier eras had cast in Picturesque and Arts and Crafts styles. Many building styles of the 1920s and 1930s looked back to the colonial and European past, to western pioneer days, or to the recently unearthed Egyptian tombs; others created visions of the future. Even formally symmetrical buildings designed as monuments of civic architecture, buildings like city halls and courthouses assisted by the Public Works Administration (PWA) and the Works Progress Administration (later, Work Projects Administration; WPA), partook of this era's romanticism through the use of applied terra-cotta ornament. Period styles became popular: revivals of British and Spanish colonial houses; fanciful versions of Pueblos, Tudor houses, and Spanish missions; and renditions of Egyptian and Gothic monuments. Rustic architecture — what is sometimes called the Rustic or Adirondack style — was used by the U.S. Forest Service and National Park Service and by the builders of recreation homes. At the same time, some architects and clients preferred new trends that in their day ap-

peared futuristic or modernistic: the Art Deco and Art Moderne styles, and late renditions of the Prairie style.

Standard building plans were used in many different sectors of society during the 1920s and 1930s. House plans continued to be available through publications, contractors, and lumberyards. J. O. Jordan and Son of Boise, for example, began business in 1922 by building houses of the company's own design but based on pattern-book plans available in publications like *Dixon's Book of Plans*.[2] The Jordans translated these basic plans into substantial Tudoresque and Colonial Revival houses in Boise's North End neighborhood and went on to become a major contracting firm for commercial and institutional projects in southwest Idaho. Radford's plan books and popular magazines like *Sunset*, *Ladies Home Journal*, and *House Beautiful* provided compendiums of simple plans in the period revival styles.

Pattern houses of this period mark a shift in domestic architecture from two- to one-story plans, from vertical to horizontal massing, and from formal room arrangements derivative of the Georgian plan to organic plans arranged in two blocks, one for public activities (living room, dining room, kitchen) and one for private (a bedroom and bathroom block). Also, the scale of houses generally became smaller. Various period styles could be imposed on this two-block system with changes in exterior features like roof profile, wall finish, and type of window. A balloon-frame Tudoresque house,

Frank H. Paradice, Jr., designed an Art Deco style concrete storefront for Safeway companies that was to be cast in place at several Safeway groceries. (Photograph by Cuzzin's Photos, Pocatello.)

for example, could have a steep gable roof, a clinker brick veneer, and multipaned casement windows. A Pueblo house with the same plan and the same balloon-frame construction could have a flat roof with canales (water spouts at the roof line), a pastel-colored stucco veneer, and multipaned steel-frame windows with casement openings.

During the agricultural depression of the 1920s and the years of the Great Depression, agricultural agencies extended their concern from the proper barn and outbuilding to the proper farmhouse and outhouse. Plans for agricultural outbuildings continued to be part of the University of Idaho's Extension and Experimental Station bulletin series, and the Extension Division added bulletins about turkey ranching and indoor plumbing. Turkey growing, often a project taken on by farm women for extra income, was one of the supplemental industries that helped many farm families through the depression years. The extension agency's bulletin of 1930 provided plans for home-built roosts, pens, and brooder houses designed for proper sanitation.[3]

Governmental concern over rural housing increased during the depression years as rural conditions became better publicized in WPA-sponsored writers' and artists' projects and as government-subsidized regional surveys and scholarship focused on issues like housing and nutrition. The U. S. Department of Agriculture's farm-housing survey, a Civil Works Administration project, inquired into such mat-

ters as the age and construction of rural houses. The architectural profession responded with a theme issue of *The Architectural Record* (April 1934) that included a preliminary report of the farm-housing survey and articles giving architects information about farm-building design. According to the editors, the farm-housing survey revealed "clearly and emphatically a number of insufficiencies in the construction and equipment of American farmhouses."[4] The final report, is-

sued in 1939, pointed to a high percentage of farmhouses built of logs, for example. (In the Rocky Mountain states nearly 6 percent of the houses surveyed were log.) The survey data helped justify initiation of federal loan programs for farmers.[5] Among the projects aimed at improving Idaho farm housing was the University of Idaho extension service's 1926 publication "Running Water in the Farm Home," which provided details for systems for heating water and for pumping it into farmhouses.

The WPA also assisted farmers by constructing sanitary, ventilated outhouses for $18.75, the cost of materials.[6]

In town, the new commercial chain stores used standardization to establish a facade and an interior layout that their customers would come to recognize. For the Safeway grocery stores, for example, Frank H. Paradice, Jr., designed a generic plan for interior details (1940) and a "cast monolithic concrete store front"[7] in the Art Deco style for identical use on stores in Rigby (1940), Idaho Falls (1941), and Pocatello (1941). Similarly, oil companies adopted standard Spanish Mission, Art Deco, and Art Moderne style buildings for their 1930s service stations, providing motorists with a means of identifying their brand from a distance.[8]

The government agencies and community groups constructing institutional buildings during this time used standard plans to their advantage, sometimes avoiding architectural design fees but also insuring that their new buildings would be safe and functional. In 1914 the U. S. Treasury Department began standardizing plans for its post offices in an effort to save architectural costs and to categorize building needs by size of community. Partly as a result of this scheme and partly as a result of the depression, buildings constructed for the small communities of states like Idaho were plainer than their counterparts elsewhere. But the number of post offices was doubled through standardization and New Deal monies. By 1920, only six federal buildings had been constructed in Idaho towns. The following two decades saw the construction of fourteen new buildings. On the exterior these plans expressed a simplified Art Deco style or equally simplified classicism. Two notable exceptions are the Georgian Revival design for the 1934 Weiser post office, locally commissioned to Tourtellotte and Hummel, and a unique Spanish Mission design used for the Sandpoint building (1928).[9]

Idaho's State Board of Education published bulletins in 1921 and 1927 with plans for one-, two-, and three-room schools. The Board of Education set forth its bulletins to make it as simple as possible to satisfy the state law requiring board approval of local school designs: adopt one of the published plans, and a local school board could be guaranteed to meet the requirements for sanitation, ventilation, lighting, water supply, and safety. Preapproved plans were provided on request, and they were accompanied by specifications and a contract form. In the event that the published plans were not sufficient, boards were admonished to hire architects, find competent contractors, and use the best materials:

No school district can afford to build a new building or remodel an old one without first securing good plans and specifications.

They are a saving and safeguard, both in getting bids and in checking up on the completed work. . . .

By all means select the most competent architect you are able to secure. All architects make practically the same charges and it is not economy to select a man that does not know his business.[10]

The state board's regulations and advice were designed principally to meet safety and health requirements, but the board's concern also extended to "the public conservation of childhood."[11] Its specifications included comments on well-landscaped lawns and well-drained playgrounds, individual and adjustable desks, schoolroom colors (cream, white, light green, and gray), heating systems, water closets and outhouses, individual drinking vessels and towels, and methods for cleaning the building (no dry sweeping).

As Susanne Lichtenstein's study of Boise public schools has shown, the very specific requirements for safety and lighting reflect the educational philosophy of the period, which was more concerned with safety and health issues than with developing, for example, art and music programs. In the Boise schools, one can see many of the features recommended by the state board. Windows were banked along one wall, and desks were arranged so that students' work was lit over the left shoulder. The front and right walls were reserved for large blackboards. To satisfy fire safety regulations, doors opened outward, and stairs were at least

Standard plans and the Colonial Revival style were adopted by the Mormons for church buildings beginning in the 1920s. This church building in north Boise displays a number of Colonial Revival motifs: multipaned windows, a large pedimented portico, a low roof profile, classical columns, and a round oxeye window. (ISHS 80-87.50.)

five feet wide, had handrails, and led directly to outside doors.[12]

Religious institutions, which already preferred certain styles associated with a particular creed and liturgy, continued to patronize architects but also recycled church plans. Construction by the Mormon and Catholic churches during this period exemplify this general trend toward standardization in church building. The Mormon church had had a superintendent of public works and a church architect as early as 1850, and tithing of cash or labor was an important source of support for church construction. Although many of the early ward and stake buildings resembled each other in style and plan, it was not until the period 1924–1929 that church architect Willard Young began providing standardized plans for ward meetinghouses. Historian Allen D. Roberts notes that the standard plans "took on a 'Colonial' appearance, supposedly reflecting the colonial heritage from which the church took root."[13] Colonial historicism is illustrated in numerous Mormon church buildings from this period, the seminary building in Paris (circa 1932), for example, or the ward building in the Fort Street neighborhood in Boise (1924).[14] The seminary is a simple version reflecting Colonial Revival styling with its low hipped roof, eave returns on the gabled entry bay, brick pilasters, and coffered wall panels. The ward building in Boise is a more explicit rendition of the Georgian-period colonial church.

The Mormon church's use of standard plans should not be overstated, however, as this was an era of transition for Mormon designers. At the same time standard plans were being put to use, locally hired architects were designing church buildings and remodelings that exhibited a range of styles. Pope and Burton's two very similar designs for tabernacles in Montpelier (1918) and Blackfoot (1920–1921) made playful use of Georgian motifs on a semicircular plan. The Blackfoot building's oversize oxeye windows and Palladian entry (with a simplified All-seeing Eye in its round arch) seem parodies of the Colonial Revival. For congregations in Idaho Falls and Ammon, Sundberg and Sundberg designed Tudoresque remodelings of ward buildings. The Idaho Falls design, for the fifth ward meetinghouse (1936), featured a large Tudor Gothic entry, casement windows, and half-timbering in which the panels had a herringbone brick veneer. The Ammon design, drawn one year later, detailed the addition of similar Tudoresque features to a late nineteenth-century Romanesque Revival building. Tudoresque was an unusual style in the work of Sundberg and Sundberg; in designs for wards in Ashton and Mud Lake the firm turned to Art Deco and Art Moderne, styles that it favored in its secular commissions. Undated plans for the Ashton building depict an Art Deco spire reminiscent of the Mormon Temple at Idaho Falls

Sundberg and Sundberg designed Mormon church buildings for many southeast Idaho communities. Here is their rendering of a Tudoresque remodeling for the Idaho Falls fifth ward. (Photograph by Cuzzin's Photos, Pocatello, reproduction courtesy of Sundberg and Associates, Idaho Falls.)

(1939–1945). Plans for the Mud Lake church (1940) include corner and entry piers with numerous setbacks. Streamlined Moderne styling was achieved economically by specifying a cement stucco veneer over a wooden frame construction. The architects' drawings provided the contractor with details for the profile of the piers and the Art Moderne overdoor panel.[15]

For plans like these, designed outside the Mormon church architect's office, the local designer received initial advice, and plans went through a review by the supervisor of church buildings in the Presiding Bishops' Office. When the Sundbergs were planning their remodeling of the Idaho Falls fifth ward building, the Presiding Bishop's Office's "Form 84 — Instructions to Architects" provided advice aimed at producing economical buildings with the proper decorum and quality. However, the instructions were general enough to allow for a range of designs:

Plan dignified buildings of appropriate architectural design. Simplicity of design is desirable. Avoid elaborate, decorative features. Avoid sameness in exterior. Individuality should be consistent with purpose of building. Economy in design and construction, consistent with good practice, should be carefully followed.[16]

The gradual shift in Mormon church-building styles can be viewed today by touring the

St. Mary's Catholic Church in Moscow is one of the many Tudor Gothic style buildings that Tourtellotte and Hummel designed for the Catholics during the 1930s and 1940s. Distinctive features of Tudor Gothic include the building's casement windows (swinging windows that are hinged at the side) and wide pointed arches with shoulders. (ISHS 80-5.184; Duane Garrett, photographer.)

many ward buildings of southeast Idaho's small towns, where Colonial Revival remodelings or additions contrast with earlier Picturesque designs.

Church building by the Roman Catholics joined a standard plan for small churches with a preference for the Tudor Gothic style. Tourtellotte and Hummel captured commissions for many Catholic churches during the 1920s, 1930s, and early 1940s. They accomplished most of these designs using a restrained Tudor Gothic style in red brick with white terracotta detailing, and they recycled their own simple plan for "A Catholic Church" in designing the smaller churches.[17] The firm's castellated Gothic design for the University of Idaho's administration building (1907–1918) was a precedent for these later, rather more subdued neo-Gothic designs, and the firm also found the style appropriate for its Boise Junior College buildings and the dairy science building at the University of Idaho (1940–1941).

Tourtellotte and Hummel's association with Catholic church construction may have begun as early as 1902 with a commission for St. Bernard's Catholic Church in Blackfoot, attributed to the firm. During the depression years Tourtellotte and Hummel designed twenty churches, parish schools and houses, rectories, and remodelings for the church. The neo-Gothic designs include St. Theresa's in Orofino (1937), St. Mary's Church and rectory in Boise (1937), St. Mary's in Moscow

(1930), and St. Anthony's in Pocatello (1941). The firm's association with Catholic church building was renewed after the war, and at least sixteen postwar designs by Hummel, Hummel, and Jones survive in the church's blueprint collection from the 1940s and 1950s, many of them Gothic in inspiration. An excellent example is Holy Rosary Catholic Church in Idaho Falls (1947).[18]

The Forest Service used standard plans and styles to fit summer homes and administrative sites to the forest landscape and to establish a public image for its programs. The development of standard plans progressed at a different pace in each of the service's regions, but the second edition of the service-wide "Use Book," put out in 1906, set an early preference for log construction. "Wherever possible cabins should be built of logs," the manual stated, "with shingle or shake roofs."[19] In addition to the Use Book, advice and plans were disseminated locally by the rangers themselves, who were expected to build their own housing and administrative buildings through "contributed time," by which was meant time out of the ranger's regular work hours. Ranger Philip Neff of the Coeur d'Alene National Forest wrote "Suggestions on Ranger Cabin Construction" (1913). Ranger Clyde Blake, Sr., drew plans in 1922 that were used at Avery Ranger Station and perhaps elsewhere.[20] During this same period the Forest Service also purchased homestead and ranch buildings for reuse as administrative sites.

Plans were being drawn for region-wide use by the late 1920s, and in the early 1930s Clyde Fickes of the Region One (northern Idaho and surroundings) Operation Section prepared a construction handbook for the region's rangers that was reproduced in other regions.[21] Administrative sites from the 1920s were a mixture of standard and nonstandard plans. On the Boise National Forest, at least three administrative sites survive with buildings from this era: Cottonwood Ranger Station (1928–1936), Deadwood Guard Station (1929–1935), and Third Fork Guard Station (1927–1940).

During the 1930s Forest Service construction handbooks became a standard part of Civilian Conservation Corps (CCC) projects. Region One favored Rustic style exteriors for these basic plans, and Region Four, which took in the rest of the state, imposed the Rustic style and Colonial Revival exteriors that still conveyed a sense of rustic woodsiness in their detailing and use of color. CCC construction crews worked under the supervision of LEMs (local experienced men), and so drew upon the skills of vernacular builders who could create rustic effects through masonry and log construction.

Regional construction manuals of the CCC era provided plans for every sort of administrative building, including ranger housing, barns, blacksmith shops, fire lookouts, and barracks. They also provided sample site plans and considerable advice concerning

maintenance, procuring materials economically, requirements of the CCC program, and the aesthetics of color schemes and alternating roof lines. Only standard plans were allowed, although alterations to plans were apparently made without approval, and only certain materials and certain colors were considered appropriate to create the Rustic style desired by the service. Region Four builders were advised

If the timber on the site or near is preponderantly conifer, a log building is the type; if broadleaf, a frame building is the proper one. If there is neither conifer nor broadleaf near nor plainly in view from the site, a frame building is the type.[22]

Similarly, color schemes were required to match the site's environment, whether coniferous or deciduous forest, sagebrush, rock outcrop, or an urban neighborhood.

The number of headquarters, ranger stations, and guard stations increased severalfold during the CCC era, ranging from large compounds located in towns and used yearlong, like Challis Ranger Station (1933–1937) and the Salmon National Forest headquarters (1931–1938), to temporary stations like Seafoam Ranger Station (1930–1933) in Challis National Forest and Caribou Basin Guard Station (1936) in Caribou National Forest.

The degree to which the Forest Service plans incorporated earlier vernacular design is remarkable. Not only was traditional log

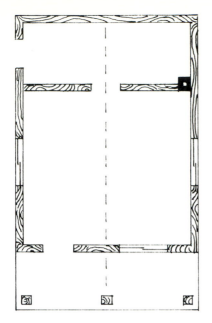

The Forest Service's standard R-4 series included plans for guard stations, housing, and barns and other outbuildings. The R4-5 plan, a one-room house with an inset front porch, was used for guard stations. (Drawing by Cheryl Marshall.)

construction used for many buildings but also traditional house types like the Rocky Mountain Cabin were used for the service's R4 plans. When it was built of logs, plan R4–5, a one-room guard station with a rear storeroom and a front porch covered by a roof extension, was indistinguishable from a miner's or rancher's Rocky Mountain Cabin or a Rustic style resort home.[23]

For CCC workers, the Forest Service manual had barracks plans, which were constructed to house the corps at its many Idaho camps. These were simple frame buildings after the manner of United States barracks everywhere — a linear plan, an entry on one or both gable walls, windows along the side walls, and ventilators on the roof and in the gables. Buildings of this description went up quickly for Japanese-Americans confined at Hunt in 1942 and for the armed forces stationed at Pocatello, Mountain Home, Boise, and Farragut during the war years. Because of their mobility and specialized function, few barracks survive to document this sort of rapidly constructed temporary shelter. The Brown's Camp CCC barracks at Weippe, reused as a public library, remains as a good example of the barracks plan.

The Forest Service had been established to manage the forest reserves under a policy of regulated conservation and use of forest, pasture, and water resources. During the 1910s, however, the public began to visit the national forests in greater numbers for recreation, and

after 1920, when automobiles became cheap enough for middle-class ownership, recreational use of the public lands grew, along with the growth of private resorts. As a result, the Forest Service found it necessary to develop campgrounds and other recreational facilities. The service also responded to public pressure by establishing a special-use-permit system for summer homes on the national forests. Permits for resorts were allowed by the General Land Office beginning in 1902, and when the Forest Service took over that office's duties in 1905 the permit policy was expanded to include summer home permits. A federal act of 1915 allowed the service to grant permits for long terms (up to thirty years).[24]

Forest Service oversight of summer homes on the public land included furnishing plan ideas, approving designs, and reviewing buildings to insure their maintenance by owners. In 1937 the Ogden office provided a manual of plans, "Suggested Designs for Summer Homes,"[25] to forest supervisors in Region Four, with the advice that "you should not hesitate to insist on special use permittees selecting a plan which is appropriate to the place they propose to build."[26]

The corner of Idaho bordering on Yellowstone National Park had some of the earliest recreational use in the state. Island Park and Targhee National Forest saw the development of private fishing resorts like the North Fork Club (1904), of private ranch-resorts like Railroad Ranch (1910s), and of summer

homes grouped along the tributaries to the Snake River, such as Targhee Row (circa 1920–1927) and the Big Springs complex, which includes the Johnny Sack Cabin (1932–1934) and the Burland/Rinetti-Capitolo summer home complex (1925). Log construction, combined with Rustic, bungalow, Colonial Revival, or even Tudoresque motifs, was almost ubiquitous in the Island Park area, where proximity to Yellowstone had made the Rustic style synonymous with recreation.[27]

Elsewhere in the state, hot springs, which had been used as resorts since prehistoric times, received new attention. The Bald Mountain Hot Springs at Ketchum, for example, was developed as a Rustic style pool and tourist-cabin complex, designed by Tourtellotte and Hummel in 1929. Lakeshore property also became desirable for summer homes. By 1930 the State Land Department was moved to urge that no new lakeshore plots should be sold at Payette Lake, arguing that "Payette lake is the most available mountain resort for all of southwest Idaho, and provision should be made for its use and enjoyment by those who are unable to build large homes."[28] The Rustic style flourished at the lake and at nearby McCall and Smith's Ferry, where two Southern Idaho Timber Protective Association complexes (1937 and 1927), constructed under the supervision of Finnish carpenters Gust Lepinoja and John Heikkila, illustrate the cross-influences between Rustic style construction and traditional craftsmanship.[29]

The rough lumber forms used in construction of Sun Valley Lodge gave the building's concrete walls a rustic texture. The effect was enhanced with a stone veneer on the rear terrace, shown here. (Environment West, Ketchum, Idaho.)

At Priest Lake in the Idaho panhandle resorts were established as early as 1914, when Sam Byars built his Forest Lodge at Mosquito Bay. Further guest cabin and hotel development followed in the 1920s and 1930s. As at Payette Lake, building lots were sold by the State Land Board, but many were not developed until after World War II. Forest Service special-use permits began at the lake in 1910 when the Vinther and Nelson family was granted a permit for their 1898 cabin, a traditional log-constructed building.[30]

A trend in the early development of summer homes was the combined ranch-resort. On Payette Lake, for example, Harry and Beulah Soulen built a small cabin in the 1920s for the family's use while they had sheep on their upper pasture. In 1934 they replaced it with a larger Rustic style log house built with a nontraditional even-tiered construction. The Rustic style of the building is borne out on the interior with carved rams' horns on the ends of ceiling joists and stair beams. Similarly, sheep ranchers John and Martha Skillern maintained a summer home at Big Creek for summer pasture on Soldier Mountain. Martha's design for the Rustic style log house, built 1920–1921, was inspired by Old Faithful Inn at Yellowstone.

Railroad Ranch near Island Park was a hobby ranch and sporting resort established by wealthy easterners, most of them connected with the Union Pacific Railroad. By 1918 the Guggenheim and Harriman families had consolidated controlling interest in the ranch. Construction there in the 1910s produced a complex of one- and two-story stockholders' cottages, guesthouses, barns, and other outbuildings built with traditional log construction and trimmed with moldings and other detailing painted white or green.[31]

One of the Harrimans established Idaho's most famous resort during this same period. The Sun Valley ski resort (1936–1939) was the dream of W. Averell Harriman, who as chairman of the Union Pacific board set out to establish the United States' prototypical ski resort. Publicized by the railroad as the "St. Moritz of America," Sun Valley was modeled after European resorts, a self-contained village of hotels and dormitories with restaurants and sports and entertainment facilities. The ski slopes incorporated an important improvement over the rope tows used in the eastern United States and over the gondolas used in European resorts: the first chair lifts, developed by Union Pacific engineers. Sun Valley Lodge, the first of the village's structures, was a distinctive Rustic design by Gilbert, Stanley, Underwood and Company of Los Angeles.[32] The building's concrete walls, poured in rough wood forms and painted brown, combine the texture and appearance of rough wooden siding with the durability of concrete construction.

Standard plans, New Deal programs, and the recreation boom combined to support new construction during two decades of hard times. They also were essential in assisting architects and builders through the depression years. In the firm of Tourtellotte and Hummel, for example, Frederick C. Hummel was

For their WPA-era courthouse designs the Sundbergs used the Art Deco style. In the entrance to the Oneida County Courthouse Art Deco piers with multiple setback layers are ornamented with foliage cast in terra-cotta. (ISHS 78-5.400/b; Duane Garrett, photographer.)

One of the state's first and most ambitious Art Deco designs is the Hotel Boise by Frank K. Hummel (right). Hummel used multiple setbacks, vertical piers, and decorative concrete panels to create the building's style. (ISHS 61-122.8.)

absent from the firm between 1935 and 1947 while he was chief architect and then chief underwriter for the Federal Housing Administration in Idaho. His brother Frank K. Hummel designed several PWA and WPA buildings for the firm during this time. When the United States entered World War II, the brothers closed the firm in 1942, and Frank worked for the Army Corps of Engineers.[33] PWA- and WPA-sponsored construction also provided many commissions for the firms of Frank H. Paradice, Jr., and Sundberg and Sundberg.

The depression combined with licensing requirements to reduce the number of architects working in Idaho and to reduce the growth of new firms. During 1917 to 1920, immediately after passage of the licensing act, eighty-six applicants were licensed to practice in the state, including many who applied under the grandfather clause. Between 1921 and 1945, sixty-two applicants received licenses, and only fourteen of them were state residents.[34]

One of the few successful firms established during the depression years was Sundberg and Sundberg of Idaho Falls.[35] The original principals of the firm were brothers Howard M. Sundberg and Clinton A. Sundberg, born in 1887 and 1892 at Pleasant Grove, Utah. They acquired early exposure to construction since their father was a carpenter in Pleasant Grove.

Howard, the senior partner, began his building career as a young man in Utah, ob-taining on-the-job experience in carpentry, laying and casting concrete, steel framing, millwork, plasterwork, and architectural drafting. His formal training included courses in architecture at the University of Utah and apprenticeship with an architectural firm in Salt Lake City. From 1909 to 1915 he taught drafting and mechanical arts at Ricks Academy.

The junior member of the firm, Clinton A. Sundberg, attended the University of Utah and received architectural and engineering experience working with his brother Alvin. Clinton moved to Rexburg, where he served as a principal in the public schools and taught at Ricks Academy. Between 1919 and 1925 he practiced architecture under the name C. A. Sundberg, Architect, based in Rexburg. Plans survive for his designs for an eight-room school, a Victor school building addition, a Driggs high school remodeling, the First National Bank in Driggs, and the 1925 Power County Courthouse. County courthouses for Teton County (1924) and Madison County (1921) are also attributed to him.[36] In this early work, especially in the courthouses, Clinton demonstrated his fondness for classical symmetry, for surface texture expressed in color and materials, and for decoration, often modeled in terra-cotta when the client could afford it. These trends continued to be evident in the firm's later work, whether the building style was Beaux Arts classicism, Prairie, Tudoresque, Art Deco, or Art Moderne.

Sundberg and Sundberg, Architectural Engineers, Rexburg, produced at least two plans for Rexburg buildings before moving its practice to Idaho Falls in 1926 or 1927. There the firm established a successful regional practice whose influence reached from Burley to Driggs and from Salmon to Preston. When Howard retired in 1947, Clinton continued his practice as C. A. Sundberg, working until his

death in 1967. Clinton was joined in the firm by his son Keith, and a successor firm still practices in Idaho Falls.

The range of Sundberg and Sundberg's commissions was typical of architectural practice during the depression years. In addition to their work for a major client, the Mormon church, the Sundbergs designed three similar WPA courthouses for Jefferson (1938), Jerome (1939), and Oneida (1939) counties; numerous school additions and remodelings; and a few commercial remodelings and additions. Residential commissions were scarce, and the firm's plans for a Tudoresque remodeling of the T. J. Johnson house in Blackfoot (1930) was a rare project. By contrast, Sundberg and Sundberg's postwar work included a good deal more new construction.

With a decided taste for Prairie, Art Deco, and Art Moderne designs, Sundberg and Sundberg made a mark in southeast Idaho rivaled only by the work of Paradice. The three styles also link the brothers' work with Utah architecture, in which the same preferences can be seen during the depression years. Among the firm's best designs are the three WPA courthouse designs, all of them two-story, five-bay buildings with outset entry bays. On each building this entry is embellished with unique Art Deco terra-cotta ornamentation. Undoubtedly these were drawn for manufacture by a terra-cotta factory. Correspondence with the Denver Terra Cotta Company and drawings for other terra-cotta

Picture palaces of the 1920s and 1930s expressed exotic styles like Egyptian Revival in their exterior and interior design. The architect's rendering of the Egyptian Theatre in Boise depicts the style's battered (tapered) piers, flared cornices, and colorful decorative motifs drawn from Egyptian art. (ISHS 80-163.20/b.)

projects show that the Sundbergs drew their own terra-cotta designs and inspected the factory's work as it was being modeled.

The few major Idaho commissions of the depression years—government buildings, hotels, theaters, and schools—became a forum for the exposition of various romantic styles. When architects had a budget to work with during this era, they created some of the state's most dramatic buildings. Large hotels were built in Lewiston, Boise, and Idaho Falls, and Pocatello's Bannock Hotel received a major addition. The Lewis and Clark in Lewiston (1922), attributed to Kirtland K. Cutter,[37] and the Bonneville in Idaho Falls (1927) were Spanish Mission Revival style hotels located along axial boulevards at the center of their respective towns. The Hotel Boise, designed by Frank Hummel of Tourtellotte and Hummel and completed in 1930, was the state's first skyscraper, an Art Deco building fashioned of concrete and modeled with spirelike Deco piers cresting its setback upper stories.[38] Its stark concrete geometry and its use of Deco setbacks anticipated two much later buildings in southeast Idaho, Hyrum C. Pope's Franklin County Courthouse (1939) and the Mormon Temple at Idaho Falls, designed by John Fetzer, Sr., of Salt Lake City and erected during the period 1939 to 1945.[39] In 1919 the Bannock Hotel in Pocatello commissioned Frank Paradice to design three tower additions, but only one was constructed.[40] Paradice's terra-cotta-encrusted

tower, resplendent with Renaissance detailing, dwarfed the rest of the building. Standing well above their surroundings, these new multistoried hotels anticipated postwar Modernism by breaking with the style, scale, and materials of the architecture in their communities.

Architects could also stretch their creative skills in designs for theaters and railroad depots. The Egyptian Theater in Boise (1926) was one of Frederick C. Hummel's major works. Always intrigued by Egyptian art, Hummel returned to sources from his college days to create the colorful Egyptian motifs

found within and without the exotic building.[41] Picture palaces of the new cinematic age were typically designed in eye-catching styles that were expressed on the building's interior as well as its facade. Other Idaho examples are the Spanish Colonial Revival style Panida in Sandpoint (1927), the Art Deco style Nuart in Blackfoot (1929), and the Chief in Pocatello (1938), an Art Deco design by Denver architect Walter H. Simon using motifs from Southwestern Indian cultures. A building that reinforced the popularity of the already well known Spanish Mission Revival style was the Union Pacific Railroad Depot in Boise

The Union Pacific Railroad constructed modern depots in Boise and Nampa during the 1920s. The Nampa building, shown here, was a Sullivanesque building employing Sullivan's distinctive round arch and heraldic ornamentation. (ISHS 63-211.39.)

(1925), designed by Carrère and Hastings of New York.[42] Like the theaters, the depot expressed its style on exterior and interior alike, with a lofty wood-trussed ceiling that duplicates the painted beams of the California missions. An equally outstanding building in its local setting was the Union Pacific depot in Nampa (1924–1925), a design that reproduced the dramatic, single round arch that Louis Sullivan employed in his late work in the Midwest.

A mixture of classicism and Art Deco or Art Moderne style was used so consistently for architects designing buildings sponsored by the PWA and WPA programs that some historians call it "PWA Moderne."[43] In Idaho, however, architects gave Deco and Moderne the flavor of their personal interpretations. Government programs offered architects like

Frank K. Hummel, Frank H. Paradice, Jr., and the Sundbergs the opportunity to design some of their finest essays in terra-cotta or cast-stone ornamentation for Art Deco and Art Moderne buildings. The Sundbergs' courthouses were matched by Hummel's simpler Moderne designs for courthouses in Gem (1938), Owyhee (1936), and Washington (1938) counties and Paradice's Deco designs for the Pocatello High School remodeling (1938) and Graveley Hall (1939) on the Idaho State College campus, in which his taste for Sullivanesque and Renaissance Revival ornamentation lingers.

The essence of Prairie, Art Deco, and Art Moderne was a break with the architecture of the past, represented by the revival styles that had dominated American architecture from Georgian times. But designing in the new,

modern styles was not the only way to break with one's history. Demolition, rebuilding, and radical remodeling began to have an effect on the state's building stock during the depression years and were held in check mainly by lack of building funds. In the Forest Service's standardized building program, for example, Boise's 1872 Italianate style assay office nearly underwent a thorough remodeling. The assay office was taken over as offices by Region Four of the Forest Service in 1934. In his specifications for the proposed remodeling, the regional architect commented that

the sketch contemplates tearing off of the present structure the unsightly cupola at the vertex of the roof and also the heavy, bulky cornice, and modernizing the appearance with a Portland cement stucco on the exterior.[44]

The resulting Colonial Revival style building would have harmonized with the many Colonial Revival designs in the region's manual. Two wings were to be added flanking the original structure, which without its cupola would have had a shallow pyramidal roof. The whole was to be stuccoed and trimmed with standard-issue shutters bearing pine tree cutouts. Coach lamps either side of the main entry completed the design.

Although many period revival styles were popular during the 1920s and 1930s, those styles had little to do with Idaho's past. The

One of Frank H. Paradice's WPA era projects depicts his adoption of the Art Deco style. The Student Union Building at Idaho State University employs terra-cotta for its ornamental panels and coping. (Photograph by Cuzzin's Photos, Pocatello.)

The Forest Service's proposed remodeling of the assay office in Boise would have added stucco veneer, side wings, and Colonial Revival shutters and coach lamps. (ISHS, MS 23.)

immediate past of western settlement was reflected only in the Rustic style, which represented a nostalgic, not a realistic, revival of pioneer architecture. Dissociation from the past was a trend that continued after the end of World War II, when new internationalism and an expanding economy created the means for replacing and rebuilding. The assay office escaped redesign in 1934; in the postwar era its lot would have been different.

Notes

1. Epigraph from "Record of Automobile Trip Made by the Anketell Family, 1922," MS 2.667, Idaho State Historical Society (hereafter ISHS), Boise.

2. Walter W. Dixon and Wayne Tharp, ed., *Dixon's Book of Plans: Homes of from Three to Six Rooms Designed in Colonial, English and Spanish Types of Architecture* (Oakland, California: W. W. Dixon Plan Service, n.d.). For information about Jordan's career, see "Jordan-Wilcomb Company"

[promotional brochure], n.d., author's personal collection; and the Jordan-Wilcomb papers, ISHS, Boise.

3. Pren Moore, et al., "Turkey Growing in Idaho," Extension Bulletin, no. 79 (Boise: University of Idaho, 1930), 38–49.

4. "Survey of Farm Conditions," *The Architectural Record* 75, no. 4 (April 1934):301.

5. *The Farm-Housing Survey,* Miscellaneous Publication, no. 323 (Washington, D.C.: U. S. Department of Agriculture, March 1939).

6. M. R. Lewis, "Running Water in the Farm Home," Extension Bulletin, no. 66 (Moscow: University of Idaho, June 1926). For WPA outhouses, see (Sandpoint) *Northern Idaho News,* 31 January 1936, 4; 15 May 1936, 1; 15 May 1936, 7.

7. Architectural drawing for Safeway store in Rigby, 4 October 1940, Paradice drawings on file in private collection of Wallace-Hudson and Associates, Pocatello. The collection also includes drawings for Safeway stores in Idaho Falls, Buhl, and Pocatello, and a generic plan for interior details.

8. For examples of service station design from this period, see "Continental Oil Company Complex, Twin Falls," Idaho Historic Sites Series, no. 554 (Boise: ISHS, n.d.); and Patricia Wright, *Twin Falls Country: A Look at Idaho Architecture* (Boise: ISHS, 1979), 62.

9. Institute for Urban and Local Studies, "Historic U.S. Post Offices (1900–1941) Thematic Resources Nomination: Idaho," (1989), National Register nomination on file at Idaho State Historical Society, Boise, and National Park Service, Washington, D.C.

10. *School House Plans: One, Two and Three Room Buildings,* Idaho Bulletin of Education 13, no. 4 (June 1927), 5–6.

11. Ibid., 3.

12. Susanne Lichtenstein, "Boise Public Schools," (14 September 1982), National Register of Historic Places nomination form, part 8.

13. Allen D. Roberts, "Religious Architecture of the LDS Church: Influences and Changes since 1847," *Utah Historical Quarterly* 43, no. 3 (Summer 1975):326.

14. The seminary is discussed in Lisa B. Reitzes, *Paris: A Look at Idaho Architecture* (Boise: Idaho State Historic Preservation Office, 1981), 95. Unless otherwise specified, the buildings mentioned in this chapter are docu-

mented in National Register of Historic Places forms.

15. Drawings, specifications, and correspondence for the work of Sundberg and Sundberg are on file in the private collection of Sundberg and Associates, Architects, Idaho Falls.

16. "Form 84 — Instructions to Architects — Church Buildings" (The Presiding Bishopric, [circa 1937]), Idaho Falls Fifth Ward file, private collection of Sundberg and Associates, Architects, Idaho Falls, 2.

17. Patricia Wright and Lisa B. Reitzes, *Tourtellotte and Hummel of Idaho: The Standard Practice of Architecture* (Logan, Utah: Utah State University Press, 1987), 28–29.

18. Ibid., 48–49, 78–81, 87–105; and Roman Catholic blueprint collection, on file at ISHS, Boise. The collection includes the post–World War II designs of Hummel, Hummel, and Jones.

19. Quoted in Cort Sims, *Ranger Stations on the Idaho Panhandle National Forests* (Coeur d'Alene, Idaho: Idaho Panhandle National Forests, 1986), 13.

20. Ibid., 12–15.

21. Ibid., 18–21.

22. R. H. Rutledge, *Building Construction Manual* (U. S. Department of Agriculture, Forest Service Region Four, 1934, rev. ed. 1935), BP–25. Information about standard plans and their use in Idaho is also compiled from Sims, *Ranger Stations*, 22–28; Joseph G. Gallagher, "A Report on the Historical Significance of Forest Service Administrative Structures in Southern Idaho Located on the Boise, Caribou, Challis, Payette, Salmon, Sawtooth and Targhee National Forests" (draft, 1986), on file at ISHS, Boise; and Linnea Keating and Karl Roenke, *Fixed Fire Detection Lookout History on the Clearwater National Forest, Idaho* (Orofino, Idaho: Clearwater National Forest, August 1987).

23. Rutledge, *Building Construction Manual*, Plan R4–5.

24. William C. Tweed, *Recreation Site Planning and Improvement in National Forest, 1891–1942*, Forest Service FS–354 (Washington, D.C.: U. S. Department of Agriculture, November 1980), 2–3.

25. *Suggested Designs for Summer Homes* (Ogden, Utah: U. S. Department of Agriculture, Forest Service Intermountain Region, [1937]).

26. J. H.(?) Stokes to Forest Supervisors [memorandum], 30 June 1937, on file at supervisor's office, Targhee National Forest, St. Anthony, Idaho.

27. For the North Fork Club, see James L. Allison and Dean H. Green, *Idaho's Gateway to Yellowstone* (Mack's Inn, Idaho: Island Park-Gateway Publishing, 1974), 109; for the Railroad Ranch, see Keith Petersen and Mary Reed, "Harriman State Park and the Railroad Ranch: A History" (January 1984), report prepared for the Idaho State Department of Parks and Recreation, Boise; and for Targhee Row, see Mildred Pacina Hoggan, *The Targhee Row Story* (Elgin T. Gates, 1985).

28. *Twentieth Biennial Report* (Idaho State Land Department, 1930), 14.

29. I am indebted to Elizabeth Egleston for sharing with me her research regarding the Southern Idaho Timber Protective Association.

30. Nancy F. Renk, "Priest Lake Planning Unit: Cultural Resource Overview," Report 118, Idaho Historic Sites Inventory, ISHS, Boise, 7–8.

31. Petersen and Reed, "Harriman State Park," 20–21, 35, 41, 171–78.

32. Doug Oppenheimer and Jim Poore, *Sun Valley: a Biography* (Boise: Beatty Books, 1976), 54.

33. Wright and Reitzes, *Tourtellotte and Hummel*, x, 6; and Frederick C. Hummel, interviewed by Arthur A. Hart, 4 May 1974, OH498A, ISHS, Boise.

34. See file cards for architectural license applicants, on file at the Bureau of Occupational Licenses, State of Idaho, Boise.

35. Information about Sundberg and Sundberg is compiled from drawings, plans, specifications, and correspondence on file in the private collection of Sundberg and Associations, Architects, Idaho Falls; license application
for Howard M. Sundberg, on file at the Bureau of Occupational Licenses; and an obituary for Clinton A. Sundberg, *The* (Idaho Falls) *Post-Register,* 1 January 1968, 1, 11.

36. (Driggs) *Teton Valley News,* 10 July 1924, 1; 14 February 1924, 1; 27 March 1924, 1; and 31 January 1924, 1; and David Crowder, *Rexburg, Idaho: the First 100 Years 1883–1983* (Caldwell: Caxton Printers, 1983), 203–4.

37. *Lewiston Tribune,* 16 January 1920, 12; 17 January 1920, 12; 19 April 1921, 10; 1 January 1922, sec. 2, 1; 7 March 1922, 12; 9 March 1922, 10; 6 July 1922, 10; 23 July 1922, 7; 13 August 1922, 10; 15 August 1922, 10.

38. Wright and Reitzes, *Tourtellotte and Hummel,* 70–71.

39. Delbert V. Groberg, *The Idaho Falls Temple* (Publishers Press, 1985), 62.

40. The architect's presentation drawing of the Bannock with the proposed three towers is in the private collection of Wallace-Hudson and Associates, Pocatello.

41. Wright and Reitzes, *Tourtellotte and Hummel,* 68–69; and Frederick C. Hummel, interviewed by Arthur A. Hart, 18 May 1974, OH498B, Idaho State Historical Society, Boise.

42. The Boise depot's relationship to other Mission style buildings in Idaho is discussed by Arthur A. Hart in "The Mission Style and Eclecticism in Idaho," in *Space, Style and Structure: Building in Northwest America,* 2 vols. (Portland, Oregon: Oregon Historical Society, 1974), 2:509–13.

43. See, for example, Thomas Carter and Peter Goss, *Utah's Historic Architecture, 1847–1940* (Salt Lake City: University of Utah Press, 1988):170. Users of the IMACS system for recording historic sites have also adopted this term. In *Tourtellotte and Hummel,* Wright and Reitzes present a good argument against such terminology, 12.

44. "Specifications; Sketch Showing Proposed Addition to Forest Offices at Boise, Idaho" (July 1934), MS 23, ISHS, Boise. This manuscript file contains many other documents pertaining to Forest Service management of the assay office.

7

Modernism and the Historic Preservation Movement, Architecture after World War II

175 Buildings Razed

Like a woman fixing up her face, Pocatello is gradually removing the blemishes — in the form of dilapidated buildings — which blemish its municipal complexion.

— 1957, Pocatello *Idaho State Journal* (Centennial Edition, 21 June 1982)

Cataldo Dedicated As Historic Park

The inclusion of the mission in Idaho's state park system insures that for the next 40 years . . . the [Sacred Heart] mission will continue to stand as part of Idaho's heritage.

— Pocatello *Idaho State Journal,* 14 June 1976

Wartime Idaho experienced renewed economic growth, and at the war's conclusion returning Idaho servicemen and -women were ready to rebuild their towns in a new Modernist image. Modernist architecture, the outgrowth of work during the 1920s by European architects Walter Gropius, Mies van de Rohe, and Le Corbusier, was based on simple geometric forms and on new technological developments in reinforced concrete, hollow steel tubing, aluminum framing, laminated wood, preformed composition panels, and concrete block. Because Modernism grew out of an international culture and avoided using ornamentation derived from older periods, it was the least place-specific of styles. But Idahoans embraced the new aesthetic of anonymity and homogeneity as readily as other Americans during the postwar era.

The mark of Modernism is all around the people of Idaho, wherever they live, for no other period has reshaped the Idaho landscape quite so thoroughly as the modern period. Postwar prosperity was matched only in the economic boom of the early decades of the century, when Beaux Art classicism reshaped city streetscapes. The postwar boom had an overwhelming effect on architecture and on city and rural planning. Development of a restructured and renewed education system, for example, began in 1947 with consolidation that abandoned 900 school districts and continued into the 1960s with expanded university campuses to educate the post-war gener-

ation. Construction of the interstate freeway system began in 1956, eventually resulting in a new pattern of freeway-exit commercial zones for restaurants, motels, and service stations and construction of shopping malls located at major highway and freeway intersections.[1] Reliance on the private automobile also made residential developments located on former farmland near town a popular alternative for postwar housing. As malls grew and suburban families patronized them, downtowns suffered. Efforts to renew downtowns under programs sponsored by the U. S. Department of Housing and Urban Development led to complete destruction of some commercial neighborhoods and successful rehabilitation of others.

Modernism lay at the core of all these developments, but this recent and influential movement has not been studied much by Idaho historians. The only survey of modern buildings in Idaho was done by J. Meredith Neil and David Nels Reese as a project of the Idaho Bicentennial Commission in 1976. On the basis of their material, published in *Saints and Oddfellows*,[2] at least two strains of Modernism in Idaho architecture can be identified. One might be called "organic"—that is, growing out of regional forms and materials—and the other might be called "international"—that is, inspired by the work of international architects.

Organic Modernism is site-specific: buildings are designed to fit their setting. This philosophy of architecture is well represented in

The Sacred Heart Mission Church near Cataldo underwent a major restoration in 1973. During the work flooring was temporarily removed, exposing the building's timber floor joists. (ISHS 73-208.0/c.)

an Idaho building designed by its principal advocate, Frank Lloyd Wright. The Teater studio was designed by Wright in 1952–1953 for artists Patricia and Archie Teater. Patricia, who managed her husband's successful career as a western landscape painter, also managed commissioning the design and overseeing construction of the house and left a thorough account, in letters and photographs, of the house's prolonged construction between 1953 and 1957. The difficulties encountered and caused by Patricia Teater constitute a case study in poor client-contractor-architect relationships. But the house was completed; and even though parts of it were modified in construction by the Teaters and their friends, the building successfully reflects the principles of Wright's organic architecture. Built of Oakley stone with a prowlike wall of glass that juts over the Snake River Canyon to give spectators in the studio a magnificent view, the building appears an outgrowth of the canyon itself. Yet its plan, based on a repeated parallelogram, is plain and geometric—that is, essentially Modernist.[3]

During the late 1930s and 1940s a group of Northwestern architects also adopted local materials and simple geometry, but employed what they saw to be vernacular forms borrowed from the architecture of Northwestern barns, farmhouses, and industrial structures like fish canning sheds. These Northwest regionalists—including Oregon architects Pietro Belluschi and John Yeon—employed

Archie and Patricia Teater's studio and house, designed by Frank Lloyd Wright, fit its Snake River canyon setting through the use of Oakley stone and through its low, angular massing. (ISHS 85-5.33/a; Arthur A. Hart, photographer.)

natural-wood siding, stonework, and simple gable and shed roofs with projecting eaves in buildings designed to fit their wooded or grassland sites. Their work influenced Idaho architecture beginning in the mid–1950s. Architect-designed examples first appeared then, and at about the same time simple tract housing began to reflect Belluschi and Yeon's work as well as the influence of Frank Lloyd Wright's small single-family Usonian houses of the 1930s.[4] In suburban housing developments of the 1970s, regionalism devolved into the clichés of diagonal wooden siding and shake roofs, entirely losing the original link between site and design. The distribution of Idaho buildings influenced by the Northwest regionalists suggests a continuing link between the Northwest coast and northern and southwestern Idaho. The style is rarer in

southeastern Idaho than elsewhere in the state.

The earliest buildings noted by Neil and Reese to suggest the influence of the Northwest regionalists are the 1955 Troutner house in Boise and the 1958 St. Thomas Episcopal Church in Ketchum.[5] The Troutner house is a flared cylinder with a very shallow roof. In materials and massing it relates well to its rocky setting in the Boise foothills, where it was among the first foothill dwellings. The house was designed by its owner, Arthur Troutner, who founded the Trus Joist Company in Boise with entrepreneur Harold Thomas in 1960.[6] The St. Thomas Episcopal Church, designed by Boise architect Nat Adams, is a stone, wood, and glass composition that Adams linked to its mountain setting through steep intersecting A-frame roofs as

well as through natural materials.

Mountain and lakeshore resort areas like Coeur d'Alene, McCall, and Sun Valley — in short, the resorts of the wealthy — called for organic designs to suit the scenic beauty. In those areas, where clients could afford quality materials and architectural expertise, Northwest regionalism supplanted the Rustic style beginning in the 1960s. The Wood River valley between Ketchum and Hailey became dotted with large summer homes, some of them by local Ketchum designers and builders. Neil Wright of Ketchum, for example, produced the 1970 Chapman Root house, which makes playful use of overlapping shed roofs to fit the building to its setting near the Sun Valley hills. Other Idahoans who created imaginative designs for resort clients included R. G. Nelson of Coeur d'Alene and Nelson Miller, who was associated with the successor firm to Hummel, Hummel, and Jones. R. G. Nelson designed the 1966 Post Falls Library, the 1967 Silverhorn Ski Lodge near Kellogg, the 1971–1972 St. Rita's Catholic church in Kellogg, and the 1972–1973 Hagadone Building in Coeur d'Alene, all directly influenced by Northwest regionalism. Nelson Miller's work from this period included departures into Modernist Brutalism (a mode that uses rough concrete and exposes piping and other innards), but his designs in McCall for the 1968–1969 Stanley Young house and the 1971–1972 Idaho First National Bank branch office resemble Yeon and Belluschi's Oregon

R. G. Nelson's design for the Hagadone Building in Coeur d'Alene drew upon Northwest regionalism to set the building in the local context of vernacular lakeshore piers and warehouses. (ISHS Neil collection.)

work in their use of multiple shed roofs, wooden siding, stonework, and clerestory windows.[7]

Overlapping with the organic Modernism of the 1950s through the 1970s was international Modernism. Examples of work in this mode abound in Idaho; one can see its influence in the most modest cinder-block strip developments. International Modernism can be traced directly to the designs of Gropius, Mies van der Rohe, and Le Corbusier in western Europe. In the United States, Richard Neutra in California was designing early Modernist buildings in the late 1920s. The impact of Modernism was felt nationwide with the late buildings of the WPA period, in which decorative motifs were rendered with a plain and formal geometry, or were discarded altogether. Then, during the 1940s and 1950s, the Art Moderne style hybridized with international Modernism to create streamlined designs for storefront remodelings, bus depots, and automobile showrooms. Moderne-Modernist buildings were built in Idaho well into the 1950s, and the 1965 Central Facility Building at State Hospital South in Blackfoot represents a very late use of the hybrid style. The building has been attributed to C. A. Sundberg's Idaho Falls firm.[8]

Designs that fully reflect the work of the Modernist architects — in massing, scale, materials, and proportions — begin to appear in Idaho by 1965–1967, when the new Federal Building went up in Boise.[9] A commission by

Hummel Hummel Jones and Shawver (the successor firm to Hummel, Hummel, and Jones) the building epitomized the design principles of Modernism in its use of a simple elongated cube cantilevered over a glass-walled first-floor lobby. The concrete structure of the building is clearly expressed on its exterior, where floors and bays are demarked by a matrix of piers and beams. Typical of Modernist buildings, the structure and its materials pay no deference to its backdrop of the Boise hills.

The Hummel successor firm also designed an education building (1967–1968) for the University of Idaho that features a "kiva," a

cylindrical auditorium separate from the rest of the building.[10] The state's university system began a period of rapid expansion in the 1960s, when Southern Idaho Community College was established in Twin Falls, when Lewis-Clark Normal School split from the University of Idaho to become Lewis-Clark State College, and when Boise Junior College became Boise State College. In private education, the College of Idaho in Caldwell, Northwest Nazarene College in Nampa, and Ricks College in Rexburg also experienced unprecedented growth.

Campus construction created a number of monolithic Modernist classroom and office

Many Idaho buildings of the 1950s and 1960s were equally influenced by Modernism and by the Art Moderne style (a latter-day, streamlined, horizontally massed version of Art Deco). C. A. Sundberg's Central Facility Building at State Hospital South in Blackfoot (left) is an extremely late example of Moderne-Modernism. (ISHS Neil collection.)

Boise's Federal Building (below, left) is a classic example of the simple geometry of international Modernism. The building's main cubical mass is cantilevered (supported by projecting beams) over a glassed lobby. (ISHS Neil collection.)

buildings. Because the scale of the new buildings was much larger than the turn-of-the-century buildings that dominated the old campus quadrangles, these were challenging commissions. The best effort to unify the architecture of a campus was at Boise State College, where campus buildings designed by Hummel, Hummel, and Jones and its successor firms were harmonized in materials (red brick and white terra-cotta or concrete) and restricted in scale within the main campus.

A more frequent response to campus expansion was the destruction or radical remodeling of old buildings and dismemberment of the original quadrangle. Plans for destruction of Sterry Hall at the College of Idaho were made when the college adopted a 1963 master plan designed by John Graham and Company of Seattle.[11] The 1910 building survived the college's expansive years and was eventually repaired instead in 1981 with a federal matching grant keyed to the building's listing in the National Register of Historic Places.

One of the most remarkable university buildings in Idaho demonstrates the new expertise in engineering that was required of the postwar designer. The roof of Kibbie Stadium at the University of Idaho (1975) spans 400 feet with trusses adapted from Arthur Troutner's lightweight steel-and-wood Trus Dek roof system. Designed by KKBNA, Structural Engineers, of Denver (in association with the building's architects, Cline Smull Hammill Shaw and Associates, Boise), the roof won an

Idaho's Supreme Court Building is an elegant example of Modernism in which simple lines are enhanced by a warm marble veneer. (*Idaho Statesman*, Boise.)

Outstanding Civil Engineering Achievement award from the American Society of Civil Engineers.[12]

At its best, Modernism could achieve an aesthetic of clarity and formal dignity. Terteling Library (1967) on the College of Idaho campus, designed by John Graham and Company of Seattle, achieves that effect through minimal reference to the classical Greek temple: piers ring the building supporting an entablaturelike, flat projecting roof. The Idaho Supreme Court Building, designed by Victor Hosford of Dropping Kelly Hosford and LaMarche, Boise, has a similar clarity produced with slotted inset and outset bays that manage to avoid the monotony of many Modernist buildings. Part of the building's beauty is its veneer of travertine marble from southeast Idaho. A dramatic interior is achieved in the Boise-Cascade Building (1971), designed as the company's corporate headquarters by Skidmore, Owings and Merrill (SOM), an American firm famous for having perfected the Modernist office tower, in association with Morganelli Heremann and Associates. In its plan for the building, SOM employed an atrium, a feature that became popular in 1970s office buildings. The Boise-Cascade atrium creates a landscaped indoor plaza appropriate to Boise-Cascade's role in

Campbell and Wayland's First National Bank of Idaho building in Boise was one of many historic buildings destroyed in the city's Urban Renewal project. Across Main Street was the Eastman Building (shown here behind the bank), long endangered by urban renewal and eventually destroyed by fire in 1987. (72-100.86/B.)

the lumber industry and resort housing.[13]

As Idahoans embraced the Modernist movement, organic or international, they often came to see the ornamented buildings of earlier periods as ugly. As they accepted the virtues of concrete and steel, they came to believe that brick and even stone were insubstantial. Certain types of buildings seemed outmoded as society redirected itself to the automobile, the suburb, and the shopping mall, and as a growing population expected more government services. City halls, courthouses, downtown churches and hotels, railroad depots, and farms were especially vulnerable, as was the downtown commercial core, where neglected and abandoned buildings were blamed for unsolved societal problems like poverty and racial inequity. Buildings that had served community needs for decades were demolished and replaced with modern construction or with parking lots.

Considering their commercial building stock expendable and easily replaced, Idaho cities followed the lead of cities all over the nation by acquiring downtown property for redevelopment through funding from the U.S. Department of Housing and Urban Development. In the capital city the Boise Redevelopment Agency (BRA) began to organize in the spring of 1965. By 1970, with plans to redevelop downtown Boise as an enclosed mall similar to contemporary suburban developments, the agency was acquiring and demolishing buildings. Eventually it leveled four

city blocks just south of Main Street.[14]

Demolition of four blocks did not go unnoticed. The BRA's actions inspired debate on all sides for at least two decades, during which the Idaho historic preservation movement became a viable force for developing alternative uses for old buildings.

Idaho's historic preservation movement had its beginning as early as 1909. Packer John's cabin (1862) near New Meadows, Idaho, had served as a meeting place for Idaho's early territorial conventions. By 1899 it was seriously

endangered by natural decay. The 1909 legislature appropriated $500 for its acquisition and rehabilitation by the Idaho State Historical Society. Society director John Hailey accomplished the work with $126.85 left over. Hailey reported that

the old Cabin [was] taken down and rebuilt, new logs were put in where needed, a new roof and a new floor put in. It is now in good shape and makes a nice summer resort.[15]

Except for its state funding, the Packer John cabin project was typical of Idaho's early preservation efforts. Local pioneer groups, seeing the rapid deterioration of their community's earliest buildings, made efforts to move and restore them. Usually their attention was drawn to log buildings, rather than other sorts of early construction, because the log cabin had become a potent symbol of the pioneer past. In Boise, for example, the 1863 John A. O'Farrell cabin was moved by the Daughters of the American Revolution in about 1910. In 1958 the Sons and Daughters of the Idaho Pioneers built a protective roof over the cabin and gave it to the city. The Sons and Daughters organization also moved the I. N. Coston cabin, another log building from the 1860s, to Boise's Julia Davis Park in 1933. Similarly, the 1860s Robert McKenzie cabin was moved from its location on the Boise River near Caldwell to the Caldwell park in 1949.[16]

By 1966, when Congress enacted the National Historic Preservation Act (NHPA) establishing a federal-state historic preservation partnership through the agency of state historic preservation offices (SHPO), the preservation movement in Idaho had not grown beyond these small grass-roots projects. When NHPA became law in 1966, Gov. Robert E. Smylie designated the Idaho State Historical Society as Idaho's historic preservation office, one of the first such designations in the nation. In 1969 federal matching grants became available to the SHPOs, and Idaho's historic pres-

ervation program prepared the state's first preservation plan in 1970. In that plan Merle W. Wells, who acted as Idaho's historic preservation officer for two decades until his retirement in 1986, set forth priorities for survey and restoration projects. The office's accomplishments during Wells's tenure included programs that had a direct effect on saving and restoring historic buildings.

A restoration program was an early priority of the Idaho SHPO. This program provided federal matching grants to organizations and individuals who wanted to acquire and restore historic buildings. Some of the grant money went to preserve buildings that had been deeded to the state historical society. In 1972 the society received two historic buildings of statewide importance, the 1862 Shoshone County Courthouse at Pierce and the 1872 assay office in Boise. In 1974 the society became the agency responsible for an interpretive program at the recently vacated state penitentiary in Boise.[17] Restoration work at the three sites proceeded in several phases beginning in the late 1970s and has continued since the last round of federal restoration grants (in 1981) with funding from other sources.[18]

One of Idaho's first federally underwritten restoration projects was directed by the Idaho Bicentennial Commission's Boise office and funded partly with SHPO monies. The Sacred Heart Mission at Cataldo had not received major attention since 1928 when stabilization work had been accomplished through

efforts by private organizations throughout the Coeur d'Alene valley. The Bicentennial Commission project began with fund raising in 1973, with Henry L. Day of Wallace serving as chairman of the fund drive. Restoration architect Geoffrey W. Fairfax of Hawaii directed the four-phase project, which included archaeological investigation of the site to locate and protect evidence about the mission complex, restoration of artwork and wallpaper, stabilizing the building's structure, and replacement of deteriorated parts with matching materials. When it was completed in 1976 the project was the most detailed and thorough building restoration yet undertaken in Idaho. Administration of the site by the state parks department was an important final aspect of the project, providing for its long-term maintenance and interpretation.[19]

Adaptive reuse became a preservation strategy in the 1970s as it became apparent to preservationists that not all old buildings could or should be turned into museums. Acquisition, restoration, and adaptive reuse of the Standrod house in Pocatello was another bicentennial project. Using federal matching grants from the SHPO, the city of Pocatello purchased the house in 1974 and the Pocatello-Bannock Bicentennial Commission restored the building, opening it to the public for use as a community center in 1976.[20]

During the 1970s Idahoans gained a new awareness of historic preservation as an alternative to destroying and rebuilding. The state

The Capitol Terrace by Hummel LaMarche Hunsucker Architects PA is a Post-Modernist structure combining retail and parking facilities. Behind the building is James King's Boise City National Bank, slated for rehabilitation as part of downtown redevelopment. Post-Modernism attempts to reconcile the simple geometries of Modernism with the more decorative styles of the historic Victorian streetscape. (Idaho State Historic Preservation Office.)

historical society and bicentennial commission projects were visible proofs, as were privately funded projects. In Boise, for example, building owners in Old Boise just outside the BRA area began rehabilitation of their historic buildings in 1974. After Old Boise was listed in the National Register of Historic Places in 1977, further rehabilitations were encouraged by the new availability of tax deductions under the 1976 Tax Reform Act.[21]

Boise gained an eloquent spokesperson for historic preservation in Arthur A. Hart, who had come to the Idaho State Historical Society in 1969 to serve as museum director.[22] Hart's columns in *The Idaho Statesman* and illustrated lectures around the state stimulated new public interest and awareness of historic buildings. A private Boise-based historic preservation group also formed in the 1970s, the Idaho Historic Preservation Council. The group addressed controversial issues in the debate over downtown Boise buildings during its early years and established annual awards — Orchids and Onions — for good and bad treatments of historic buildings statewide.[23]

In 1975 the Idaho legislature passed an act recognizing the importance of historic buildings and enabling local governments to establish historic preservation commissions that could designate and protect local historic districts and buildings. The legislature declared that

the historical, archeological, architectural and cultural heritage of the state is among

the most important environmental assets of the state and furthermore that the rapid social and economic development of contemporary society threatens to destroy the remaining vestiges of this heritage.[24]

Passage of the state law represented a considerable change in the public attitude toward old buildings. In 1965 the BRA organizers could not have anticipated that it would be twenty more years before effective revitalization of downtown Boise was underway, nor would they have predicted that rebuilding Boise would hinge on a new historic preservation movement that directly opposed the Modernist streetscape they sought to build. At this writing a reconstituted BRA board, the Capital City Development Corporation, is overseeing the reconstruction of downtown Boise in a Post-Modernist era. Benefiting from new ideas developed during the twenty-year hiatus, the BRA is creating a multiple-use downtown with a central, public open space and a mixture of new Post-Modernist and rehabilitated historic buildings.

Like all the other movements that have affected Idaho architecture, Post-Modernism — a 1980s trend that uses simplified, oversize decorative elements from the past — is a fashion from out of state. Historians have generally maintained that western architecture is essentially derivative of outside trends. This view was summed up by Arthur A. Hart in 1974:

The failure of a regional style to emerge in Idaho must be viewed in part within the context of the rapid communications available over the past 80 years. . . . Since the first professional architect came to the state (in 1889) there has been no isolation from the mainstream of architectural ideas in the rest of the country.[25]

Regarding the development of new styles, it is certainly the case that Idaho has not developed a regional architectural style of its own. In fact, the course of Idaho architecture has been to shy away from regional expression, as if things regional were somehow inferior. Beginning with a varied Native American, missionary, and fur-trade architecture that bore a direct relationship to the regional environment, Idaho architecture has become increasingly more national and more homogeneous with each period of its development.

No one will find a distinct Idaho architecture by looking for an original style or by attempting to claim as uniquely regional an invention like the Trus Dek. In Idaho, the styles are indeed familiar to anyone visiting from elsewhere in the country. But the particular recombinations of structure, materials, plan, motifs, and function are as distinctive in Idaho as anywhere. It is clear that in Idaho, architecture has *regionalized*. That is, through the winnowing of ideas brought into the state; through the use of indigenous materials; and through the tastes of architects, builders, and clients for particular styles and plans, architecture in Idaho has taken on a regional flavor. Nowhere else are there buildings quite like Ravalli's Sacred Heart Mission, the shingle and Boise sandstone Temple Beth Israel, the basalt well houses of south-central Idaho, the Mormon Tabernacle at Paris, or even Paradice's Sullivanesque business blocks. As for the new downtown Boise: one can expect that, although inspired by models in Portland and Seattle, it will develop its own Idaho character.

Notes

1. For information about Idaho development in the modern period, see [Merle W. Wells, et al.], *Idaho: An Illustrated History* (Boise: Idaho State Historical Society, 1976), 237–43; Merle W. Wells, *Boise: An Illustrated History* (Woodland Hills, California: Windsor Publications, 1982), 109–49; and Merle W. Wells and Arthur A. Hart, *Idaho: Gem of the Mountains* (Northridge, Calif.: Windsor Publications, 1985), 137–52.

2. J. Meredith Neil, *Saints and Oddfellows: A Bicentennial Sampler of Idaho Architecture* (Boise: Boise Gallery of Art Association, 1976). Where information about modern buildings does not come from Neil or the other sources cited below, I am relying on my own observations.

3. The story of the Teater studio is told in detail by the current owner, Henry Whiting, II, and historian Robert G. Waite in *Teater's Knoll: Frank Lloyd Wright's Idaho Legacy* (Midland, Michigan: Northwood Institute Press, 1987).

4. A good summary of the work of Northwest regionalists appears in Rosalind Clark, *Architecture Oregon Style* (Portland, Oregon: Professional Book Center, 1983),

215–19. Wright's term "Usonian" derives from "United States of North America."

5. Neil, *Saints and Oddfellows*, 182–83, 130–31.

6. John Corlett, et al., "Partners in Progress," in Merle W. Wells and Arthur A. Hart, *Idaho: Gem of the Mountains* (Northridge, Calif.: Windsor Publications, 1985), 219.

7. Neil, *Saints and Oddfellows*, 12–15, 20–21, 56–57, 132–33.

8. Ibid., 86–87.

9. Ibid., 172–73.

10. Ibid., 30–31; and Keith C. Petersen, *This Crested Hill: An Illustrated History of the University of Idaho* (Moscow, Idaho: University of Idaho Press, 1987), 59–60.

11. Master plan [1963], on file at The College of Idaho, Caldwell.

12. Petersen, *This Crested Hill*, 60–61, 139; Neil, *Saints and Oddfellows*, 32–33; and Lillian W. Otness, *A Great Good Country: A Guide to Historic Moscow and Latah County, Idaho*, Local History Paper, no. 8 (Moscow, Idaho: Latah County Historical Society, 1983), 65.

13. Neil, *Saints and Oddfellows*, 150–51, 160–61, 168–69.

14. This summary of Boise redevelopment and the historic preservation movement is based on conversations with Merle W. Wells, 20, 21 October 1989; Wells, *Boise*, 146–47; "Environmental Assessment, Financial Settlement of Urban Renewal Projects, Idaho R–4 and R–5," City of Boise, May 1979, II–5–6, II–14–15; and "Amendment—Environmental Assessment, Financial Settlement of Urban Renewal Projects, Idaho R–4–Idaho R–5," City of Boise, September 1986, 8–9. I am indebted to Rick Greenfield, Executive Director of the Capital City Development Corporation, for locating the latter two documents for me.

15. [John Hailey], "Real Estate," report on file in MS 2.6, ISHS, Boise. Other documents in this manuscript provide the basis for my summary of the Packer John cabin restoration. See also [Merle W. Wells], "Early

Idaho Historic Preservation" [September 1988], a one-page commentary on file at the Idaho State Historical Society (hereafter ISHS), Boise.

16. "The John A. O'Farrell Cabin Rehabilitation Report," Report 82, Idaho Historic Sites Inventory, ISHS, Boise, 2; Neil, *Saints and Oddfellows*, 182; and "Pioneer McKenzie Cabin Moved to Caldwell Park," *Boise Valley Herald*, 7 July 1949, 1.

17. Merle W. Wells, "Twenty Years of History," *Idaho Yesterdays* 20, no. 4 (Winter 1977), 14.

18. Project files for these restorations and for the federal tax projects mentioned later in the text are on file at ISHS, Boise.

19. See Wells, "Early Idaho Historic Preservation"; and Cataldo files, Idaho Bicenntenial Commission manuscripts, AR61, boxes 7 and 8, ISHS, Boise.

20. Bobbi Rahder, "Report to the Historic Preservation Commission and the City of Pocatello" (17 August 1988), on file at Community Development and Research Department, City of Pocatello, 1; and J. Meredith Neil, "Bicentennial in Idaho," *Idaho Heritage* 1, no. 3 (Winter 1976):19.

21. Donald W. Watts, "Private Preservation Efforts Contrast with Urban Renewal in Old Boise," *Small Town* 13, no. 3 (November-December 1982):55–56.

22. Conversation with Arthur A. Hart, 22 October 1989.

23. See, for example, MS 2.444, ISHS, Boise, a letter from the council regarding the BRA, 1972.

24. *Idaho Code* (Charlottesville, Virginia: The Michie Company, 1989), chap. 46, sec. 67–4601.

25. Arthur A. Hart, "The Mission Style and Eclecticism in Idaho," in *Space, Style and Structure: Building in Northwest America*, 2 vols., ed. Thomas Vaughan and Virginia Guest Ferriday (Portland, Oregon: Oregon Historical Society, 1974), 2:514.

The Study of Idaho Architecture:
A Postscript and Annotated Bibliography

The study of Idaho architecture began in earnest with the state historic preservation office's efforts to identify historic buildings. Many of the publications listed below were the result of surveys conducted by preservation office staff. The surveys and publications have answered some general research questions about Idaho architecture. A great deal is known, for example, about the distribution of architectural styles and the periods in which they were used. Most of the state's principal architects have been identified, and one firm — Tourtellotte and Hummel — has been studied in detail. Something about the kinds of construction used and about the availability of materials in different periods is also known.

The number of unanswered questions, though, is myriad. For instance, little is known about women's involvement in architectural design and construction. Scattered sources, some of them mentioned in the text of this book, suggest that an untold story awaits the attention of a feminist scholar. For example, Patricia P. Saviers of Sun Valley was probably the first Idaho woman to obtain a license to practice architecture in Idaho, in 1953; but how were women involved in design before her time? How have they been involved in design in the years since her licensing?

Relatively little is known about the full range of construction used in the missions, fur-trade posts, and early mining towns and Mormon villages. Are the surviving structures really typical? Possibly they are not. In this history I have tried to use documentary sources that amend the story told by the surviving buildings, but there is also a clear need for more historical archaeological excavations at the sites of early settlement. Perhaps evidence can be unearthed that will yield data about construction, materials, and plan, if not style. (I will not presume to suggest the topics that archaeology could explore to document prehistoric shelter, but clearly more work could be done in that field also.)

Beginning about 1880, Idaho's architectural remains are fairly abundant and allow for better generalizations. Few buildings, though, have been recorded in the detail needed to draw either very firm or very subtle conclusions about the types of floor plans found in Idaho, the types of construction used, or the way in which manufactured materials affected overall design (such matters as window pro-portions, for example). The details of timber framing have not been noted, nor have the differences between platform and balloon framing. Box construction is poorly recorded. Brick quality, color, and bonding patterns have rarely received attention. Stone coursing and the treatment of mortar joints have been noted only in the basalt buildings of south-central Idaho. Without these details one cannot approach such questions as: How has ethnicity been expressed in Idaho buildings? Did new house plans appear here? Have traditions or pattern-book ideas been the main influence on vernacular architecture? How have the two influences interacted?

As mentioned, one architectural firm has been studied in detail. Others deserve further study. Something about the range of work done by Wayland and Fennell, Sundberg and Sundberg, Ralph Loring, Frank Paradice, and others is known; left to guesswork are the stylistic tendencies in their work. No one has identified all or even most of their commissions, identified the signature motifs they used, or fully worked out their connections with outside influences. Little is known about architect-client relationships, collaborations between architects and contractors, or the role of contractors as designers. One can only guess at how architectural design proceeded in various periods.

Much more could be explored in regard to the availability of materials in Idaho during particular periods, especially in the period after 1910. Did Idaho architecture simply take over the technological innovations available elsewhere in the nation? Were there any significant lags in materials availability? Were there other in-state innovations — like those of the Trus Joist Company — that had an impact locally and elsewhere?

It is known that standard plans were available in many areas of society during the depression years. Not known is how they actually were employed, and exploration of the ways they were related to such matters as educational philosophy and the development of modern commerce and bureaucracies has only begun. How, for example, has the Federal Housing Administration influenced housing? Where were the earliest suburban developments in Idaho and what forms did they take? Where were the early shopping malls? A patient researcher, willing to spend hours studying FHA archival materials and tracking down suburban development plans, has an opportunity for important research regarding home building in the modern era.

In this book specific building types have been discussed only where they related to very general movements in architecture. With the exception of courthouses, the development

of architectural types in Idaho — schools or churches, for example — has not been explored in any thorough, statewide studies. Idaho architecture is ripe for histories of church building, school development, barn construction, or farm layout.

Much of the current knowledge deals with the exteriors of buildings. Trends in church iconography and office building facades can be identified, but what about church plans and office layouts? What are the patterns in interior decoration, room use, and landscape architecture in Idaho?

Many sociological questions remain untouched. What effect have class distinctions had on Idaho architecture? Is there an architecture of poverty in Idaho? How have Idahoans provided for migrant housing and housing for transients? Are there ethnic or racial neighborhoods in which architecture, landscaping, or interiors are distinctive?

Finally, practically nothing has been done to survey and analyze the architecture of the era after World War II. I have been able to discuss two major trends in Modernism, but only very generally. Developments like trailer housing, a major postwar industry in southwest Idaho, have gone entirely untouched. Exciting work lies ahead for a scholar interested in the architectural styles and technologies of the late 1940s through 1989.

These are but the suggestions of a writer who has been frustrated by the many inviting avenues of research that appeared in the prep-

aration of this book and that could not be followed up. As with any field, the number of research questions that can be asked about Idaho architecture are limited only by the imagination.

The following bibliography of secondary sources has two sections. The first, Architectural Studies, includes published works whose purpose is the description and analysis of architecture, including prehistoric and Native American construction. Since few architectural historians have studied Idaho, here the reader will find articles written by archaeologists, historians, anthropologists, and folklorists as well as architectural historians. The second section, General Studies, includes works that have information useful for the study of Idaho architecture, but which is incidental to their main focus. Works are included in this section only if they devote substantial passages to architectural subjects. With the exception of the Look at Idaho Architecture series put out by the Idaho State Historical Society and Otness's very useful tour book of Latah County, the bibliography does not include the numerous walking tours available for Idaho towns, most of which are based on information in National Register nomination forms, Historic American Buildings Survey records, or similar documentary sources. Unpublished dissertations, theses, and conference papers are included only when they provide information unavailable elsewhere. This bibliography is not intended to duplicate the chapter notes, which refer the reader to primary and secondary sources that provide only a few, highly specific items of information about particular buildings, materials, or constructions.

Architectural Studies

Allen, Harold. *Father Ravalli's Missions*. Chicago: The School of the Art Institute of Chicago, 1972.

    A history of the Coeur d'Alene Mission of the Sacred Heart and St. Mary's Mission (Montana), both designed by Ravalli. Much of Allen's information is from primary sources contained in the archives at Gonzaga University, Spokane, Washington. Allen includes information about Ravalli's training and career as well as the construction of the missions. The second half of the book contains full-page black-and-white photographs of the two missions.

Ames, Kenneth M. "Instability in Prehistoric Residential Patterns on the Intermontane Plateau." Paper presented at the Northwest Anthropological Conference, 1988.

    Identifies three separate phases of pit house construction in the area that includes northern Idaho and suggests that the pit house was not a continuous residential pattern in the period after 6000 B.P.

Anderson, Paul L. "An Idaho Variation on the City of Zion." In *Chesterfield: Mormon Outpost in Idaho*, edited by Lavina Fielding Anderson, 70–78. Bancroft, Idaho: The Chesterfield Foundation, 1982.

    Describes and discusses the architecture and village plan of Chesterfield, a late nineteenth-century Mormon settlement, in the context of Mormon architecture. A photographic essay in the same volume provides illustrations for this article.

"Architecturally Significant and Historic Buildings of Boise, Idaho." Information Sheet Series. Boise, Idaho: Idaho State Historical Society, 1970.

    Twelve numbers present information about the construction and style of Boise buildings built between 1867 and 1906 and argue for their preservation.

Attebery, Jennifer Eastman. "Courthouse Architecture in Idaho, 1864–1940." *Idaho Yesterdays* 31, no. 3 (Fall 1987):11–23.

    Divides courthouse construction into several eras based on economic and social trends and describes typical courthouse style in each era. The article is followed by a photographic essay.

———. "The Diffusion of Folk Culture as Demonstrated in the Horizontal Timber Construction of the Snake River Basin." Ph.D. diss., Indiana University, 1985.

    Describes the characteristics of log construction in the several regions of the Snake River drainage, based on obser-vation of over 1,000 examples. Discusses the sources for log construction in Idaho.

———. "Domestic and Commercial Architecture in Caldwell." *Idaho Yesterdays* 23, no. 4 (Winter 1980):2–11.

    Discusses the style and construction history of residential and commercial buildings in a railroad town from its establishment in 1883 through 1910. The architecture is seen as a reflection of economic development.

———. "Log Construction in the Sawtooth Valley of Idaho." *Pioneer America* 8, no. 1 (January 1976):36–46.

    Describes the characteristics of log buildings constructed in the Sawtooth Valley during the period 1900–1920.

———. "The Square Cabin: A Folk House Type in Idaho." *Idaho Yesterdays* 26, no. 3 (Fall 1982):25–31.

    Describes several single-pen houses in southeast Idaho and their function as pioneer or marginal housing.

———. Kenneth J. Swanson, Joe Toluse, and Frederick L. Walters, "The Montgomery House: Adobe in Idaho's Folk Architecture." In *Idaho Folklife: Homesteads to Headstones*, edited by Louie W. Attebery, 46–55. Salt Lake City: University of Utah Press, 1985.

    A detailed description of a circa 1870 house in Boise Valley and history of its builder. Discusses the probable sources for the house's construction technologies.

Attebery, Louie W. "A Contextual Survey of Selected Homestead Sites in Washington County." In *Idaho Folklife: Homesteads to Headstones,* edited by Louie W. Attebery, 129–42. Salt Lake City: University of Utah Press, 1985.

Describes subsistence farming on three Washington County homesteads, including construction of houses and outbuildings.

Brown, Sharon. "The Built Environment." In *Prospects: Land-Use in the Snake River Birds of Prey Area, 1860–1987,* edited by Todd Shallat. Social Sciences Monograph, no. 1, 63–83. Boise, Idaho: Boise State University, 1987.

Describes the remains of stone buildings constructed at Halverson Bar, a few miles downriver from Swan Falls Dam on the Snake River. There is an extended study of the house of Doc Hisom, a black settler who lived at the bar during the 1920s through 1944.

Buckendorf, Madeline. "Early Dairy Barns of Buhl." In *Idaho Folklife: Homesteads to Headstones,* edited by Louie W. Attebery, 144–59. Salt Lake City: University of Utah Press, 1985.

Describes the construction of dairy barns built by farmers who moved from Tillamook County, Oregon, to Buhl in the 1910s. Buckendorf considers the influence of tradition and pattern books on the barns' construction.

Cannon, Martha Hibbard. "The Restoration of the Lorenzo Hill Hatch House." Master's thesis, Utah State University, 1982.

Presents information about Lorenzo Hatch and his 1872 Greek Revival style house in Franklin, with emphasis on its interior plan and furnishings.

Chance, David H., and Jennifer V. Chance. *Exploratory Excavations at Spalding Mission, 1973.* University of Idaho Anthropological Research Manuscript Series, no. 14. Moscow, Idaho, 1974.

Report of excavations designed to locate the Spaldings' 1838 house and subsequent outbuildings. Includes information about foundations, construction materials, and building layout.

Fielder, George, and Roderick Sprague. *Test Excavations at the Coeur d'Alene Mission of the Sacred Heart, Cataldo, Idaho, 1973.* University of Idaho Anthropological Research Manuscript Series, no. 13. Moscow, Idaho, 1974.

Report of excavations designed to yield information about the flooring, foundation, porch, and construction materials of the Sacred Heart church and the locations and construction of other buildings in the complex, including Native American housing.

Garth, Thomas R., Jr. "Early Architecture in the Northwest." *The Pacific Northwest Quarterly* 38, no. 3 (July 1947):215–32.

Summarizes information about the architecture of Pacific Northwest fur-trade posts and missions, including data from excavations of the Whitman mission. Because there had been only limited study of American vernacular architecture by 1947, Garth's conclusions about the sources of Northwestern architecture need re-evaluation.

Gowans, Alan. "The Mission of the Sacred Heart." *Idaho Heritage* 1, no. 3 (Winter 1976):24–25.

A brief essay on aesthetics and social function of the mission church. Gowans connects the Baroque character of the church with *Il Gesu,* the Jesuit mother church in Rome.

Green, Thomas J. "Aboriginal Residential Structures in Southern Idaho." Paper presented at the Great Basin Anthropological Conference, Park City, Utah, 1988.

Describes the three basic types of shelter that have been identified in prehistoric sites located in southern Idaho: the pit house, the pole and thatch structure (or wickiup), and the pole and rock structure. Comparing these house types to those found in the Plateau and Great Basin cultures, Green concludes that a major shift in house construction occurred in southwest Idaho in about 1200–1000 B.P.

Groberg, Delbert V. *The Idaho Falls Temple.* Publishers Press, 1985.

An appreciation and history of the Mormon Temple at Idaho Falls. Illustrations include photographs of the temple under construction between 1939 and 1945. Planning, design, and erection of the temple are discussed by Groberg, a church official who was affiliated with the temple from its inception.

Hart, Arthur A. "Architectural Styles in Idaho: A Rich Harvest." *Idaho Yesterdays* 16, no. 1 (Spring 1973):2–9.

Describes architectural styles that can be found in Idaho, from Greek Revival to Moderne and Prairie style. Includes comments on the derivation of each style. Styles are illustrated with photographs of Idaho buildings.

———. *The Boiseans: At Home.* Boise, Idaho: Historic Boise, 1985. Describes the social, family, and business lives of thirty-four representative Boise families, most of them prominent in commerce or politics. Hart includes information about women's activities when they can be documented. The book is well illustrated with contemporary photographs of the people and their houses.

———. "Farm and Ranch Buildings East of the Cascades." In *Space, Style and Structure: Building in Northwest America,* 2 vols., edited by Thomas Vaughn and Virginia Guest Ferriday, 1:241–54. Portland, Oregon: Oregon Historical Society, 1974.

A historical overview of rural buildings in the Intermountain West region, with emphasis on log and frame farmhouses, barn construction and type, and stone masonry.

———. "Fur Trade Posts and Early Missions." In *Space, Style and Structure: Building in Northwest America,* 2 vols., edited by Thomas Vaughn and Virginia Guest Ferriday, 1:30–43. Portland, Oregon: Oregon Historical Society, 1974.

Describes construction used in the Pacific Northwest missions and fur-trade forts. Includes information about Forts Boise and Hall and the Spalding and Sacred Heart missions, setting them in their regional context.

———. *Historic Boise: An Introduction to the Architecture of Boise, Idaho, 1863–1938.* Boise, Idaho: Historic Boise, 1980.

A historical narrative of Boise architecture from the establishment of Fort Boise in 1863 through the 1930s. Hart emphasizes the local use of American architectural styles and the development of several Boise-based architectural firms.

———. "M. A. Disbrow and Company: Catalogue Architecture." *The Palimpsest* 56, no. 4 (July/August 1975):98–119.

A history of M. A. Disbrow and Company, a factory in Iowa that sold its millwork by catalog. The article is illustrated with examples of Disbrow millwork that was used in Idaho buildings.

———. "The Mission Style and Eclecticism in Idaho." In *Space, Style and Structure: Building in Northwest America,* 2 vols., edited by Thomas Vaughn and Virginia Guest Ferriday, 2:509–17. Portland, Oregon: Oregon Historical Society, 1974.

Discusses stylistic trends in Idaho architecture of the 1920s and analyzes the Mission style with reference to its precedents in Idaho architecture of the 1900s.

———. "Notes on Sources of Architectural Iron in the West." In *Festschrift: A Collection of Essays on Architectural History,* edited by Elizabeth Walton Potter, 41–46. Salem, Oregon: Northern Pacific Coast Chapter, Society of Architectural Historians, 1978.

Discusses the availability of cast and galvanized iron for ornamentation of commercial buildings in the West from 1850 to 1910. Includes brief histories of firms in California, Nevada, Oregon, Washington, British Columbia, Montana, Utah, and of midwestern firms that exported to the West, identifying existing examples of their work. Black-and-white photographs depict cast and galvanized iron in Montana, Oregon, Washington, and California. Idaho examples are mentioned in the text.

———. "Stone Buildings East of the Cascades." In *Space, Style and Structure: Building in Northwest America* 2 vols., edited by Thomas Vaughn and Virginia Guest Ferriday, 1:363–72. Portland, Oregon: Oregon Historical Society, 1974.

Describes the qualities and stylistic use of building stones found in the Intermountain West, including Boise sandstone, Baker County tuffs, and Spokane basalt. Stonework by Basque, Welsh, and English stonemasons is described and illustrated with black-and-white photographs, historical and contemporary.

Hartung, John. "Documentation of the Historical Resources in the Idaho Primitive Area, Big Creek Drainage." Master's thesis, University of Idaho, 1978.

A survey of homesteads located on Big Creek in the Salmon River basin. Most of the homesteads have log buildings, some of them Rocky Mountain Cabins.

Hibbard, Don. "Chicago 1893: Idaho at the World's Columbian Exposition." *Idaho Yesterdays* 24, no. 2 (Summer 1980):24–29.

A history of the Idaho building at the 1893 Columbian Exposition in Chicago. Hibbard discusses the politics of planning for Idaho's participation in the exposition, the Idaho building's design, its use after the exposition, and its meaning to Idahoans.

———. *Normal Hill: An Historic and Pictorial Guide.* Lewiston, Idaho: Luna House Historical Society, 1978.

Describes the development of the Normal Hill neighborhoods in Lewiston from 1891 to the late 1920s. Hibbard describes the hill's architecture and discusses the careers of architects and builders who worked in Lewiston. The book is illustrated with drawings and maps indicating building locations.

———. *Weiser: A Look at Idaho Architecture.* Boise, Idaho: Idaho State Historic Preservation Office, 1978.

Describes the architecture of Weiser from 1883 through the 1920s based on surviving examples. Buildings are discussed in the context of Weiser development and of the work of Weiser architect H. W. Bond and Boise architects Tourtellotte and Hummel.

Idaho Historic Sites Series. Boise, Idaho: Idaho State Historical Society, n.d.

This photocopied series provides condensed versions of the text of National Register nominations for Idaho properties proposed for registration before 1986, when the series was discontinued.

Keating, Linnea, and Karl Roenke. *Fixed Fire Detection Lookout History on the Clearwater National Forest, Idaho.* Orofino, Idaho: Clearwater National Forest, August 1987.

A brief overview of lookout construction history followed by a list of lookouts on the Clearwater National Forest and copies of selected Forest Service lookout plans from 1928, 1931, 1932, and 1954.

Koskela, Alice. "Finnish Log Homestead Buildings in Long Valley." In *Idaho Folklife: Homesteads to Headstones,* edited by Louie W. Attebery, 29–36. Salt Lake City: University of Utah Press, 1985.

Describes Finnish log construction on homesteads taken up in Long Valley between 1904 and 1925. Koskela includes information about specific Finnish builders. Black-and-white photographs illustrate the buildings and the techniques of Finnish construction.

Morrill, Allen, and Eleanor Morrill. "Old Church Made New." *Idaho Yesterdays* 16, no. 2 (Summer 1972):16–25.

Documents the 1890 remodeling of Kamiah Presbyterian Church under the instigation and direction of Alice Fletcher, E. Jane Gay, and Philadelphia philanthropist Mary Thaw. The three women also had Kate McBeth's 1894 house built.

Neil, J. Meredith. *Saints and Oddfellows: A Bicentennial Sampler of Idaho Architecture.* Boise, Idaho: Boise Gallery of Art Association, 1976.

A guidebook to Idaho architecture arranged by region. With the assistance of David Nels Reese of the University of Idaho, Neil included contemporary as well as historic buildings. Each building is illustrated with a small black-and-white photograph. Many of the older buildings in this volume have received additional documentation since the book was published, providing more accurate information about dates and builders.

Otness, Lillian Woodworth. *A Great Good Country: A Guide to Historic Moscow and Latah County, Idaho.* Local History Paper, no. 8. Moscow, Idaho: Latah County Historical Society, 1983.

A walking and driving tour guide to historic buildings and sites in Moscow and Latah County. Includes detailed information about the construction and use of buildings.

Reece, Daphne. *Historic Houses of the Pacific Northwest.* San Francisco: Chronicle Books, 1985.

A guidebook to historic houses open to the public in Alaska, British Columbia, Idaho, Oregon, and Washington. The guide includes houses in Boise, Moscow, Blackfoot, and Pocatello.

Reitzes, Lisa B. *Paris: a Look at Idaho Architecture.* Boise, Idaho: Idaho State Historic Preservation Office, 1981.

A history of Paris architecture from the settlement's beginning in 1863 through the 1920s. Reitzes discusses the local use of American styles and house types and places them in the context of Mormon social history and Paris's economic development.

Robinson, Willard B. "Frontier Architecture." *Idaho Yesterdays* 3, no. 4 (Winter 1959–1960):2–6.

Analyzes the classical elements of Ra-

valli's Sacred Heart church. Robinson errs in labeling the building Greek Revival and in suggesting that the English Renaissance was one of Ravalli's sources.

Shallat, Todd, and David Kennedy. *Harrison Boulevard: Preserving the Past in Boise's North End.* Boise, Idaho: School of Social Sciences and Public Affairs, Boise State University, 1989.

A history of the development of Boise's Harrison Boulevard neighborhood. The book includes information about the area's planning, early beautification efforts, architectural styles, histories of individual buildings, and recent preservation efforts. Excerpts from oral histories and historic photographs illustrate the book. There is also a walking tour.

Sims, Cort. *Ranger Stations on the Idaho Panhandle National Forests.* Coeur d'Alene, Idaho: Idaho Panhandle National Forests, 1986.

A history of Forest Service construction on the north Idaho forests from creation of the forest reserves through the post–World War II era. The appendices include a list of ranger stations indicating extant buildings.

Walker, Deward E., Jr. "The Nez Perce Sweat Bath Complex: An Acculturational Analysis." *Southwest Journal of Anthropology* 22 (1966):133–71.

Describes Nez Perce sweathouse architecture, contemporary and historical, in detail. Walker also discusses the use

and function of the sweathouse in modern and precontact Nez Perce culture.

Whiting, Henry, II, and Robert G. Waite. *Teater's Knoll: Frank Lloyd Wright's Idaho Legacy.* Midland, Michigan: Northwood Institute Press, 1987.

A history and appreciation of Frank Lloyd Wright's Teater studio, designed for Patricia and Archie Teater in 1952. The house's construction is described in detail based on correspondence and photographs. The book is lavishly illustrated with color and black-and-white photographs.

Wilson, Mary. *Log Cabin Studies.* Cultural Resources Report, no. 9. Ogden, Utah: U.S. Agriculture Department, Forest Service Intermountain Region, 1984.

Describes and discusses the origins of the gable-front log cabin with overhanging roof, which Wilson calls the Rocky Mountain Cabin. The volume includes a good bibliography of log construction studies.

Wright, Patricia, and Lisa B. Reitzes. *Tourtellotte & Hummel of Idaho: The Standard Practice of Architecture.* Logan, Utah: Utah State University Press, 1987.

Analyzes the commissions of a Boise architectural firm in the context of the development of the architectural profession in the West, 1896–1941. The text includes an introductory history of the firm and its work, detailed discussion of key commissions, a comprehensive list of commissions, and a chronology of events in the firm's development. The volume is illustrated with black-and-white historical photographs and reproductions of plans and elevation drawings.

Wright, Patricia. *Twin Falls Country: a Look at Idaho Architecture.* Boise: Idaho State Historical Society, 1979.

Presents Twin Falls architecture of the 1900s through the automobile age placing it within the context of national styles. Each building has a brief history, including information about architects and owners. A section deals with buildings in outlying towns and farmsteads.

General Studies

Behre, Charles H., Jr. "Volcanic Tuffs and Sandstones Used as Building Stones in the Upper Salmon River Valley, Idaho." In *Contributions to Economic Geology, 1929,* edited by E. F. Burchard. U.S. Geological Survey Bulletin, no. 811. Washington, D.C., 1930.

Explains the limitations of tuff as a building material and discusses several buildings in Challis that were constructed with local tuff. Buildings are illustrated with photographs.

Gurcke, Karl. *Bricks and Brickmaking: A Handbook for Historical Archaeology.* Moscow, Idaho: University of Idaho Press, 1987.

A history and guide for archaeologists. The historical narrative presents information about the technology of brickmaking and its development in Idaho, Oregon, and Washington. A bibliography lists references to Pacific Northwest brickmaking in city directories, newspapers, and other documentary sources. An appendix lists American brick brands and their place and date of manufacture.

"Idaho Building Stone." In *Twenty-Sixth Annual Report of the Mining Industry of Idaho for the Year 1924,* 16–19. [Boise, Idaho]: Idaho Inspector of Mines, [1924].

Describes the qualities of Boise sandstone and lists buildings where it has been used.

Liljeblad, Sven. *The Idaho Indians in Transition, 1805–1960.* Pocatello, Idaho: The Idaho State University Museum, 1972.

A study of the changes in Idaho Indian culture that have come after contact with whites. Liljeblad describes twentieth-century Indian architecture, including the modern use of precontact forms.

———. "Indian Peoples in Idaho." Typed manuscript. Pocatello, Idaho: Idaho State University, Eli M. Oboler Library, Intermountain West Collection, n.d.

Overlaps somewhat with *The Idaho Indians in Transition.* This study is based on Liljeblad's ethnological work with the Shoshoni and Bannock Indians and presents a sympathetic view of their traditional lifeways, including architecture. Published, in part, in Merrill D. Beal and Merle W. Wells, *History of Idaho,* 3 vols. (New York: Lewis Historical Publishing Company, 1959), 1:29–59.

Petersen, Keith C. *Company Town: Potlatch, Idaho, and the Potlatch Lumber Company.* Pullman, Washington, and Moscow, Idaho: Washington State University Press and Latah County Historical Society, 1987.

Describes the building of a lumber company town in northern Idaho, including information about the architect, planning the town, managers' houses, and standard house plans for workers.

———. *This Crested Hill: An Illustrated History of the University of Idaho.* Moscow, Idaho: University of Idaho Press, 1987.

Includes a chapter on planning and construction of the early campus, 1889–1906. Photographs of buildings, old and new, provide good documentation of campus architecture.

Slickpoo, Allen P. *Noon Nee-Me-Poo (We, The Nez Perces): Culture and History of the Nez Perces.* [Lapwai, Idaho]: Nez Perce Tribe of Idaho, 1973.

Provides a Nez Perce point of view on the changes wrought by white invasion. Throughout are comments about the adoption of white architecture, including photographs of twentieth-century Nez Perce buildings.

Thompson, Erwin N. *Historic Resource Study, Spalding Area: Nez Perce National Historical Park/ Idaho.* Denver: U.S. Department of Interior, National Park Service, September 1972.

Presents a narrative history of the Spalding area, followed by chronologically arranged descriptions of the buildings constructed at Spalding. Each building has its own bibliography of sources, mostly primary documents. Both the Spalding mission and Lapwai Indian Agency periods are covered.

Walker, Deward E., Jr. *Indians of Idaho.* Moscow, Idaho: University of Idaho Press, 1978.

Includes illustrated sections describing the architecture of each group before contact with white culture.

Wells, Merle W. "'A House for Trading': David Thompson on Pend d'Oreille Lake." *Idaho Yesterdays* 3, no. 3 (Fall 1959):22–26.

Discusses the establishment of Thompson's Kullyspell House with details of its architecture drawn from Thompson's journal.

———. et al. *Idaho: An Illustrated History.* Boise, Idaho: The Idaho State Historical Society, 1976.

Includes three overviews of Idaho architecture: "Nineteenth-Century Idaho Architecture," pp. 151–64; "Architectural Trends in the Twentieth Century," pp. 219–23; and "Mormon Architecture," pp. 224–25.

Index